THE HACKER
AND THE STATE

THE **HACKER** AND THE **STATE**

Cyber Attacks and the
New Normal of Geopolitics

Ben Buchanan

Harvard University Press

Cambridge, Massachusetts, and London, England   2020

Third printing

Library of Congress Cataloging-in-Publication Data

Names: Buchanan, Ben (Writer on cybersecurity), author.
Title: The hacker and the state : cyber attacks and the new
normal of geopolitics / Ben Buchanan.
Description: Cambridge, Massachusetts : Harvard University Press, 2020. |
Includes bibliographical references and index.
Identifiers: LCCN 2019033274 | ISBN 9780674987555 (cloth)
Subjects: Cyber intelligence (Computer security). | Hacking—Political
aspects. | Cyberterrorism. | Cyberspace operations (Military science). |
Cyberspace—Political aspects.
Classification: QA76.9.A25 B823 2020 | DDC—dc23
LC record available at https://lccn.loc.gov/2019033274

For Kelly

Contents

THE HACKER
AND THE STATE

Introduction

"HOW MUCH YOU PAY FOR ENEMIES CYBER WEAPONS?"
The question was posed online with no preamble and in broken English. It sounded like a prank, a thought experiment, or an internet troll shouting into the digital ether. It was none of these things.

This message, posted in 2016 by an account calling itself "theshadowbrokers," began a series of events that would send shock waves through United States intelligence agencies and beyond. During a year-long escapade, the Shadow Brokers released documents that exposed how hackers working on behalf of the American government had penetrated networks around the world to delay, disrupt, and defang their targets. Their purloined files revealed that hacking was a fundamental, though mostly secret, tool of American statecraft, one deployed clandestinely against foe and friend alike.[1]

The Shadow Brokers released more than just documents. They revealed a collection of hacking tools amassed and guarded by the National Security Agency, or NSA, that were so powerful that American hackers likened them to "fishing with dynamite." And now this dynamite had suddenly been made available to anyone for free.[2]

The result was predictably disastrous. Hackers from authoritarian regimes and criminal groups repurposed the exposed code for use in their own devastating cyber attacks. They rank as the most destructive hacks in history, wreaking more than $14 billion of damage, infecting hundreds of thousands of computers, and interfering with businesses across the globe. American spy agencies that were accustomed to stealing other's secrets and penetrating others' intelligence operations did not know what had hit them. The United States government began a massive counterintelligence investigation into the Shadow Brokers, an inquiry made much more difficult by the careful steps the group had taken to cover its tracks. Though it has not been confirmed, leaks from the investigation suggest the Shadow Brokers were Russian in origin. America's loss was Russia's gain.[3]

The Shadow Brokers' data dump and the attacks that followed were the culmination of an unmistakable trend: over two decades, the international arena of digital competition has become ever more aggressive. The United States and its allies can no longer dominate the field the way they once did. Devastating cyber attacks and data breaches animate the fierce struggle among states. Chinese hackers plunder American business secrets and steal digital consumer records while Russian hackers interfere in the power grids and electoral politics of their adversaries. Even isolated countries such as North Korea and Iran can now decimate major global corporations like Sony and Aramco. And for all the blows it has suffered, there is no doubt that the United States continues to punch back. This book shows how all these events fit together, synthesizing and interpreting two decades of modern history to show how hackers have reshaped the world.

The chaotic arena of cyber operations that this book portrays is not what scholars and military planners had long imagined. They had always envisioned cyber attacks as a kind of digital equivalent to nuclear war: devastating but rare. This notion first etched itself into American consciousness with the 1983 movie *WarGames*, which featured a young Matthew Broderick inadvertently bringing the world to the brink of nuclear Armageddon by hacking into military computers. President Ronald Reagan saw the film the day after its release and demanded that the government investigate its premise.[4] Over the five presidencies since, an endless string of Washington blue-ribbon commissions has addressed the specter of digital destruction. Books by academics and policymakers have conjured up images of hacked power plants and air traffic control networks, of food shortages and mass panic.

Rather than realizing this apocalyptic vision, however, cyber attacks have become a low-grade yet persistent part of geopolitical competition. They happen every day. Government hackers play an unending game of espionage and deception, attack and counterattack, destabilization and retaliation. This is a new form of statecraft, more subtle than policymakers imagined, yet with impacts that are world-changing.

Signaling and Shaping

The more competitive aspects of statecraft rely on two overlapping but distinct approaches: signaling and shaping. The distinction between the two is vital.[5] If international relations are like a game of high-stakes poker, to signal is to hint credibly at the cards one holds, in an attempt to influence how the other side will play its hand. To shape is to change the state of play, stacking the deck or stealing an opponent's card for one's own use.

This book argues that while cyber capabilities are increasingly versatile tools for shaping geopolitics and seizing the advantage, they are comparatively ill-suited for signaling a state's positions and intentions.

Since the dawn of the nuclear age, the theory and practice of international relations has focused on signaling, and with good reason: humankind's most powerful weapons have become so destructive that they cannot be used except in the most extreme of circumstances. The canonical scholarship of the Cold War period thus explained not how to win a conflict, but how to avoid it on one's own terms.[6] Theorists like Thomas Schelling, who received the Nobel memorial prize in economics for his studies of game theory, described how a state can gain and retain an edge without firing a single shot. To hear Schelling tell it, much of statecraft is about manipulating the shared risk of war, coercing an adversary with carefully calibrated threats so as to gain a peaceful advantage.

Military mobilization is an example of statecraft by signaling. Deploying armed forces highlights one's fighting capabilities and demonstrates resolve to adversaries. It suggests that any aggression will bring significant consequences. For this reason, during the Cold War, the United States regularly positioned forces in Western Europe. Since there were not nearly enough American troops to stop a Soviet invasion, one might have wondered what these warriors could do. Schelling had a ready answer: "Bluntly, they can die. They can die heroically, dramatically, and in a manner that guarantees that the action cannot stop there."[7] The Soviets knew that no president could suffer the loss of thousands of Americans and not retaliate. The troops lent credibility to the United States' signal of commitment to the continent. Their presence helped keep the peace.

The importance of signaling resonated in the highest levels of government. Some senior foreign policy decision-makers fancied themselves Kremlinologists who could interpret the signals of Soviet leaders and deduce how best to respond. Presidents and premiers signaled to each other, too: the most iconic moments of statecraft in the Cold War were Kennedy and Khrushchev's battle of wills in the Cuban Missile Crisis and Reagan and Gorbachev's tense negotiations at Reykjavik. Thousands of history books give weight to this kind of statecraft.[8]

Many scholars ignored how clandestine activities subtly *shaped* the global environment. These operations were hard to spot and harder still to study, but they mattered. A few American policymakers argued early on that aggressive shaping needed more attention. The famed diplomat George Kennan wrote in 1948 that American policymakers hewed too blindly to an overly simplistic worldview, in which times of war were neatly separated from times of peace, failing to "recognize the realities of international relations—the perpetual rhythm of struggle, in and out of war."[9] Kennan suggested that the inevitable conflict between states' divergent interests would lead to a constant competition for advantage—a vision that proved prescient.

Both superpowers tried to reshape the Cold War through espionage and deception. Soviet military planners wrote extensively about the practice of *maskirovka,* or "little masquerade"—multifaceted deception campaigns to mislead the enemy's political and military leadership.[10] While it is true that the adversary sometimes spotted these efforts, they were not designed to act as geopolitical signals and compel a change in behavior by threatening harm. They were operational and strategic tricks meant to gain an edge.

Without maskirovka, the Cuban Missile Crisis with all its drama and signaling would not have unfolded as it did. Deception helped get the missiles to Cuba. The Soviets began with code-names that made it seem to anyone listening to their communications as if the missiles were bound for the Bering Sea. When the time came to load the ships that would instead travel to Cuba, the Soviets covered the missiles in farm equipment to fool observers, and in metal sheets to block infrared photography. The troops on board the ships were kept below decks in stifling heat and darkness, and even the captains did not know the true destination until they were underway. The secrecy was so all-encompassing that some of the Soviet troops swore they would never leave port again.

To further the deception, the Soviets leaked accurate information about their own operation to Cuban counterrevolutionary forces likely to communicate with Western intelligence. These forces, and their friendly newspapers in Miami, had a well-earned reputation for exaggeration and poor attention to detail. When a flood of Cuban voices correctly reported the arrival of Soviet missiles, the CIA discounted their claims as hyperbole, choosing instead to believe the repeated Soviet denials. As a result, the United States failed to recognize the danger for months after the initial Soviet missile deployments began, and did so only once spy plane missions and sources on the ground produced direct evidence that policymakers could not ignore.[11]

Pushed far enough, deception can morph into sabotage. Late in the Cold War, the Soviet Union began to spy aggressively on American technological production and markets, obtaining thousands of technical documents and sample products for their engineers to study. Once the CIA realized what was happening, the agency saw an opportunity. It fed flawed designs to the Soviets, ones that looked real but would fail before too long. As a result, the CIA managed to get poor-quality computer chips installed into Soviet equipment, faulty turbines installed into Soviet gas pipelines, and much more. Duped Soviet engineers unwittingly used defective designs for chemical plants and tractor factories. The Soviet space shuttle, which never flew, was a variant of a rejected NASA blueprint. Until well after the end of the Cold War, the Soviets never knew about the CIA's program, which is just how the American saboteurs wanted it.[12] Almost always out of view, shaping mattered, too.

How Hackers Change Statecraft

Today, one of the primary ways governments shape geopolitics is by hacking other countries. Hackers' power and flexibility are underappreciated, especially by those who focus only on the most visible attacks or on an imagined civilization-ending cyber war. Government hackers continually find ways to advance their states' interests and hinder those of their adversaries. Like a boxer who wins on points rather than with a knockout blow, they can be effective without being flashy or drawing blood.

Cyber operations show up again and again in the sophisticated modern state's playbook. Hackers wiretap, spy, alter, sabotage, disrupt, attack, manipulate, interfere, expose, steal, and destabilize. They fray the enemy's social fabric and denude its hacking capabilities. To understand contemporary statecraft, one must understand these shaping operations and their cumulative strategic effects.

Conversely, cyber operations are ill-suited for signaling. When states deploy cyber operations to communicate to other states, the signals tend to lack calibration, credibility, and clarity.

This is not a view aligned with conventional wisdom, with its roots in Cold War theories.[13] Policymakers and scholars frequently present cyber capabilities as analogous to nuclear capabilities, which make signaling essential given the potentially catastrophic impacts, or as analogous to conventional military capabilities, which make signaling easier given their high visibility. For military leaders, cyber capabilities may seem like tank battalions: reliable assets that can be deployed against a wide range of targets and whose force is easily understood.

But these comparisons to nuclear and conventional weapons are misleading. Cyber capabilities are not nearly as powerful as nuclear weapons or even most conventional military capabilities. Nor are they as dependable, fungible, or retargetable as traditional arms. Maybe most vexing of all, the operational functioning of cyber capabilities is nonintuitive; while most policymakers and scholars understand what nuclear weapons and tanks can do, the possibilities, pitfalls, and processes of hacking missions are comparatively opaque.[14]

The best way to conceptualize cyber operations is not through familiar signaling-centric paradigms, but through the framework of shaping, rooted in concepts like espionage, sabotage, and destabilization. The states that reap the most benefits from hacking are the ones that aggressively mold the geopolitical environment to be more to their liking, not the ones that try to hint, coerce, or threaten.[15]

This book shows that governments hack ever more forcefully in their never-ending competition for preeminence. Each chapter will explore a distinct objective of this hacking and put forward one case or campaign as an exemplar. Many of the same operational steps appear in case after case, even as the end goals differ. To form these narratives, the book draws on firsthand interviews, government files, technical forensic analyses, leaked documents, and in-depth media reporting.[16]

These sources clearly show that government hacking has evolved and accelerated over the past two decades. It used to consist of espionage operations almost entirely out of public view. The United

States and its allies had crucial advantages in this arena, examined in Part One. Over time, as Part Two shows, states built capabilities for covert cyber sabotage, and then for overt cyber attacks. States next realized how cyber operations could have broader effects, indiscriminately disrupting adversaries' companies and destabilizing their societies. Part Three focuses on some of the biggest hacking events of the last five years, turning to the story of the Shadow Brokers and other cases of destabilization. Cyber operations are now indelibly part of international relations, and the gap between the United States and other countries has narrowed considerably.

As competition rages in this new field of global engagement, everyone on the internet is caught in the crossfire and subject to the "perpetual rhythm of struggle" that Kennan warned about. This struggle does not manifest itself in public debates at the United Nations or even the discreet summits of international leaders. It does not rely on conspicuous military mobilizations or troops that serve as human trip wires. Instead, it flows through vast server farms, ad hoc networks of unwitting participants, third-party states, and homes and workplaces nearly everywhere. The global communications links, encryption mechanisms, internet companies, and computers that individuals use every day are the new front lines of statecraft. For better and for worse, hackers—working for, against, and within states—are shaping the future of the world.

PART ONE

ESPIONAGE

1

Exploiting Home-Field Advantage

IT WAS THE MIDDLE OF MAY 2010 and a key vote was drawing near at the United Nations Security Council. The United States was pushing for tougher sanctions on Iran, which was enriching uranium in defiance of international law. The sanctions would require the world's countries to inspect ships and planes going to or coming from Iran if forbidden cargo was suspected. They would also ban certain Iranian companies from doing business overseas. A Security Council resolution was an imperfect vehicle, but it would create economic stress, further isolate Iran, and show that the world was ready to stop Iran from getting the bomb. The United States and its allies planned to follow a successful resolution with additional sanctions to ratchet up the pressure and force Iran to negotiate.[1]

But the Security Council's passage of the proposal was no sure thing. Susan Rice, the United States ambassador to the United Nations, wanted to understand exactly what the member countries of the Council were thinking. She wanted to know their goals, concerns, and negotiating positions. She and her staff had talked to their representatives, of course, but knew such discussions could be filled with misdirection and bluffing. Rice needed to ascertain the members' true sentiments so that she could develop a strategy to hammer out a deal and win their votes.

The NSA was built for moments like this. The intelligence agency, which specializes in hacking, wiretapping, and codebreaking, already had programs in place to spy on several members of the Security Council, including China, Russia, France, Japan, Mexico, and Brazil.[2] But there were four other countries—Bosnia, Gabon, Uganda, and Nigeria—which had only recently rotated onto the Security Council and would soon rotate off. Their votes were also important to win, but the United States lacked advanced espionage programs against them. The NSA would have to develop the required capabilities, and with the sanctions vote looming, it would have to do so quickly.

NSA lawyers raced to get legal authorization under the Foreign Intelligence Surveillance Act, which governs the agency's activities within the United States. They sought permission to expand the NSA's spying to target the other four countries' embassies in Washington and their delegations to the United Nations in New York. With time running short, the NSA legal team worked over the weekend of May 22–23. NSA Director Keith Alexander, a hard-charging Army general, signed off on the increased surveillance on May 24. Approval from Secretary of Defense Robert Gates and the Department of Justice followed soon after. The FISA Court accepted the four requests for increased espionage just two days later, setting a record for speed.

With the legal authorization in place, the NSA was free to act. The agency coordinated with its close partner, the telecommunications company AT&T, which counted the United Nations in New York as a client. AT&T had long provided intelligence to the NSA on the data that transited the company's network, and now it was perfectly positioned to supply key information on the agency's new targets. Using the information about the UN's communications that AT&T offered, as well as other sources, analysts at the NSA quickly built up a picture of what the key Security Council members were saying in their internal debates. The analysts then rushed that information to Rice and others, who used it to guide their negotiating strategy.

It worked. The resolution passed, twelve to two. President Obama hailed the resolution's passage as delivering "the toughest sanctions ever faced by the Iranian government."[3] The United States had deployed its espionage capabilities for insights into other countries, then turned those insights into geopolitical advantage. Rice remarked in a file later leaked by Edward Snowden that the NSA's intelligence effort had "helped me to know when the other [state's representatives] were telling the truth . . . revealed their real position on sanctions . . . gave us an upper hand in negotiations . . . and provided information on various countries' 'red lines.'"[4]

This case reveals an important fact: the United States and its allies have what some in the NSA call a "home-field advantage" when it comes to cyber operations. They are well-positioned along the key hubs and cables that connect the globe. United States telecommunications providers such as AT&T serve a gigantic variety of clients. Other American corporations are also central to the modern digital ecosystem. Individuals, corporations, and governments all over the world voluntarily give data to Google, Facebook, Amazon, and other firms. These companies are subject to American law and are compelled partners of the intelligence community, meaning they must turn over information on foreign intelligence targets to the government.[5]

The two parts of this home-field advantage—collection from telecommunications sites and access to data from internet firms like

Google and Facebook—work together to play a significant role in the American intelligence apparatus. They represent a shift from the millennia-old form of espionage, in which a well-placed human source steals a few vital secrets at a time, and also differ from the most common type of cyber operation: hacking an individual target or device. Together, the two parts of this advantage feed powerful analytic tools that provide intelligence analysts with near-real-time insights on targets, offering powerful new means of finding people of interest. Using these tools, the NSA has enabled missions that have killed hundreds of terrorists, thwarted foreign hackers, informed international negotiations, and produced many thousands of intelligence reports for policymakers at the highest levels of government.[6] The details of particular cases are not always known, but the aggregate impact on statecraft is unmistakable.

But the home-field advantage requires secrecy. These activities do not attempt to signal to other states or change their behavior; indeed they may only succeed if the other states remain unaware and continue typical operations. They hinge on using the United States' favorable position, powerful partnerships, and overseas alliances to better understand the world as it is—and give policymakers the tools to remake it into the world they want it to be. These are *shaping* missions through and through.

Why History and Geography Matter

Porthcurno is a tiny village at the southwest tip of Britain. Though the village is now obscure, in 1870 it became host to the most important telecommunications hub in the world. Its Cornwall beach location made it an ideal termination point for undersea telegraph lines.

An army of workers maintained these cables and transmitted millions of messages. When World War II broke out, the British considered this telecommunications equipment so vital they rushed to build bomb-proof tunnels to keep it safe from German air raids. For a hundred years, it was through Porthcurno that people throughout the far-flung British Empire kept in touch.

When electronic messages travel, they do not take the shortest path as the crow flies; they pass along whatever path the network permits, through switchboards, hubs, and clearinghouses, crossing borders and sometimes even continents. In the early days of telecommunications, their paths frequently ran through the hub of Porthcurno. Messages from one part of the world to another transited through the town's cables, even though neither sender nor receiver was located on the British Isles. Great Britain enjoyed a home-field advantage for accessing electronic communications long before the United States did: the world's secrets came through Britain. British spies set up shop right alongside the technicians, intercepting communications as they transited across the telegraph lines. From this small coastal village and other hubs like it, they listened in on the world.

The spies got results. Most notably, on January 17, 1917, amidst the ongoing stalemate of World War I, British intelligence intercepted a message from Germany on its way to Mexico. The author was Arthur Zimmerman, the German foreign secretary. The intended recipient was the German embassy in Mexico. In the telegram, Zimmerman proposed plans for a German-Mexico alliance if the United States entered the war, promising Mexico the return of Texas, Arizona, and New Mexico. British intelligence quietly helped to make the telegram public, while concealing the cable-tapping effort so as to preserve its future efficacy. After the telegram's publication, Americans were outraged, further turning opinion in the United States against Germany. Five weeks later, the United States declared war, to the great relief of Britain. The full role of British intelligence in this geopolitical shaping operation was not known until many years later.[7]

Collecting secrets from telecommunications cables and hubs is now known as passive collection. It contrasts with the active collection in hacking operations that sneak malicious code onto a target computer—though passive collection can help with these operations, too.

Passive collection is fundamentally about access to information. The most valuable collection points in the world are the ones where the best intelligence flows by. The globe's telegraph and phone networks required huge amounts of capital to construct, and thus their main hubs are in the richest and most economically interdependent states. This is one reason, among many others, that the alliance known as "the Five Eyes" matters so much.

The precursor to the Five Eyes was the American and British cooperation during World War II that was formalized in 1946 in a deal known as the UKUSA Agreement. Later this was expanded to include the British Commonwealth countries of Canada, Australia, and New Zealand. In each of these five countries, major contributions to the alliance are made by "signals intelligence" agencies like the NSA—so called because they intercept communications, hack computers, and steal secrets all over the world. These *intercepted* messages should not be confused with the sorts of signals countries *send* to influence each other's behavior.

The Five Eyes members have a common language and democratic heritage, but they also share something else: terrific placement along the coasts of the world's major oceans and ownership of some of the world's most important telecommunications sites. The United States and United Kingdom are well-positioned on either side of the Atlantic; the Government Communications Headquarters (GCHQ), the British signals intelligence agency, identifies Great Britain's favorable location as one of its "unique selling points" for intelligence collection.[8] In the Pacific, Australia and New Zealand also enjoy good access to key cable landing spots and switchboards.

Unlike telegraphs, modern digital communications feel ephemeral. Cellular networks are wireless. The cloud filled with emails and files is invisible. Yet, while geography may seem unimportant, it still matters tremendously. All digital messages must take a physical route. Whether they go through the air or along cables, whether they travel short distances or long, they nonetheless have a real presence and must pass, however briefly, through some points on Earth between sender and receiver.

The central nervous system that ties together all the far-flung parts of the internet builds on what came before: the same telephone and telegraph networks that spies from the Five Eyes have long targeted. As a result, the geography of the United States and its partners is just as favorable now as it has been for more than a century. Even as technology evolves—there are now 750,000 miles of undersea fiber-optic cables—the contours of the Earth stay the same.[9] An analysis of 2.5 billion modern internet routing paths suggests that just under half of the observed traffic traveled through at least one more nation than would be geographically necessary, often a Five Eyes country.[10] To steal other countries' secrets, the Five Eyes just need to bring the right technology to the right spot.

Spying on the Backbone of the Internet

At 33 Thomas Street in New York City, there is a tower that can withstand an atomic blast. Built in the architectural style of brutalism, it cuts an imposing figure as it stretches twenty-nine floors above ground and three below. Its original designs outlined how it could serve as a city unto itself, hidden in the heart of the country's largest metropolis. Those plans called for storing 250,000 gallons of fuel and two weeks of food for the facility's fifteen hundred technicians. Despite its size, the tower has no windows.

Computers do not need windows, and they are the most important tenants of 33 Thomas Street. The building is a modern communications hub. Giant banks of telephone and internet switches, the kind that whisk data all over the world, fill the floors. Large satellite dishes on the roof pluck signals out of the sky. In the 1970s, the tower's architects aspired to devise a "20th century fortress, with spears and arrows replaced by protons and neutrons laying quiet siege to an army of machines within."[11] Today, the internet depends on this AT&T-operated building in lower Manhattan and others like it scattered across the world.

On the "No Standing" street signs that keep cars from lingering at 33 Thomas Street, there is a curious notation: AWM. Other similarly marked signs are scattered across the city, mostly by sensitive government sites; this notation permits parking by secretive government officers on official business. A New York City traffic commissioner came up with AWM—which does not stand for anything—in the 1980s after an embarrassing incident in which officers had an FBI vehicle towed while agents were inside a government building making an arrest.[12]

The signs suggest that more than just telecommunications business happens inside. The NSA calls 33 Thomas Street by the code name

TITANPOINTE, using its typical all-caps style.[13] The task of extracting information from the site and others like it falls to the NSA's Special Source Operations division.[14] The seal of the secretive group, a bald eagle holding the world's fiber-optic cables in its talons, alludes to its global reach. The team includes many technical experts with specialization in modern telecommunications systems. Working in close partnership with AT&T, the group collects intelligence from the massive amounts of information that flow through 33 Thomas Street's cables and antennas. While technical limitations restrict how much the spies can gather at once, the opportunity is still enormous.[15]

Intelligence collection happens at other telecommunications hubs, too, thanks to the NSA's partnership with AT&T. At one point, AT&T installed collection devices in at least seventeen of its facilities, more than its similarly sized competitor, Verizon. But the company's willingness to help did not stop there. On numerous occasions, AT&T proactively rolled out new surveillance techniques ahead of other NSA industry partners. AT&T was a leader in turning over phone and email data—sometimes without a warrant—as well as hundreds of billions of internet records, billions of domestic cell phone records, and enormous amounts of data passing through the United States.[16] Some of the NSA's classified files also note that, due to AT&T's own corporate relationships, the firm has access to the data of other telecommunications companies, as well. The company's long reach gives the agency's spies access to even more information.

In addition to supporting espionage before the Iran sanctions vote in 2010, AT&T helped the NSA with other targets at the United Nations. The United Nations maintains that spying on it and on diplomatic sites is illegal under international law, but the United States and other countries ignore this; there are just too many foreign intelligence targets conveniently located in one place to pass up.[17] AT&T

continually gave the NSA voice and data communications from its client, filtering them to provide information of most interest. In 2011, even as it charged the United Nations almost two million dollars per year for telecommunications services, the company quietly compromised its secrets.[18] Using this access, the NSA gathered the talking points of the secretary general before his meeting with President Obama, enabling the United States to better position itself in negotiations.[19] Among other targets, in 2012 the NSA focused on surveilling the United Nations official in charge of a monitoring mission overseas, presumably in a region of strategic importance to the United States.[20]

Another legal authority the NSA uses to access information traveling through AT&T's network is known as "transit authority."[21] Under this justification, the agency can target communications that pass through the United States but do not originate or terminate within its borders. At American sites of collection, the agency and its partners first employ technical filters to attempt to ensure that the collection sweeps up only foreign-to-foreign communications. But some domestic data does get misclassified and included. The on-site collection systems cull the information down to the communications of most interest, sending these back to NSA headquarters for further storage and analysis. In general, the agency is much less interested in Netflix binge-watching or Spotify streaming than in messages between potential intelligence targets. Since the former take up so much data, it is often best for the agency not to store them at all.[22] When looking for a needle in a haystack, the solution is rarely to add more hay.

Much of the hard data on passive collection, including that done using transit authority, comes from the documents leaked in 2013 by Edward Snowden, a contractor to the NSA. This means that the evidence of NSA activities is ample but imperfect. On the one hand, some of the leaked documents are likely to overstate NSA capabilities and successes; just as in every organization, employees have incentives to make their programs look good. On the other hand, since most of the leaked files are over five years old, it is likely that NSA capabilities have gotten much better in the intervening years as technology has progressed.

Yet, with these caveats, it is possible to explore the vast scale of the passive collection program. In 2012, the NSA used its transit authority on AT&T's network only to gather emails. From AT&T, the agency collected an enormous number of foreign-to-foreign emails, about sixty million per day, or more than twenty billion messages per year, of which the agency focused its systems on only a subset. Even then, the smaller percentage totaled almost two billion messages annually—a massive volume of communications flowing through the United States that neither originated nor terminated there.[23]

Hidden within this huge haul are insights that previous forms of espionage would have missed: the messages of foreign ministers and officers, terrorists, and extremists, all located overseas and whose authors are almost certainly unaware that their communications boomerang through the United States. Like the British at Porthcurno, from 33 Thomas Street and other hubs, the Five Eyes can watch the modern world. In a one-year period, NSA analysts used foreign-to-foreign communications intercepted from AT&T's network in more than eight thousand intelligence reports.[24]

Passive collection has its limits, however. The unpredictable nature of internet routing sometimes causes communications to take an unexpected or obscure path, and there are too many cables and hubs for even the most well-funded signals intelligence agencies to tap them all. Sometimes, therefore, the NSA must deploy a technique called traffic shaping to make sure that the internet traffic of most interest passes through chokepoints monitored by the agency.[25] AT&T assisted with this task, expanding the power of passive collection a little bit more; the NSA praised the company for being "highly collaborative," and showing "an extreme willingness to help."[26]

Other telecommunications firms also partner with the NSA. Verizon works with the agency at seven major chokepoints where the company's US hubs connect to overseas cables. One of these cables links the US west coast with China, Japan, and Korea. The NSA set up a ten-thousand-square-foot collection facility on Verizon's site and deployed fifteen specially designed systems for sorting through internet traffic. Funds earmarked for American cyber defense appear to have paid for the efforts.[27]

These tight ties between the United States government and telecommunications companies are not new. AT&T has long been a federal government partner. During World War II, its research labs made major contributions to the invention of radar, aircraft communications systems, and cryptography, and the research cooperation continued during the Cold War. It was the rise of internet communications, however, that supercharged AT&T's value to the intelligence community. Other companies have developed their partnerships more recently. For this assistance, the United States government pays the companies hundreds of millions of dollars per year out of its classified black budget.[28]

When asked about its activities at 33 Thomas Street and elsewhere, AT&T says that it does not "allow any government agency to connect directly to or otherwise control our network to obtain our customers' information." Instead, the company says its practice is to "simply respond to government requests for information pursuant to court orders or other mandatory process and, in rare cases, on a legal and voluntary basis when a person's life is in danger and time is of the essence."[29] Other telecommunications companies, including British firms, have given similar answers when questioned about their activities.[30] For all the techno-utopian talk of a borderless internet, cyberspace is still physical space.[31] National laws compelling corporate cooperation still apply—a fact that the Five Eyes are happy to use for their geopolitical benefit.

Partnering with Internet Platforms

A century ago, communications were fleeting. Telegrams moved from sender to receiver, at which point they disappeared into whatever paper files the recipient kept, if any. When intelligence officers wanted to intercept a message electronically, they had to do so as it traversed the network, not afterward. But if telegrams once traveled with barely a ripple, today's online events leave pronounced wakes in the servers and data centers of private companies.

This modern system creates an intelligence opportunity. Some of the users of internet platforms are foreign individuals of great interest to the NSA. Luckily for the agency, the dominance of American firms means that these foreign targets will likely send their emails, online messages, and other data through internet platform companies that are legally required to cooperate with the United States government. Under the Foreign Intelligence Surveillance Act, the agency can compel internet companies operating in the United States to turn over data on a target if two criteria are met. First, the NSA must "reasonably believe" that a specific intelligence target is foreign; former agency director Michael Hayden suggested that the threshold for this is a 51 percent chance that the target is not an American and is not located in the United States. Second, analysts must determine that the target fits into one of the broad categories of permitted intelligence collection, the full list of which is not public.[32]

The mechanism for getting this desired data from American technology companies, a program the NSA code-named PRISM, began in 2007 as an arrangement between the United States government and Microsoft.[33] It quickly expanded over the next five years to add eight more internet companies, including Google, Facebook, Apple, and Yahoo. Also included are some companies, such as Paltalk, that are little known in the United States but popular in the Middle East and other regions of strategic interest.

When NSA analysts are tracking foreign intelligence targets, they can use PRISM to gather more information. The analyst usually begins with what the agency calls a selector, which is often an email address or an IP address that corresponds to the target. With the target's virtual identity in hand, PRISM enables two kinds of collection: surveillance and stored communications. The former provides forward-looking collection of the target's activities online. It can give analysts great insight into what a target is up to, enabling a response if warranted. The latter is backward-facing, and arranges for the transfer of a company's records on a target to the government. This kind of collection sheds light on past activities, including messages the target sent to other possible accomplices, messages received, and files the target uploaded, such as photos and videos. Between the two methods, analysts can gain extraordinary insight into the target's digital and even physical life.

As of 2012, the last complete year for which data is available, analysts used the system to surveil more than forty-five thousand email and IP addresses. In a one-week period for which granular data is available, PRISM contributed to 589 intelligence reports on a wide variety of targets. For analysts focused on Mexico, it provided information relating to counternarcotics, internal security, and political stability. For those looking at Japan, it revealed data on trade negotiations and internal Japanese discussions about Israel. Analysts whose remit was India used PRISM to look into the country's nuclear and space programs. Investigators watching Venezuela used PRISM to examine oil issues and military procurements, while those interested in Colombia analyzed what PRISM returned about the terrorist group FARC. Almost certainly, PRISM supported spying on non-democratic countries, as well, such as China and Russia, though the details have been redacted.[34]

That week's activity level seems not to be exceptional. Annually, PRISM informs tens of thousands of intelligence reports on a wide variety of subjects, including counterterrorism, counterproliferation, weapons development, space programs, cyber defense, regional assessments, counterintelligence, and much more. Across the broad US intelligence mission PRISM provides incredible insight, all because foreign intelligence targets rely on American businesses to communicate and coordinate. Perhaps most crucially, PRISM serves as one of the most significant sources of information for the President's Daily Brief—a sign of just how important the Five Eyes home-field advantage is to the intelligence community's top priority of informing senior policymakers.

PRISM supplements, but does not replace, passive collection from fiber-optic cables and telecommunications sites. Given the unpredictability of internet routing, it provides the NSA with a valuable second chance at gathering sensitive data, as well as older data predating a target's arrival on the agency's radar screen. This is why NSA analysts are told to rely on both passive collection and PRISM.

One incident offers an example of how PRISM and passive collection, working together, can give the United States an edge vis-à-vis its adversaries. In December 2012, a team at the NSA used PRISM to watch a group of foreign hackers who were targeting American systems. They realized that the hackers had successfully breached a domestic defense contractor that handled large amounts of classified information. Having placed malicious code inside that company's network, the hackers had gathered large amounts of sensitive information—more than 150 gigabytes in all—and prepared to exfiltrate it from the company back to their home network. With the intelligence provided by the United States' home-field advantage, the NSA tipped off the FBI, which rushed to the defense contractor, blocked the adversary's activity, and helped remove the malicious code from the network. In the never-ending struggle for advantage in cyber operations, the United States won that round.[35]

Wiretapping the World

Costas Tsalikidis was dead. Many years later, this is the one key fact upon which everyone agrees. He died in Athens on March 9, 2005, at age thirty-eight. His death marked the abrupt end of a career as a network-management expert at the phone company Vodafone. It had been a fitting job for someone who had loved technical systems and had an aptitude for math and physics.

Tsalikidis died seven months after Athens had hosted the first Summer Olympics held after 9/11. The Games had been lauded as a return to the roots of international athletic competition. Much of the rhetoric before the Opening Ceremony emphasized that the world community, frightened by the specter of terrorism and fractured by the American invasion of Iraq, would come together.

But the United States government worried about the Greek government's counterterrorism abilities and its capacity to protect the crowds coming to Athens. In the run-up to the 2004 Olympics, American officials offered to help. In particular, they presented a plan to lend their extensive signals intelligence apparatus to the task. All they would need was access to key parts of the Greek telecommunications system. Though it was of questionable domestic legality, Greek government officials agreed to collaborate in secret. American spies set about penetrating the core of Greek phone networks, including key systems and hubs. Perhaps to alleviate privacy concerns, the United States promised the Greek government that it would remove its espionage technology once the Olympics were over.

But when the Games ended and the athletes went home, the United States did not dismantle its collection capabilities as it had promised.[36] Instead, it used the well-positioned spying apparatus for its own ongoing missions. The job, for the most part, was well done. The American espionage software built upon the lawful interception mechanisms that Greek law enforcement used but, crucially, it bypassed key auditing and oversight systems.[37] This made possible the secret wiretapping of more than a hundred targets, including the prime minister and his wife, cabinet members, the mayor of Athens, and various Greek journalists.

Espionage is a tricky business. Bad luck or a single mistake can blow an entire operation. In January 2005, it appears that the American operators attempted to make a routine update to the wiretapping software they had placed in the Greek phone network. The software update process went amiss, and the phone system failed to deliver hundreds of text messages sent by legitimate users. The disruption in service caused Vodafone and others to investigate, and they soon found the espionage capabilities hidden inside their network.

The shadowy intelligence collection operation was thus thrust into the light of day. The story started to gain widespread coverage in the media. Tsalikidis's boss at Vodafone ordered the removal of the sophisticated American eavesdropping software, obscuring key evidence of what had happened. One day later, Tsalikidis was dead. His mother found him hanging from a rope tied to pipes in his bathroom.

Given the circumstances, Tsalikidis's death immediately attracted attention. A disputed coroner's report ruled the death a suicide and there is no conclusive evidence that he was murdered. Vodafone denied any link between his death and the espionage operation that had targeted its networks. A senior Greek prosecutor was having none of it: "If there had not been the phone tapping," he declared, "there would not have been a suicide."[38] But despite the Greek investigation, much of the case still remains shrouded in mystery.

For all its tragedies and complexities, the Greek wiretapping incident underscores an important fact: some data of great interest to the intelligence community does not make it to the shores of Five Eyes countries or to the servers of American firms. If the Five Eyes' signals intelligence agencies want access to this information, they will have to proactively get it, as they did in Athens. Through a series of partnerships, alliances, and deceptions, the Five Eyes have extended their home-field advantage to other friendly countries around the world. The alliance spends tens of millions of dollars per year to work with other friendly countries to increase the reach of its collection.[39]

There are at least thirty-three countries that secretly partner with the Five Eyes on cable access. One of these is Denmark. Internet companies like Facebook and many others locate their data centers in Denmark because its cold weather and cheap renewable energy make it easier to cool hot computer servers. As a result, when individuals in Russia or Western Europe use the internet, their data often flows along Danish cables to these data centers, providing an opportunity for passive collection. This sort of cable-tapping collaboration between the United States and Denmark goes back many years. Leaked NSA files indicate that the United States and Denmark have cooperated on a longstanding program with "special access."[40]

Another partner is Germany, where the NSA once very narrowly avoided accidental exposure. The agency had placed a secret collection system in the German telecommunications network, codenamed WHARPDRIVE, which monitored messages as they flowed by.[41] The system had worked for some time, but bad luck reared its ugly head in March 2013. Just as Greek technicians had found the collection systems in Athens, some employees at the affected German site realized that something was amiss. They began to investigate, raising the potential of another media spectacle. But individuals on the scene who knew of the agency's top-secret effort quickly removed the evidence. They provided an acceptable cover story, averting the danger—until evidence appeared in the Snowden leaks.[42]

These highly classified arrangements rest on a conceptually simple trade. The partner countries provide the NSA (or sometimes another intelligence agency from a Five Eyes country) access to key telecommunications facilities in their territory. In return, the NSA provides the sophisticated equipment required to process and transport the collected data, some of which is eventually sent back to the United States for storage and analysis. The NSA usually also agrees to share intelligence about some of the targets of its espionage and not to use the access to spy directly on the partner country's residents.[43] Internally, the NSA claims that the program is valuable, noting that this sort of collection has contributed to more than nine thousand signals intelligence reports per year.[44]

The Greek and German cases suggest that countries can be both partners and targets. Other examples of overseas passive collection demonstrate that tension. There are some indications that the NSA uses its Danish access points to target Germany and its German access points to target Denmark. If this is the case, the agency would technically be upholding its pledge not to use a partnership to directly spy on its partner's citizens, while still spying on them when inclined.[45] With its range of overlapping partnerships, the sum total of the agency's collection arrangements is substantial and far-reaching. One internal NSA description bluntly claims that it "has access to international communications from anywhere around the world."[46] Another boasts that one partner-enabled passive collection program can collect three terabits of data, or more than the amount of data on a normal computer's entire hard drive, every single second.[47]

Due to the risk of American duplicity, some potential partner countries reject the NSA's overtures. To overcome this obstacle, the NSA piggybacks on relationships that the CIA and Drug Enforcement Administration (DEA) have established with foreign governments and firms. The extent of these previously developed connections can be substantial. While the CIA has a famously global reach, the DEA has a surprisingly large remit, as well, with more than eighty international offices. Under its counternarcotic auspices, it can go places the NSA cannot. One former DEA agent explained why, saying "countries let us in because they don't view us, really, as a spy organization."[48] The NSA turns this access to its own advantage, using an international relationship established for one purpose to secretly serve another.[49]

The Bahamas provides a prominent example. The United States government—seemingly using DEA relationships—established a partnership with an unnamed private firm in the country that installed equipment for police and counternarcotic investigations on the country's phone network. Using the covert arrangement with this firm, the United States developed and deployed an enormous passive collection operation. The program stored the audio of every cell phone call in the Bahamas for approximately thirty days after it was collected.[50] This kind of lengthy storage lets intelligence analysts uncover the calling history of newly discovered targets. NSA documents suggest that the Bahamas program was a model that could be replicated in other countries; it is unclear if that expansion ever happened or if the Bahamas program is still operating.[51]

The United States has another way to extend its home-field advantage overseas: through its embassies and consulates all over the world. Many of these buildings have antennas hidden on their roofs or behind facades. Small teams of intelligence officers from both the NSA and CIA run collection programs that steal secrets in foreign lands.[52] In one of the operations that sparked the most controversy when it became public, the NSA apparently tapped German Chancellor Angela Merkel's cell phone, using the secret listening devices on top of the United States embassy in Berlin.[53] That the United States would spy on an allied leader, particularly one so tightly aligned with President Obama, shows how friends and enemies are all sometimes targets of intelligence collection.

Other spying sites are in much rougher territory. The Five Eyes' wide network of listening stations includes posts made possible by secret partnerships with less savory foreign governments.[54] Some of these stations, like the one in Saudi Arabia, are well-positioned to intercept communications from adversaries, such as Iran and Al Qaeda in the Arabian Peninsula.[55] In pursuit of their intelligence gathering mission, the NSA and its Five Eyes partners want to make sure their targets have nowhere to hide.

But sometimes the need for overseas access is high and no realistic partner is in sight. The Five Eyes then go it alone, taking the techniques they are accustomed to deploying on friendly or neutral turf and using them in unilateral operations.[56] The Five Eyes have spent years analyzing the network architectures of key internet cables all over the world so that they can better access them without external assistance. One example is the so-called SEA-ME-WE-4 cable system, a massive group of fiber-optic connections that links parts of Europe with North Africa and Asia. It is one of the most important cable systems outside of the Five Eyes. With its signals intelligence capabilities, the NSA gained access to the management systems for the cable and acquired information about its design. This access and insight could enable eventual tapping of the cable using a variety of methods, potentially including advanced submarines.[57]

One of the NSA's largest cable-tapping endeavors has the internal code-name DANCINGOASIS. It is unclear which specific cable the program taps. It might be SEA-ME-WE-4, as NSA documents indicate that the targeted cable links Western Europe and the Middle East, and other documents describe the program as "non-corporate," meaning the NSA does not have a relationship with the telecommunications provider that operates the cable.[58] The amount of data flowing through the tapped cable is enormous, around 25 petabytes per day, or about two thousand times the storage capacity on an average computer's hard drive. The agency scans a percentage of this and stores a smaller percentage for future use. All told, the DANCING-OASIS collection effort gathered almost sixty billion internet records during a one-month span beginning in 2012, the last period for which leaked data is available.[59] The staggering number—which has likely only grown as wiretapping has advanced and internet usage has increased—suggests the power of passive collection.

"Just Plain Awesome!"

Surveying the landscape of passive collection and corporate access, one Five Eyes staff member bluntly summed it up: "our ability to pull bits out of random places of the Internet, bring them back to the mother-base to evaluate and build intelligence off of is just plain awesome!"[60] The statement's first half speaks to the power of the signals intelligence apparatus to collect a wide variety of information, but its second half hints at another important truth: data only becomes intelligence once it is evaluated and analyzed. Just as prospectors panning for gold must make sense of what they find in order to profit, so too must analysts sort through, identify, and understand the information they have acquired. The Five Eyes have developed some ingenious tools to do this.

Once the prospector has plunged a scoop into an area of interest, the first goal is to figure out what is in the pan. The global mass of internet users can be hard to differentiate, especially when collection is imperfect. Many look alike. But the NSA is not the only party interested in cataloging them; advertisers are, too. To provide better targeting to marketers, ad-serving platforms like Google carefully track what their users do online by placing small files called cookies onto their computers. When users move from one website to the next, the cookies help identify them. As a user interacts with multiple sites, the NSA can intercept the cookie information as it is transmitted, enabling it to track that user just as Google does.[61] This kind of tracking can help sidestep some internet anonymization tools.[62]

The NSA also piggybacks on the tracking efforts of a variety of mobile app developers, further helping to identify the same users as they appear again and again.[63]

The second goal is to figure out which potential gold dust is worth a second look and which can safely be ignored. GCHQ devised an analysis program called KARMA POLICE, a name that might have been borrowed from a Radiohead song with the refrain "This is what you'll get when you mess with us." KARMA POLICE tries to evaluate "every visible user on the internet," sifting through the wealth of collected information to let GCHQ analysts study potential new targets of interest and where they go online. In addition, when investigators find a web site of interest, KARMA POLICE aims to identify and catalog all of the site's visitors. If the agency knows a particular site is suspicious—perhaps it is a forum frequented by terrorists or a server used by a foreign intelligence service for relaying secret instructions—passive collection and KARMA POLICE can help determine who is visiting the site.[64] Where there is gold dust, there may be a gold mine.

The third goal is to understand what has been found, building a picture of where it has come from and what its value may be. One tool, sometimes known as "the NSA's Google," but officially called XKEYSCORE, helps with this.[65] XKEYSCORE categorizes collected information for easier investigation. For example, it separates intercepted attachments in Gmail from intercepted instant message chats. It also fingerprints the intercepted communications based on language, the encryption used, and other factors, with more than ten thousand possible categorizations in all.[66] Using these categories and other search terms, analysts can ask XKEYSCORE for intelligence on specific foreign targets or types of targets.[67] If, for instance, the NSA has obtained the email address of a foreign party, analysts can query XKEYSCORE for all the available collected data associated with that address, and thereby gain insight into a geopolitical competitor.[68] XKEYSCORE can also provide proactive alerts to analysts about what targets are doing online.[69]

But the analysis can extend offline, too. One relevant Five Eyes program, ROYAL CONCIERGE, replete with a crown-wearing and scepter-carrying penguin for its logo, extracts hotel reservation confirmations from emails collected by the signals intelligence apparatus. Analysts use it to track the travels of foreign diplomats and other targets, enabling intelligence agencies to position additional electronic and human intelligence gathering capabilities in advance if needed.[70] In this way, cyber espionage can beget physical espionage.

The fourth goal is to extract the gold. For the Five Eyes, sometimes this involves hacking the target, which can provide information and access even beyond what passive collection and corporate partnerships offer. To deliver malicious code to the target's computer, the Five Eyes use a suite of tools known as QUANTUM, which depends on the Five Eyes' partnership with telecommunications companies. With these companies' access, QUANTUM can detect when one of the Five Eyes' targets is making an ordinary internet request to a common site, such as LinkedIn. The system then responds more quickly than the legitimate web server and impersonates it. In addition to delivering the desired web site, though, it also delivers malicious code tailored to the vulnerabilities of the target's browser. The technique has a success rate of over 50 percent when impersonating LinkedIn, according to the NSA; as a result, QUANTUM has become one of the most important mechanisms in the NSA's hacking arsenal.[71]

An even easier method of gaining additional access to users' systems is to make copies of their passwords as they log into servers, routers, and other important machines. Provided the Five Eyes can break the encryption that protects these credentials, hackers can use the usernames and passwords to get access to the target machines and accounts. Training slides show how XKEYSCORE can be queried to return every email password for government users in Iran that the NSA can find. Another slide appears to show how password theft and guessing enabled access to the Iraqi Ministry of Finance. Still other slides show how analysts use XKEYSCORE to find intercepted passwords for terrorist web forums and Chinese mail servers.[72]

Sometimes, these operations turn deadly. As of 2008, NSA files claim that "over 300 terrorists [were] captured using intelligence from XKEYSCORE."[73] These targets in many cases communicated through internet links or companies that the NSA could access. The content of their messages helped the Five Eyes better track and find them. So, too, did the existence of the communications themselves, which analysts call metadata—who is talking to whom, from where, and so on. With enough intercepted metadata, analysts can assemble a detailed picture of members of a terrorist group, enabling the targeting of drone strikes or commando raids. As Michael Hayden, the former director of the NSA and CIA, noted, "We kill people based on metadata."[74]

Whatever the goal, this combination of passive collection and corporate access plus massive storage and rich analytical tools gives intelligence analysts a lot of power. When they develop new questions, the signals intelligence system can provide answers. Analysts tracking foreign hackers can better observe the command and control infrastructure they employ and the hacking tools they use.[75] Analysts with a focus on a particular country can gather large hauls of emails flowing out of its presidential palace or defense ministry.

And those supporting military activities can quietly keep an eye on an enemy's communications or watch for a neutral state's spies sending reports back home.

The shaping value of these cyber operations is unmistakable, but these tools and capabilities all require secrecy. Passive collection and corporate access are not useful for signaling, since revealing the capability diminishes it. This is as true now as it was in 1917, when the British carefully used the fruits of their cable-tapping program without revealing its existence. States will adapt if they learn their adversaries' collection mechanisms. One of the most common criticisms of the Snowden leaks is that they revealed the extent of the NSA's passive collection and corporate access programs, alerting America's enemies and causing them to change their behavior.[76] It is likely that adversaries take more care now to avoid American cables and companies, although evasion remains difficult and there will always be some careless targets.

But target adaptation is not the only hurdle that increasingly stands in the way of much of the Five Eyes' collection efforts. All targets, from the cautious to the careless, are protected more and more from prying eyes by one thing: math.

2

Defeating Encryption

ON DECEMBER 2, 2015, husband and wife Syed Rizwan Farook and Tashfeen Malik entered the holiday party for the San Bernardino County Department of Health, where Farook had worked for the past year, carrying firearms and pipe bombs. The couple killed fourteen people and wounded twenty-two more before fleeing in an SUV. Four hours later, they died in a shootout with police, ending what was at the time the deadliest terrorist attack on United States soil since September 11, 2001.[1]

The urgent investigation that followed attracted widespread attention. Farook and Malik had destroyed their electronic devices before the attack, but one phone had survived intact: the iPhone 5C that San Bernardino County, Farook's employer, had issued to him for work use. The FBI wanted to access the contents of the device to determine if they would point to any other members of a terrorist cell or shed light on foreign sources of radicalization. Yet the bureau made a key mistake in the immediate aftermath of the shooting: they tried to force a password reset of Farook's iCloud account. This move locked the account, eliminating access to backups and seemingly leaving the government with no choice but to try to get data off the locked phone itself.[2]

But Farook's iPhone, like all iPhones, had a layer of cryptography that secured its data from unauthorized access. Cryptography, Greek for "secret writing," is used to communicate or store information such that, even if an eavesdropper accesses it in full, the content will remain meaningless to all but the intended party. Encryption is the art and science of transforming readable information into an indecipherable form; decryption is the process of reverting it to comprehensibility, either as the intended party or as an eavesdropper. This sort of selective protection seems magical, but it is only mathematical.

As a result of Apple's encryption, unlocking Farook's phone required either knowing his passcode or hacking the device. Neither option looked promising, according to the United States government. Farook was dead and no one else seemed to know his passcode. The FBI said that it lacked the capability to hack the phone. The Department of Justice demanded that Apple create the software to remove the encryption and provide access to Farook's data.

Apple refused. Even if the company could hack the phone and bypass the cryptographic protections, it said, to do so would be irresponsible and dangerous. The same kind of encryption that secured Farook's phone also protected hundreds of millions of phones all over the world. If Apple devised encryption-bypassing software for the FBI and it fell into the hands of foreign hackers, the hackers could use it to target anyone with the same model of iPhone. Instead, Apple thought it was better to make encryption as strong as possible so that everyone would be more secure—even if it meant that the FBI could not get access to a dead terrorist's data.

This was not the first time this debate had raged. The United States government had been worried about what encryption might do to its investigative capabilities for several decades before the San Bernardino shooting. Cryptography poses an obvious threat to espionage and some law enforcement efforts. It reduces intercepted communications to gibberish, preserving the secrets within. Wiretaps can intercept vast quantities of data by functioning at an enormous scale, but advanced encryption can match them bit for bit, securing the true contents of messages from even court-authorized prying eyes. Seizing the device of a suspect can bring investigators tantalizingly close to the next clue, but encryption can leave them stymied.

The San Bernardino case was an opportunity for the bureau to take a stand and establish a favorable precedent. With fourteen dead Americans, winning the support of the public seemed easy. This is perhaps why the FBI does not appear to have tried all of its options for hacking the phone and instead viewed the case, in the words of one senior FBI official, as the "poster child" that could be used to force a change in encryption policies.[3] The two sides prepared for a legal showdown over Apple's refusal.

Perhaps surprisingly, Apple came out better in the national debate that followed. The value of the phone's data seemed minimal, as it was unlikely that there would be much useful information on Farook's work device. Cryptographers weighed in en masse, warning about the dangers of trying to weaken encryption—a theme they had emphasized in policy debates for decades.[4] Perhaps most amazing of all was how popular culture turned against the FBI and toward Apple; John Oliver's HBO show *Last Week Tonight* ran a lengthy segment explaining the cybersecurity benefits of Apple's position.[5]

On the eve of the court battle, the FBI backed down. It withdrew its demand that Apple hack its own products. Instead, the bureau said, it had employed another company to find a weakness in the iPhone 5C, bypassing the encryption and providing access to Farook's data.[6] Further investigation later showed that there was nothing of interest on the phone.[7] The public moved on, though law enforcement and the intelligence community continued to emphasize how much of a threat encryption posed.

The San Bernardino case was hardly the first time that cryptography has mattered to national security. Leaders and governments have always tried to guard their secrets. Julius Caesar used a simple substitution cipher, consistently replacing each letter with another letter, always the same alphabetical distance away. In a simple Caesarian cipher, this distance serves as a key, since it is the vital bit of knowledge that enables decryption and unlocks the true message. If, for example, this key is positive four, every A in the original message becomes an E in the encrypted version and every B becomes an F. The American Founding Fathers used encryption to protect their communications from post office workers they suspected were loyal to Britain. Thomas Jefferson even invented a series of discs to make the letter substitution process easier and more elaborate. The United States military later independently discovered Jefferson's system and used a variant of it for decades.[8]

In the twentieth century, cryptography continued to shape world events. Indeed, the British success with the Zimmerman telegram described in Chapter 1 was possible only because, during World War I, the Germans were so confident in their encryption that they sent the telegram over a widely used cable. After the British intercepted the message, an elite unit of the Admiralty known as Room 40 broke the code with several weeks of effort. It was British mathematical skill that revealed the Germans' geopolitically explosive secrets for all the world to see.[9]

During World War II, code-breaking and code-making took a central place in the military struggle. The Nazis deployed the most famous encryption mechanism in history: Enigma. Its whirring rotors and complex mathematics yielded 158 million million million possible keys and obscured the true meaning of intercepted German communications. After an extensive effort involving some of the world's most impressive mathematicians and the forerunners to today's computers, the Allies broke Enigma's codes. Their triumph was one of the most significant signals intelligence successes in history, so important that then-General Dwight Eisenhower called it "decisive" in the overall Allied victory.[10]

The Allies' own mechanism for encrypting messages was called SIGABA. American forces guarded SIGABA machines with extreme caution, taking care to destroy the devices when endangered, all to ensure that the Nazis would never capture one. Through the careful protection of the military and the strength of the underlying mathematics, SIGABA survived the war unbroken and American communications remained secure. While the Allies were able to gain enormous insight into German military thinking and planning, better positioning their own forces and saving countless lives as a result, the Nazis remained in the dark.

This stark difference in outcomes highlights how clearly the intelligence battle lines were drawn. The Allies had to secure SIGABA and crack Enigma while the Nazis had to secure Enigma and crack SIGABA. There was no overlap between the users of the encryption systems. The mission for both sides was unmistakably clear, even as it remained very difficult. This was typical; such a clear distinction between signals intelligence offense and signals intelligence defense had been the status quo for millennia.

But the San Bernardino case shows that the modern era is different. Whereas cryptography was once the domain of only governments and high-profile targets, in the internet age it is omnipresent.

With the dawn of widespread digital communications and the security risks that accompany them, major technology companies deploy cryptography on their software platforms by default. They rely on ever-faster computers to create more complex and more secure codes. Internet users and cell phone owners, including many in government, depend on their devices every day, but most have no idea that math keeps them safe. While militaries and intelligence agencies might at times use their own proprietary cryptographic protocols, a small number of encryption algorithms handle the security for everyone else.

This cryptographic convergence has its benefits. Online financial transactions are possible only because of the mathematical protections that reduce the risk of identity theft. Just one encryption system, AES, provided more than $250 billion of economic growth over a twenty-year period and helped secure top-secret United States government data.[11] Newer and even stronger algorithms continue to protect the communications and devices of untold numbers of American citizens and officials every day.

But cryptographic convergence poses a problem, too: most of the time, the math works either for everyone or for no one. The same AES system that secured top-secret data was widely available for anyone to use. The same encryption that secures the iPhones of citizens all over the United States also secures the iPhones of terrorists and intelligence targets. This ubiquitous encryption reduces to nonsense many of the communications that law enforcement and the intelligence community intercept. Whereas weakening Enigma did nothing to endanger SIGABA's codes, to weaken modern encryption for one target risks weakening it for all, including one's own side. Signals intelligence has become much messier than it used to be.

Savvy foreign intelligence targets almost always secure their communications with some form of encryption. If the NSA wants to be able to read the Chinese or Russian secrets it has acquired through its passive collection program, the agency first has to defeat the math that protects those intercepted communications from prying eyes. Only after this is done can analysts determine what the adversary knows and thinks. The same is true for thwarting terrorist plots. Though terrorists are far less adept than foreign intelligence officers at deploying strong encryption, default mathematical protections can obscure vital details of interest to the American intelligence community.

Signals intelligence agencies thus need to be able to defeat or bypass encryption, a fact they recognized long before the San Bernardino case. In 1996, a House Intelligence Committee study noted that clandestine human capabilities would be necessary to break encryption and support signals intelligence collection. The committee argued that compromising cryptographic systems might be the "greatest contribution" a clandestine service could make.[12] In a 2007 document, the NSA concluded that developing a robust crypto-busting capability was the "price of admission for the US to maintain unrestricted access to and use of cyberspace."[13] The government subsequently prioritized the need to "counter the challenge of ubiquitous, strong, commercial network encryption."[14]

The United States intelligence community uses its computational power, hacking capabilities, signals intelligence programs, and commercial relationships to achieve this goal; this chapter discusses the first three of those elements, while Chapter 3 discusses the last one.[15] The NSA makes these efforts because it believes they are essential to modern statecraft. Thwarting encryption is, just as it was for the British in 1917 or the Allies in World War II, sometimes the difference between victory and defeat.

Nobody But Us

To manage the problems posed by cryptography's convergence, the NSA settled on an approach that is often informally referred to as "Nobody But Us," or NOBUS (unlike the other all-caps terms the agency uses, this is not a code-name for a secret program, but just an acronym for a phrase).[16] Originally, the idea behind the term was that there were mathematical ways to ensure that only the United States could use certain espionage capabilities. In current usage, though, it often refers to a more general policy goal: when there is tension between the offensive and defensive missions—perhaps because both targets and citizens use the same kinds of encryption—the NSA tries to secure communications against all forms of eavesdropper decryption except those decryption capabilities that are so complex, difficult, or inaccessible that only the NSA can use them. In other words, if the NSA is the world's best high-jumper, then the agency wants to set the bar just an inch above where its competitors can jump but low enough that it can still clear it. Achieving this goal requires solid intelligence and careful risk calibration, especially when it comes to understanding adversary capabilities.[17]

The NOBUS discussion also suggests the tremendous technical capabilities that the agency can wield. In its classified black budget requests, the NSA has placed a priority on "investing in groundbreaking cryptanalytic capabilities to defeat adversarial cryptography and exploit internet traffic."[18] One of the top-secret efforts to achieve this goal was code-named BULLRUN, and was described by a 2010 NSA briefing as "aggressive" and "multi-pronged," costing around a quarter of a billion dollars per year.[19] The name BULLRUN, a reference to the famous battlefield in the United States Civil War, hints at some of the inherent tensions in the code-breaking effort, including that BULLRUN undermines cryptographic systems built and used by Americans. The United Kingdom's counterpart program, called EDGEHILL, derives its name from a battle in the English Civil War and suggests the same sort of internal tension.[20]

The computational power and mathematical skill the NSA wields in its decryption program contribute to some NOBUS capabilities. For example, internet users rely every day on a vital encryption mechanism called Diffie-Hellman key exchange, which is an example of a technology called public key encryption. Diffie-Hellman provides a way for users' devices to agree on a cryptographic key that no one else can use to decode communications between them. Conceptually, this is similar to how the two people using a Caesarian cipher must agree on a key distance to shift the letters of their message, though Diffie-Hellman is much more complicated. Unlike the Caesarian cipher, even if an eavesdropper intercepts the shared key, the messages encrypted with the key will remain protected; this protection is achieved by splitting the key into multiple mathematical components, some of which are never transmitted.

The underlying mathematics of public key encryption are complex. It suffices to say that the technique represents a conceptual breakthrough and a massive improvement over previous methods of encryption, which required keys to be prearranged and failed when the keys were intercepted. Diffie-Hellman and technologies like it enable secure and easy communication between two individuals who have never interacted before, such as an online seller and buyer. It is no exaggeration to say that this sort of public key technology is fundamental to making modern digital communications work.

But even though the Diffie-Hellman system appears secure in its complex mathematical design, it can have fatal weaknesses in its practical use. To work, Diffie-Hellman requires that the sender and receiver of a message agree to use a gigantic prime number with a particular mathematical form as they establish their secure communication. Theoretically, it is not a major problem if many implementations of Diffie-Hellman use similar prime numbers, but in practice it creates an opportunity for eavesdropping by large and advanced agencies like the NSA. An eavesdropper with enormous supercomputing power could use brute force to, in the parlance of cryptographers, "crack" a group of prime numbers that many Diffie-Hellman key exchanges use. By guessing again and again at top computational speed, the agency can eventually get the key.

If the NSA successfully cracked such a group of primes, it would then be a lot closer to breaking all the encryption that relied on primes in that group. Estimates from one group of computer scientists indicate that successfully cracking one group would enable an eavesdropper to decrypt data sent and received by two-thirds of a popular kind of Virtual Private Network used to secure online communications all over the globe, though other computer scientists estimate that the number of vulnerable systems is lower. Successfully cracking another group would enable the decryption of one-fifth of the world's secure internet traffic.[21] Just as the math of cryptographers can protect secrets, better math on the part of eavesdroppers can strip those protections away to decode the meaning of intercepted communications.

The NSA is one of a fairly small number of organizations that possess the computational power and mathematical skill required to achieve such a feat. Estimates indicate that building a computer capable of cracking one Diffie-Hellman prime per year would cost around $250,000, a small fraction of the NSA's more than $10 billion annual budget.[22] The agency is also the United States' largest employer of mathematicians.[23] While it is unclear how successful this decryption program might be in practice, prominent computer scientists who have studied the NSA's capabilities consider it likely that the agency uses its resources to target Diffie-Hellman through this kind of brute force. The NSA prioritizes collecting the type of information that would enable such an effort.[24]

Former NSA Director Michael Hayden seemed to confirm the possibility to the *Washington Post*. By targeting cryptography using mathematical skill and computing power, he noted, the NSA could strike an effective balance between its offensive and defensive missions. Other states without the same kinds of prowess were unlikely to be able to keep up and target encryption in the same way. When a vulnerability is known to exist, Hayden said, "you look at a vulnerability through a different lens if . . . it requires substantial computational power or substantial other attributes" to exploit. If the bar is high, the agency will size up its competitors.

In such a case, Hayden continued, the NSA has "to make the judgment who else can do this? If there's a vulnerability here that weakens encryption but you still need four acres of Cray [super]computers in the basement in order to work it you kind of think 'NOBUS' and that's a vulnerability we are not ethically or legally compelled to try to patch—it's one that ethically and legally we could try to exploit in order to keep Americans safe from others."[25] In other words, if only the NSA and its unique computational abilities could clear the bar, the agency could keep exploiting the vulnerability. But while a supercomputer-enabled mathematical assault is one of the pieces of the BULLRUN cryptography-breaking effort, it is far from the only one.

Defeating Cellular Encryption

The GSM Association is one of the most important organizations that most people have never heard of.[26] A London-based trade group of phone companies, it counts among its members more than 750 mobile network operators from 220 countries, including major American and European firms. Among other tasks, the group handles the design, interoperability, and functioning of the world's cell phone networks. Without its standards, roaming and international calls would be much more difficult. The group needs to make sure not just that phones from around the world can talk to one another, but that they can do so securely.

Encryption, at least in theory, provides this needed security. To stop eavesdroppers from intercepting cellular communications as they travel through the air, phones and tablets often encrypt their messages before relaying them to nearby cell towers. But, because ever-faster code-cracking computers keep increasing eavesdroppers' abilities to decrypt intercepted communications, experts like those working at GSM and other standards-setting organizations must constantly devise new ways to stay ahead.

Contemporary cryptography has by necessity grown much more complicated and counterintuitive. Designing a new, modern cryptographic system is a little like designing a next-generation jet. It requires an enormous amount of complex work, the perspectives of a wide range of specialists, and many consultations to agree on important principles and details. The process can take more than a decade, with individual components requiring years of their own.

As a result, setting modern cellular standards is time-consuming and laborious. Members of the GSM Association routinely share obscure technical documents with one another as they develop and implement these specifications. The documents contain a great deal of proprietary information about the members' mobile phone networks, including details on technical architecture, cell phone roaming, compatibility between networks, and more. They also contain insight into the encryption implementations the companies will deploy in the future. In short, these files contain the sort of granular information seemingly of interest only to technical experts who make the telecommunications networks function.

But another group cares about these documents, too: the spies interested in tapping the world's phone and data networks. The technical files provide a roadmap to the digital terrain on which the NSA and others will in the future carry out cyber operations. By understanding how the landscape is changing and what is coming next, especially in terms of encryption and security upgrades, the agency can better prepare to develop and deploy decryption capabilities—ideally ones that are NOBUS in nature. For this reason, the NSA calls these documents "technology warning mechanism[s]" and spies on groups like the GSM Association to get them.[27]

The NSA uses a secretive unit, the Target Technology Trends Center, to do this. The unit's logo, a giant telescope superimposed on a globe, and its motto—"Predict, Plan, Prevent"—give a sense of its mission: to make sure the agency is not rendered blind by the network operators' security upgrades and advances. The mobile communications experts and analysts in the unit spy on phone companies all over the world to ensure that future collection remains unimpeded.[28]

The Target Technology Trends Center builds and maintains a database of mobile phone operators. As of 2012, the database included around seven hundred companies, about 70 percent of the world's total.[29] The group focuses on gathering information that the agency can use to defeat security mechanisms and gain access to cellular calls, messages, and data.[30] The NSA maintains a list of around twelve hundred email addresses associated with employees at mobile phone operators around the world.[31] Using its signals intelligence methods—almost certainly including passive collection—the NSA makes its own surreptitious copy of some of the information sent to and from these addresses. It uses these intercepted technical documents to anticipate what sorts of encryption its targets will use in the future, and to find vulnerabilities in those systems so that it can eavesdrop as needed.[32]

As a result of these and other efforts, the NSA and its partners can crack a great deal of the encryption that protects cellular communications. In an effort that one NSA file described as "a very high priority," the agency devised mechanisms to break the security on 4G cell phone systems several years before those systems were actually in widespread use by mobile phone customers.[33] Prior to that, the Five Eyes used specialized computers and invested millions of dollars to successfully break the encryption used in 3G cell phone networks.[34] They also broke the most widely-used encryption system in the world, called A5/1, which protects billions of phones in the developing world.[35]

But sometimes it is not practical even for the Five Eyes to break the cryptography by finding mathematical weaknesses. In these cases, there is another option: impersonating the legitimate recipient by stealing the key that enables decryption. In the case of cell networks, this is the secret information baked into cell phones' SIM cards.[36] A large Dutch firm called Gemalto produces these small cards by the billions, each with its own unique encryption key. The company contracts with more than 450 mobile phone operators all over the world, including all the major American companies, providing them with SIM cards and, at least in theory, improved security.

The mechanism through which Gemalto's system works is called symmetric key encryption. With symmetric key encryption, the two sides agree on a key in advance. In this respect, symmetric key encryption is somewhat akin to a pitcher and catcher arranging signs before a baseball game. Gemalto determines this pre-shared key, puts one copy of the secret key in the SIM card, and sends another copy to the mobile operator.[37] With one reproduction of the key on each end of the communication, it thus becomes possible to encrypt and decrypt communications while leaving the messages secure against passive collection in transit. The eavesdroppers in the middle who lack the key cannot figure out what is being said.

In baseball, a batter who has figured out the key—which pitch corresponds to which sign—can intercept and decrypt the catcher's codes. He or she will know which pitch is coming next and will stand a much better chance of hitting it. The same holds true for symmetric key encryption. If a signals intelligence agency can get a copy of the secret key in symmetric key encryption, it can decrypt communications.

Through a sophisticated, multistage hacking effort, GCHQ gained access to millions of keys that Gemalto produced and shared with some of its wide range of mobile phone company clients, particularly those in developing countries.[38] This gave the agency the code-breaking edge it desired. Many targets might have used the cell networks assuming that encryption secured their communications, but the GCHQ program enabled analysts to sidestep these protections.

One analysis suggests that the SIM card hack might have been most useful in tactical military or counterterrorism environments, perhaps enabling the agency to acquire insight into adversaries' activities and quickly share the information with those who could act on it.[39] In an internal status report, the agency described the result of its key theft triumph in language that was bureaucratic yet hinted at the scale and success of the mission: analysts were "very happy with the data so far and working through the vast quantity of product."[40]

Cable Taps and a Smiley Face

From 2011 to 2014, John Napier Tye was the section chief for internet freedom in the State Department's Bureau of Democracy, Human Rights, and Labor. In March 2014, he wrote a speech for his boss to deliver at an upcoming human rights conference. Tye, a Rhodes Scholar and Yale Law graduate, wanted to emphasize the importance of checks and balances in the American system when it came to surveillance. "If U.S. citizens disagree with congressional and executive branch determinations about the proper scope of signals intelligence activities," he wrote, "they have the opportunity to change the policy through our democratic process." It seemed like a boilerplate, feel-good statement, one designed to respond to criticisms of NSA overreach.

But the White House legal office disagreed. The lawyers called Tye and instructed him to change the line. Instead of stating specifically that the practices of the intelligence community were subject to democratic process, they wanted him to make only a broad reference to how American citizens could change laws. He was not to mention Americans' power to change intelligence activities.[41] At the White House's insistence, Tye changed the phrasing.

To most people, this distinction might seem meaningless. But Tye drew an alarming conclusion from the White House's modifications: some American intelligence activities were beyond the reach of citizens' democratic process. As Tye knew, intelligence agencies' overseas activities against foreign targets are most closely governed by a presidential executive order signed by Ronald Reagan, known as EO 12333, and updated several times since. EO 12333 gives the NSA and other intelligence agencies a much freer hand in their overseas programs than they have on American soil.

Historically, EO 12333's clear foreign versus domestic distinction might have made some sense. In the Reagan years, comparatively fewer pieces of data on Americans ended up overseas. In the internet age, however, the world's digital networks are bound ever more closely together, and the lines between foreign and domestic activities become blurrier. Just as foreign-to-foreign traffic travels through the United States, enabling the NSA to passively collect other countries' data from American hubs and cables, so too does the data of Americans travel through other countries.

Major technology companies routinely back up and mirror information in data centers all across the world, both for redundancy and to ensure the fastest possible retrieval of the information when needed. When an American's data resides in a foreign data center or travels along a foreign cable, the privacy protections that restrict the United States government from collecting the data diminish, so long as the government is not directly targeting Americans. Intelligence agencies have partially classified guidelines that stipulate how they interpret this condition.[42]

Long before Snowden's leaks and Tye's amended draft, technology companies took some steps to try to protect this data overseas. Google and Yahoo encrypted users' connections to their sites, blocking eavesdroppers who could not break the encryption. This might have posed a problem for the NSA, especially if BULLRUN's encryption-busting tools could not work against the technology companies' systems.

If the NSA wanted the data and could not decrypt it, it had several options. The agency could, under its interpretation of the authority of the Foreign Intelligence Surveillance Act, use the PRISM program described in Chapter 1 to compel American companies to turn over the desired information about their users. But, as previously discussed, this was a program that operated on American soil under at least some oversight and constraint. Under the law, the agency's target had to be foreign and fit into one of the broad categories of permissible intelligence collection.

So the Five Eyes instead found a different way to get the information they wanted. They targeted the series of fiber-optic links that Google and Yahoo had built to connect their data centers outside American borders. These private cables gave the companies the capacity to move information quickly and securely—they thought—between different parts of their expansive digital infrastructure. These were the cables and centers that made the cloud possible.

Google protected its data centers very carefully, with round-the-clock guards, heat-sensitive cameras, and biometric authentication of employees.[43] But because the connections were privately owned and only between data centers, Google and other companies had not prioritized encrypting the communications that flowed through the cables. Google had planned to do so, even before the Snowden revelations, but the project had moved slowly.[44] This delay left large amounts of users' data unencrypted; getting access to these cables would be almost as good as getting into the heavily protected data centers themselves.

Like a quarterback drawing up a play in the dirt, someone at the NSA hand-diagrammed the plan for targeting the technology companies and copied it onto a slide. The image showed the unencrypted links between data centers that the Five Eyes would target. Near the text highlighting the unencrypted areas, the artist had included a mocking smiley face.[45] Through their telecommunications partners, the NSA and GCHQ gained access to the cables. The agencies then reverse-engineered the targeted companies' internal data formats, a technically complex task. They then built their own custom tools, just as if they worked for the firms, so that they could make sense of their massive new trove of data.

And what a trove it was. As with other passive collection programs, this one yielded too much data for the Five Eyes to handle. Even after filtering the fire-hose spray of data for the most useful information, the flow was still a torrent. In just a thirty-day period, the NSA collected and sent back to headquarters almost two hundred million records of internet activities, including website visits, records of emails and messages sent and received, and copies of text, audio, and video content.[46] It was an immense haul made possible by the interconnected global architecture of technology firms and the agency's secret access to their cables.

Much of this data was from foreigners. But other data was from Americans whose information had ended up overseas thanks to the complexity of the technology companies' clouds. In the parlance of the NSA, this data on Americans was "incidentally collected." Even though the data was American in origin, because the NSA had incidentally collected it overseas under EO 12333, the agency could hang onto it for five years with certain restrictions, and sometimes longer.

When the Snowden leaks revealed the NSA's tapping of private cables, Google and Yahoo were apoplectic. To Silicon Valley, it appeared that the NSA had used a legal loophole to do an end run around oversight. It seemed as if the NSA had hacked American companies either to gather data on Americans or to gather data on foreign targets that the agency could have collected, with more oversight and accountability, through the PRISM program. Google Chairman Eric Schmidt said the company was "annoyed to no end" about what the Five Eyes had done.[47]

Google engineers were more direct. When the *Washington Post* showed two Google-affiliated engineers the NSA's smiley-face diagram, they "exploded in profanity."[48] Another wrote an online post condemning the Five Eyes operation and expressing his sentiments plainly: "Fuck these guys."[49] Google and other firms had built their security systems to try to keep out Chinese and Russian hackers, and many considered the United States government a partner, even if that partnership was legally compelled. Finding out that the Five Eyes targeted them and bypassed their encryption felt like a betrayal to their engineers.

Even government employees were concerned by the activities conducted under EO 12333. After his speechwriting experiences, Tye came to believe that the United States intelligence community was using the workaround provided by EO 12333 to authorize vast collection programs that existed almost entirely outside of congressional and judicial oversight. After eventually leaving government, he strongly suggested in a *Washington Post* editorial that Americans should be concerned about the impact on their privacy.[50] But, unlike Snowden, he leaked no classified information to support his warnings about the government's abuse of EO 12333.

The post-Snowden signals intelligence review commission was similarly alarmed, and recommended reform.[51] As part of new legislation authorizing intelligence activities in 2015, some overseas collection procedures were amended and codified, though the NSA retained a great deal of flexibility. Regarding data incidentally collected on Americans, the law authorizes the NSA to retain it for five years, and also includes a broad exception allowing data to be held longer if the agency determines it is "necessary to understand or assess foreign intelligence or counterintelligence."[52]

Within the NSA's broader effort to gain unencumbered access to the world's data flows, its EO 12333 operations made a direct contribution to success. Though encryption would always pose a threat, the Five Eyes' efforts were actively defeating it and preserving the power of global espionage. An internal Five Eyes document boasted that, thanks to the multi-pronged efforts, "vast amounts of encrypted Internet data which have up till now been discarded are now exploitable."[53]

Defeating encryption like this required complete secrecy. There was no value for the alliance in signaling or posturing about its decryption capabilities. To do so would cause adversaries to change their tactics, perhaps by avoiding the encryption mechanisms the Western spies could crack or circumvent. Even within the Five Eyes, where almost every significant employee had a security clearance, guidelines instructed those who were not working on the cryptologic capabilities not to speculate or ask about how those capabilities worked.[54]

As long as the decryption capabilities were still hidden, times were good. The Five Eyes' intelligence targets all over the world knew enough to use computers, but did not know how to secure them. Whether operating against countries like Russia or China or terrorist groups like al Qaeda, the NSA had the capacity to uncover meaningful secrets and bring them to US government policymakers in time to act. While details of these operations are almost entirely hidden from view, their success was so significant that senior officials in the NSA refer to this period, up until 2013 or so, as "the golden age of signals intelligence."[55]

But all golden ages must end. Snowden's revelations exposed the decryption capabilities and put forward a public debate the NSA did not want to have. Others, like Tye and the post-Snowden review commission, lent additional credibility to the concerns about the agency's activities. Even worse, as the NSA grappled with the exposure of its tactics, foreign adversaries lurked, waiting for an opportunity. For as much as the Five Eyes aspired to live in a world of Nobody But Us, they were not alone.

3

Building a Backdoor

ESPIONAGE, LIKE FOOTBALL, IS A GAME OF INCHES. The smallest details can make a world of difference. Selecting the appropriate business cards and accessories for a spy's jacket pocket is essential to maintaining one's cover overseas. Choosing the wrong dead-drop location for a package with stolen documents inside can blow an entire operation. Placing a cable tap in the right spot can unearth a gold mine of intelligence.

It is sometimes hard to notice these little make-or-break features. The art of intelligence and counterintelligence is to identify them in real time, thus uncovering any hallmarks of an adversary's operation or dangerous giveaways of one's own efforts. Luck is always a factor in espionage, but good operators make their own luck by getting the nuances right. During World War II, for example, the Nazis used to airdrop their spies into British territory with British-issue army boots, replica ID cards, and genuine wallets taken off the bodies of dead British soldiers—replete with letters from worried girlfriends. Every detail made the cover more convincing.[1]

The revelations that come from minutiae are especially powerful in cyber operations. Intelligence efforts carried out with great care and at significant expense play out in computer networks all over the world. Close examination of the malicious code employed by signals intelligence agencies and of the commercial products they exploit provides substantial insight into what happens between states in this sometimes-hidden world.

The instructions that make up software are known as source code. This code, which software engineers write in human-readable programming languages like C++, determines what the software does and how it functions. When the source code is ready for use in products, whether those products are espionage tools or commercial security software, it gets converted through a process called compilation into the binary form that computers understand. New versions of software contain newly compiled code. In some cases, companies distribute the new code to customers all over the world through software updates. For a software company, nothing is more important than what is in the source code.

Cybersecurity researchers, like paleontologists, dig through layers of compiled code looking for artifacts. These small details yield a timeline of what happened and when. By reverse-engineering the compiled code and looking at changes, researchers can determine what modifications occurred in the source code; these modifications include official updates and improvements, but also sometimes reveal illicit manipulation of the code. Alternatively, by observing the evolution of hackers' malicious code over time, researchers can understand its purpose and methodology. To a careful observer, digital fossil records reveal the stories that lie within.

Minding P's and Q's

The last chapter showed how the Five Eyes use brute force, key theft, and encryption bypassing to develop NOBUS decryption capabilities. But there is an even more powerful option: intelligence agencies can secretly build deliberate weaknesses into the computer code that makes encryption work. They can craft these weaknesses, which are usually called backdoors, to be subtle enough to avoid detection but exploitable enough to be broadly useful.

The geopolitical payoff of a successful backdoor can be huge. Targets use encryption to secure their communications as a matter of routine. Military strategists use it to outline their contingency plans heading into a conflict. Diplomats use it to debate their negotiating positions before international summits. Companies use it to protect their trade secrets and strategic priorities. Intelligence agencies use it to share what they know with those they trust. All have faith that the math of their preferred encryption system is keeping their messages safe.

But an illicit backdoor can strip that mathematical armor away. If the encryption system trusted by so many is in fact insecure by design, an intelligence agency that knows of the flaws can once more uncover information that their targets most want to secure. The backdoor can turn a trusted system into a single point of failure, exposing all that the system protects. As long as no one else can use the backdoor, it remains a NOBUS capability—powerful but hidden.

Just as the United States holds a home-field advantage, thanks to geography and history, in passive collection, it also enjoys a natural edge when it comes to backdooring encryption. Much of the world's cryptography is American-made, and NSA files indicate that the agency attempts "to leverage sensitive, co-operative relationships with specific industry partners." It uses these relationships to gather "cryptographic details of commercial cryptographic information security systems" and to alter the systems in ways that benefit the agency. These modifications introduce weaknesses into the companies' products with the aim "to make them exploitable" by the NSA's cryptographers.[2]

When the agency cannot rely on a partnership, it tries to introduce weaknesses covertly.[3] The right flaw in the right spot can offer dramatic geopolitical advantage; just a single tainted encrypted component, endowed with a backdoor known only to its creators, can render entire systems of encryption insecure. Even without having significant mathematical knowledge, it is possible to understand how the backdoor process works, at least at a simplified level.[4]

Randomness, or at least the illusion of it, is fundamental to encryption. In the simple Caesarian cipher described at the beginning of Chapter 2, the sender and receiver of the message need to agree on a key: how many places to shift the letters. If this key is predictable, it is easy for an eavesdropper to figure it out through mathematics, or even just guess what it is, and then break the code. Cryptographers therefore employ randomness in choosing encryption keys and in many other processes. In short, eavesdroppers use patterns to break codes, and randomness breaks patterns. If an eavesdropper can crack a particular encryption mechanism's foundation of randomness, all the math that cryptographers have built on top will also tumble.

But where does this randomness come from? While creating perfect randomness is difficult, cryptographers have long hunted for sources of information with few predictable patterns. During World War II, British codemakers used to hang a microphone outside their office on London's busy Oxford Street. In their search for randomness, they used the cacophony of any given moment. The street's assortment of erratic noises, from car honks to conversations to sirens and beyond, was random enough, since no one could guess exactly what sounds would be heard. The recordings were then converted to a mathematical form and used as a source of randomness in codes.[5] In the modern era, one major internet company uses continuous video of a wall of one hundred lava lamps to generate random inputs for its encryption mechanisms.[6]

But true randomness is not always required. Often, cryptographers settle for what they call pseudorandomness, which is not truly random but functions in key respects as if it were. This is where a type of software known as a pseudorandom number generator comes in. Pseudorandom number generators take a single random starting point and then continually devise a series of numbers that appear random but are actually derived from the original starting point. Much more complex encryption processes can then rely on this stream of pseudorandom numbers as a basis for security. But there is a danger: if an eavesdropper can consistently predict the numbers that come from a pseudorandom number generator, they can often crack the encryption that depends upon those numbers.

The United States National Institute of Standards and Technology, or NIST, has a vital role in writing technical specifications adopted by the United States government and others around the world. As such, it is an important player in the world of cryptography. In 2004 and 2005, the institute recognized the need for additional pseudorandom number generators that met the criteria for government use.[7] Drawing in part on the NSA's cryptographic expertise, NIST developed a series of four generators. It named one generator, the oddest of the bunch, Dual_EC_DRBG, or Dual_EC for short.

Dual_EC relies on a type of curved line known as an elliptic curve. On this line are two points, which cryptographers call *P* and *Q*. The generator uses these points, along with a seed number that varies by user, to begin the process that eventually produces the output of pseudorandom numbers. Once picked, the two points never change, and so are called constants; this mathematical architecture is unusual in a pseudorandom number generator, but it is not necessarily insecure. When an organization decides to implement Dual_EC, it can pick its own *P* and *Q*. As long it chooses *P* and *Q* randomly, it is nearly impossible to predict the pseudorandom numbers that Dual_EC will generate, even if an eavesdropper knows the values chosen for *P* and *Q*. This is as it should be.

The cryptographers studying the early drafts of Dual_EC, however, found something curious. Unlike most pseudorandom number generators, Dual_EC works in such a way that, under certain circumstances, it can lose its pseudorandomness and become dangerously predictable. This is a failure that risks jeopardizing the secrecy of all the encrypted communications that rely on Dual_EC for pseudorandom number generation.

Three things are required for this backdoor to appear. First, the two starting constants *P* and *Q* need to be chosen deliberately, in a way that is not random. Second, the eavesdropper needs to know the mathematical relationship between the two points, which is not difficult to determine if the eavesdropper already knows that the two points are not random. Third, the eavesdropper needs to intercept a small amount of the pseudorandom numbers generated by Dual_EC to uncover the relevant mathematical patterns.

If these three criteria are met, the eavesdropper can, with a bit of math, determine the future numbers that Dual_EC will generate—and thus can gain the ability to decrypt a target's communications.[8] In other words, there is the possibility to backdoor the pseudorandom number generator and then exploit that backdoor to read others' messages.

At the end of 2005, NIST published a more detailed draft document that defined the specifications for Dual_EC. Academic cryptographers quickly spotted flaws in the draft. They noticed that Dual_EC exhibited small tendencies in its supposedly random numbers, a worrying sign that something was amiss.[9] They also suggested that there might be a backdoor involving the points P and Q. Two other cryptographers found similar irregularities and filed a patent claiming as much.[10] Nonetheless, in 2006, NIST published the finished Dual_EC specifications. Despite the warnings, it did not fix the identified flaws.[11]

The final published document from NIST included a pair of default values for P and Q. Many of the organizations that implemented Dual_EC used these values rather than selecting their own. They assumed that, since the government's experts provided them, the numbers must have been chosen through a process that was suitably random. Yet the NIST specification provides no insight into how its authors determined the P and Q values provided, nor does the specification offer verification that the numbers were the result of a random process. The specification authors simply wrote that P and Q should be "verifiably random" and that organizations should use the P and Q that NIST helpfully offered.[12]

In 2007, two researchers warned of Dual_EC's backdoor in a talk on the sidelines of a cryptography conference.[13] But because their short discussion was informal, complex, and somewhat arcane, it attracted comparatively little attention.[14] Observers struggled to determine if the problem was a backdoor or just, as some thought, "laughably bad" cryptography.[15] Yet the United States government and the International Organization for Standardization, with 163 member countries, incorporated flawed versions of Dual_EC into their standards, ensuring widespread implementation all over the world.

The Snowden leaks, which began several years later, shed more light on Dual_EC's flaws and how they came to be. With the benefit of hindsight and internal documents, the NSA's subtle hand becomes visible throughout Dual_EC's creation and standardization process. Initially, the agency worked to influence the design of the number generator. "Eventually," an in-house memo states, the "NSA became the sole editor" of the Dual_EC specification, and presumably had enough free rein to manipulate the requirements to suit its espionage purposes.[16] It was likely here that the NSA managed to introduce the backdoor and pick faulty default versions of P and Q.[17] If this is the case, the agency fulfilled the first and second requirements for enabling the backdoor: choosing non-random points and knowing the mathematical relationship between them.

But that technical trickery was not by itself enough. The NSA also pushed for the formal adoption of the flawed specification by the United States government and by organizations overseas. Agency documents describe this process as "a challenge in finesse."[18] More importantly, in order for the backdoor to be useful, companies had to use Dual_EC in their products. If they did not, the entire effort was nothing more than an academic mathematical exercise. Fortunately for the NSA, some companies did use the standard. Very few changed the default P and Q to verifiably random constants.[19] Indeed, some organizations' procedures obliged them to employ the government-chosen points and not ones of their own selection. OpenSSL, which protects everyday Web traffic and is one of the largest cryptography projects in the world, was a prominent example.[20]

The NSA also worked in secret with American corporations to encourage them to use Dual_EC. Little is known about this, except for one vivid report from Reuters: the NSA paid $10 million to the cybersecurity company RSA. After reportedly receiving the money, RSA used the Dual_EC system as its default pseudorandom number generator and made a number of odd engineering decisions that appeared to make some of the company's products—including ones designed to protect key systems and networks—more susceptible to NSA decryption.[21] Though the company at first denied working with the NSA, RSA's chief executive later fiercely criticized the agency, saying that it had "exploit[ed] its position of trust," but he did not provide specifics.[22]

A Series of Unfortunate—Or Malicious—Events

RSA was not the only business that would fall, willfully or not, into the Dual_EC trap. In 2008, an American technology company called Juniper Networks decided to add Dual_EC to the new version of ScreenOS, the software that runs many of its security products. These include firewalls, designed to keep hackers out of networks, and Virtual Private Networks, or VPNs. VPNs protect sensitive communications all over the world by encrypting internet traffic between two points in such a way that eavesdroppers cannot understand it unless they can break or bypass the encryption.

Some of the company's big customers are foreign governments, including targets the Five Eyes have in their sights. For example, in Pakistan, Juniper firewalls protect government and military networks, and Juniper routers steer traffic for some of the country's telecommunications companies. Juniper products also serve China's internet. The vendor's VPNs are in widespread use in companies around the globe, with one internal GCHQ document praising them as the "ablest competitor" on the market.[23]

The United States federal government uses many products that rely on ScreenOS, too, including for sensitive organizations that handle personnel records.[24] More generally, the government authorizes Juniper to build cryptographic systems that protect top-secret information.[25] Other Juniper customers are spread throughout nearly every sector of American society; the company's website lists technology companies, telecommunications firms, local governments, universities, consumer-facing businesses, sports teams, data retention specialists, and many other types of clients.[26] Juniper's annual revenue is measured in billions of dollars, much of it coming from within the United States.

Juniper has long known that cybersecurity is vital to its customers. By 2008, ScreenOS had for years used an established pseudorandom number generator, one that was formally called ANSI X.9.31. There was no public indication of any security danger from ANSI and no obvious need for a change, yet Juniper chose to add Dual_EC, an odd and worrying choice. In addition to the concerns about its flaws in reliably choosing pseudorandom numbers and possible backdoors, Dual_EC had a glaring problem: the new generator was very sluggish, about a thousand times slower than its counterparts. Inexplicably, the company did not seek federal government certification that its use of Dual_EC was secure, a practice that would have been expected and would have made it clearer to customers that the company had changed its design.[27] Nothing about the opaque decision to add Dual_EC made sense.

Mathematically, the way the company went about implementing this change was even more bizarre. To start, Juniper used the P point provided in the NIST specification but generated its own Q point. Yet the firm provided no mechanism to verify that it had chosen its new Q point randomly. This absence of proof left open the possibility that Juniper had chosen the point in such a way that would enable it (or the NSA) to decrypt messages. It was thus plausible—and many expert cryptographers say very likely—that Juniper's code intentionally made the backdoor embedded in Dual_EC exploitable by someone who had the requisite insight into the configuration of the system.[28] If the chosen points were not random but deliberately placed to compromise the encryption, anyone who knew of Juniper's Q and its mathematical relationship to P was two-thirds of the way to being able to use the backdoor. To finish the job, they would just need to obtain a certain amount of numbers generated by Dual_EC in practice.

It was here that the already-strange story took another unexpected turn. Juniper did not entirely replace the well-regarded ANSI generator that it had long used. Instead, the company tried to use both the older ANSI and the newer Dual_EC generators together. In this new approach, the ANSI generator supposedly took the number generated by Dual_EC as a start and then used it as a seed to generate another pseudorandom number. In so doing, Juniper set up a cascade of the two generators. This is a fairly unusual practice—since only one pseudorandom number generator is needed—yet it is not necessarily insecure.

But the next oddity was worse. Juniper changed the size of the output of Dual_EC, in effect adding more digits to the numbers it generated. This change did not appear to have any technical benefit. What it did do, however, was provide a potential eavesdropper with more information. In fact, with this larger output, Dual_EC now leaked just enough data for an eavesdropper to be able to predict what pseudorandom number was coming next and thus break the encryption. This unexpected change provided enough material to fulfill the third condition of the backdoor. It was exactly what cryptographers had warned about.

In theory, this unfortunate combination of events by itself was not an issue. The ANSI generator would, in Juniper's stated design, use what it got from Dual_EC only as a starting point for its own pseudorandom generation process. Even if the input to ANSI was somehow compromised because of a flaw in Dual_EC, the pseudo-randomness generated by ANSI should have provided protection. But Juniper's code had one final problem, and it was a big one: when the software ran, it essentially skipped the ANSI mechanism altogether and left the Dual_EC backdoor exposed.[29] If this was accidental, it was a catastrophic mistake. If it was intentional, it was deviously clever.

In short, not only did Juniper decide out of the blue to add Dual_EC, which had poor performance and contained a secret backdoor, and not only did it decide to change the configuration so that an eavesdropper would have enough information to take advantage of the backdoor, but the backdoor was next to an incredible software bug that gave the appearance of added security but actually made that very backdoor easier to exploit. Juniper's series of bizarre and illogical changes to already secure software in fact made its code substantially less secure. The company supplanted a secure number generator with a deeply questionable one under the guise of using both for more protection.

The firm provided no explanation for any of this. It simply insisted for years that its system was safe. Later, in the face of swirling controversy about weaknesses in Dual_EC—including the NIST's eventual withdrawal of the specification, brought about by Snowden's revelations—Juniper assured its customers that even if Dual_EC had a backdoor, its customers would be safe because of the second generator.[30] Due to the bug in the code that bypassed ANSI, this was false.

As a result, all of the many customers who relied on Juniper's ScreenOS for cybersecurity were in fact vulnerable. The foreign tele-communications companies and governments of interest to the Five Eyes lacked protection for their messages, but so too did many United States government agencies. Many of these organizations transmitted their messages and files over the internet, confident that Juniper's encryption was protecting them. But they were wrong. Passive collection could provide access to the data, while, in the right hands, the Dual_EC backdoor would let the NSA strip the facade of encryption away. While it is impossible to know any specifics about operations that exploited the weakness, there is no doubt that Juniper's change in code put many secrets all over the world at risk.[31]

To reiterate, it is uncertain whether Juniper did any or all of this at the NSA's behest. It is possible that Juniper decided to add Dual_EC for an unknown but benign reason. It is possible as well that the company picked its Q point randomly and did not know the danger it was courting when it increased the amount of information leaked by Dual_EC. Perhaps the catastrophic bug that bypassed the secure ANSI generator was also the result of a series of very unlucky coincidences, as was the choice not to seek federal security certification for the addition of Dual_EC. Maybe the company had only user security in mind and genuinely tried to prevent the NSA or any other eavesdropper from exploiting its products. While there are leaks that quite clearly show the NSA's hand in establishing the Dual_EC backdoor in the first place, no leaked file provides insight one way or the other on Juniper's adoption of the flawed pseudorandom number generator.

Nonetheless, the evidence is strong enough to arouse very deep suspicion of an intentional effort to weaken the encryption in Juniper's products. A tight link between the NSA and Juniper would not be unusual given the agency's deep corporate ties. GCHQ is the partner agency that knows the NSA better than any other, and in 2011 it was suggested internally there that such a connection between the United States government and the company might exist. One British document filled with other information on the possibility of targeting Juniper notes that "Juniper carries a potential opportunity and complication by being a US company. There is potential to leverage a corporate relationship should one exist with NSA. Any GCHQ efforts to exploit Juniper must begin with close coordination with NSA."[32]

The unusual bug in the 2008 code change that bypassed the secure ANSI generator adds weight to this suspicion of an intentional weakness. Matthew Green, one of the widely respected cryptographers who examined the case, said, without blaming Juniper directly, "if you wanted to create a deliberate backdoor based on Dual_EC and make it look safe, while also having it be vulnerable, this is the way you'd do it. The best backdoor is a backdoor that looks like a bug."[33] The combination of components stood out to Green. He pointed out that "this bug happens to be sitting there right next to this incredibly dangerous NSA-designed random number generator, and it makes that generator actually dangerous where it might not have been otherwise."[34] In the cryptanalysis business, plausible deniability is essential, but too many coincidences start to look intentional.

If, as seems very likely, the ScreenOS flaw was an NSA operation as opposed to a very unfortunate series of events, there is no doubt that it put American systems at risk, too. But the vulnerability of US communications, even government communications, might not have been a problem. As long as only the NSA knew of the backdoor and the details of how to exploit it, it would be a NOBUS capability. Secrecy would thus once more be paramount—but secrets are hard to keep.

Two New Backdoors

The digital fossil record of Juniper's source code shows another very important change in 2012. There were two notable things about it. First, unlike the modifications in 2008, which added Dual_EC, the original Q, and a number of suspicious bugs, the 2012 change was far subtler. While 2008's alterations reshaped the broader infrastructure of the company's code, the 2012 change modified just one line, the definition of Q, changing it from one indecipherable string of numbers and letters to another. And second, while there is every indication that Juniper itself made the 2008 change—very likely in coordination with the NSA, but possibly not—outside hackers with illicit control over the source code seem to have made the 2012 modification. This means that when Juniper next shipped out its software updates, it appears not to have known it was sending a new Q to customers all over the world.

Although they have not previously been reported, there are extremely strong suggestions that a group of Chinese hackers made the 2012 change. Two individuals in the private sector with knowledge of the case indicated that a Chinese group was responsible for the redefinition of Q, though both declined to identify the specific hacking group. Such an operation would fit with a broader pattern of activity, as multiple Chinese hacking groups have successfully targeted telecommunications companies all over the world.[35]

The hackers showed enormous restraint in changing just the Q point. With the access to Juniper's systems they enjoyed, they could have made more major changes, though that might have increased the risk of detection. Instead, they played their hand with subtlety, merely inching Q along its elliptical curve. Manipulating the backdoor that was already there was likely more elegant, harder to trace, and perhaps provided the benefit of harming the NSA's intelligence collection capabilities.

Juniper's engineers did not notice the change. This is not entirely surprising, as it was probably difficult to spot unless one knew it was there. Juniper's clients who downloaded updated versions of the software would almost certainly have no idea the new Q existed. Even someone scrutinizing the source code would likely pass over the rekeyed backdoor without a second thought. But the effects may have been global.

One result was immediate. If it was Chinese hackers who changed the points, the NSA would not have known the details of the mathematical relationship between the new Q and the old P. Assuming this was the case, the new point locked the agency out of the Dual_ EC backdoor that it may have been exploiting. In all versions that came after 6.2 of ScreenOS, the old backdoor was gone. If the NSA had been relying heavily on the backdoor to decrypt passively collected information and quietly steal others' secrets, this change represented a real loss of intelligence access. Though the NSA had other means of hacking Juniper devices and exploiting information from them, this backdoor still had its unique merits, especially in its potential scale.[36] It seems unlikely any other method could let an intelligence agency silently exploit millions of Juniper devices all over the world, all while their targets thought they were secure.

The damage did not end there. A second effect was perhaps still worse: whoever changed the point probably deliberately chose a new value for Q that was not verifiably random. The hackers, after all, were likely not interested in securing Juniper's systems, but instead were trying to target them. As a result, the hackers had good reason to pick a new Q point that enabled a new backdoor, known only to whoever made the change. This would mean that the 2012 change not only locked out whoever might have known about and exploited the previous backdoor, but also aided the newer perpetrators. Juniper's customers had unwittingly traded one insecure encryption system for another.

The 2012 hackers thus could reap the decryption benefits that might have been available to the NSA in 2008. China does not have the same global passive collection reach that the United States does, but it has some. In addition, on a number of occasions it has brazenly rerouted foreign internet traffic through its own territory by using the power of China Telecom.[37] In these and other circumstances, encryption might have stopped the Chinese from reading the intercepted communications. The backdoor would have helped overcome that obstacle. With knowledge of the new Q, they could now decrypt intercepted traffic, so long as the target was one of Juniper's many customers.

At a technical level, there is a direct link between the 2008 and 2012 backdoors. Matthew Green, the aforementioned cryptographer, noted how the hackers deftly spotted the implications of the 2008 code and used it to enable their modification of Juniper's software. "They then piggybacked on top of it to build a backdoor of their own, something they were able to do because all of the hard work had already been done for them," he said. "The end result was a period in which someone—maybe a foreign government—was able to decrypt Juniper traffic in the U.S. and around the world."[38] If the NSA had once thought that the Dual_EC backdoor was a NOBUS capability, the 2012 changes proved that assumption incorrect.

As bad as this new backdoor was, the digital record of Juniper's source code shows that things only got worse for the company and its customers. In 2014, according to two individuals in the private sector with knowledge of the case, Chinese hackers made another modification. The attribution to China has not been previously reported, and the individuals caution that this group of hackers was not necessarily the one that made the 2012 changes.

This change was somewhat more obvious than the earlier cryptographic backdoors. The new code placed a secret password into Juniper's software: the seemingly incomprehensible phrase <<< %s(un='%s') = %u. But the hackers did not choose this password without careful thought. They picked this obscure string of characters to look like regular code.[39] The hackers hoped that, if someone saw it during a security audit or code review, they would pass over it without further investigation.

That unpronounceable password carried enormous might. The 2008 and 2012 backdoors made passive collection possible by thwarting encryption, but the 2014 backdoor enabled active hacking operations. Anyone who was aware of it could log in remotely to any of Juniper's vulnerable security products anywhere in the world, just as if they were the legitimate owner and operator of the product. Knowing the password would in some cases even bypass the need to find traditional software vulnerabilities and build exploits targeting

Juniper devices. Armed with the right string of characters, hackers could simply log into the device without the need for additional vulnerabilities.

This sort of access is a boon for spies who aim to learn other states' secrets. Once the hackers logged in with the hidden password, they gained control over the target. They could make changes to the security product's configuration, potentially altering mission-critical settings and shaping the digital environment for future hacking operations. They could also gather information on how the target was using the product. Maybe most important of all, using this administrative access, they could better avoid getting caught. Hackers who knew of the password-enabled backdoor could delete logs to cover their tracks, wiping away evidence of other signals intelligence operations against Juniper products. Detecting operations of this sort is fiendishly difficult, and so they all remain hidden from view even today. But there is virtually no doubt that they occurred; no hackers would create the 2014 backdoor unless they were intending to reap its benefits.

The hardcoded password that enabled the 2014 backdoor did not depend on the 2008 or 2012 backdoors and had no direct tie to the flawed Dual_EC specification. It was a bolder stroke, in contrast to the understated changes that had come before. The change to the code was potentially more noticeable than the 2012 change, but the payoff was significant, too, and different in kind from what the earlier source code manipulation had yielded. In a postmortem analysis, security researchers were unequivocal in noting the severity of the situation. One analysis put it simply and aptly: the breach was as "terrible as it gets," because of all that it let the hackers do, with near impunity and near invisibility.[40]

Beyond the tantalizing indications of Chinese responsibility from those with knowledge of the case, there is frustratingly little information about the source and motivation of the code changes. One thing is clear, however: there was far more illicit foreign access to Juniper's source code than the company wanted. As a result, the company's secrets were out in the open, a potential NSA espionage capability had disappeared, and adversarial hackers had gained the ability to decrypt many communications Americans thought were secure.

Short-Lived Victory

The record of Juniper's source code shows that both the 2012 and 2014 backdoors remained in place for a significant period of time. They eluded any code reviews and security audits at Juniper, perhaps aided by the hackers' attempts to make them look innocuous. The backdoors, powerful and stealthy, enabled the quiet decryption of supposedly protected traffic and permitted hackers to log in as administrators. Because of the hackers' clever design, it is impossible to determine how often they used the backdoors; they left no trace of malicious code and made most detection and after-action assessment impossible.

One must wonder why the NSA, which likely knew about the 2008 code changes, did not intervene in 2012 or 2014. There are several possibilities. The first is that the 2008 code changes were not an intended backdoor at all, and instead just a series of exceptionally unlucky coincidences. In this case, the NSA would have been in the dark from the start and unlikely to gain awareness of what Juniper or the hackers did. The second is that the NSA knew of the 2008 backdoor and knew that in 2012 another state's hackers had rekeyed it. In this case, perhaps to protect its sources and methods, the agency chose not to act on this knowledge by alerting Juniper or the public.

The third possibility is that the NSA did lose access to its backdoor with the 2012 software update but did not realize that it was due to the activities of other hackers. Former NSA Director Michael Hayden, speaking generally, indicated that the loss of access due to software changes is reasonably common in the world of signals intelligence. "Access bought with months if not years of effort can be lost with a casual upgrade of the targeted system, not even one designed to improve defenses, but merely an administrative upgrade from something 2.0 to something 3.0," he said.[41] Cyber capabilities never last forever.

The fourth possibility is that many users of Juniper's products did not update their software. If so, the 2008 backdoor would have continued to work against many old targets, though not new ones. If there was not a drop off in collection, a signals intelligence agency exploiting the 2008 backdoor might not have known about the later changes. Whatever the reason, the 2012 and 2014 backdoors remained in place in updated versions of ScreenOS well into 2015.

Then, out of the blue, Juniper removed them. In late 2015, the company publicly announced that a "code review" had found "unauthorized code" in its software and that it had removed it in a new emergency software update.[42] This statement may have been the full truth. The code review may have been routine and the company's security auditors may simply have found the illicit changes that were previously overlooked. If so, Juniper realized that the backdoors were certainly of high enough concern to warrant an immediate fix.

But the statement might also have omitted some key facts, such as why that particular code review was ordered. The company said nothing about whether it had any knowledge about what it might find or where to look. Perhaps the NSA eventually recognized that another group of hackers had inserted a backdoor into Juniper's systems, and it was not the only cat playing the cat-and-mouse game between network intruders and defenders. Such an assessment could have drawn on the NSA's counterintelligence capabilities (discussed in Chapter 5), which potentially would have enabled the agency to observe other states exploiting Juniper's products.

If indeed the NSA had discovered that foreign hackers had compromised Juniper, the agency might have felt an imperative to alert the company so it could issue a patch. It would be dangerous to let the company remain compromised, given its widespread presence inside US government networks and in the networks of many important organizations all over the world; one audit showed that of twenty-four surveyed government agencies, half of them were left vulnerable for years due to the backdoor, including the Treasury Department and other key entities.[43]

Yet prompting a patch might also cast attention on the irregularities surrounding Dual_EC and the agency's role in them. Given that NSA officials were overtly pushing for mandatory encryption backdoors in American products at the time, a fuller discussion of how the backdoor in Juniper went awry could have created an unwelcome public relations problem.[44] Nonetheless, despite the inevitable scrutiny the disclosure brought upon the agency, even its fiercest critic, Edward Snowden, said that the NSA likely informed Juniper of the compromise and prompted the fix, though he almost certainly did not have direct knowledge of the case.[45] There has been no official confirmation one way or another.

Juniper's 2015 code cleanup left a lot to be desired. It perhaps sheds light on what was going on behind the scenes and further suggests that something was amiss from the start. In its emergency software update, the company removed the hardcoded password, closing the 2014 backdoor. The firm also changed the new Q point that hackers had inserted in 2012, denying access to the second cryptographic backdoor. However, instead of using a verifiably random process to pick a new value for Q, the company simply reverted to the original Q that it used in 2008—the one that had long since fallen under suspicion as hiding the first backdoor. Juniper did not remove the flawed Dual_EC code, nor did it fix the catastrophic and perhaps intentional bug that made the more secure ANSI generator irrelevant.[46] It was a deeply unusual security update, one that appeared to leave a lot of very serious known security issues in place.

With this patch, all of the conditions for the exploitation of the 2008 backdoor were back in place: the unverified Q, the use of Dual_ EC, the bypassing of the secure ANSI pseudorandom number generator, and the leaking of just enough data for an eavesdropper to predict the sequence of numbers that was coming next. If it was the NSA that alerted Juniper and caused the 2015 fixes, the agency seemed to have gotten the last laugh against its adversaries: by reinstating the 2008 Q point and its associated software bugs, Juniper reinstated the original backdoor.

But the agency's victory, if it was one, was short-lived. For years, suspicion had continued to mount about the process that led to Dual_EC. A major study commissioned by NIST, the standards body, warned the institute about the dangers of working with the NSA on encryption and recommended greater independence and transparency.[47] It was an implicit rebuke of the Dual_EC affair. In an article for a mathematics journal, a senior NSA official called the failure to withdraw support for the compromised Dual_EC standard earlier "regrettable." He also wrote that the "NSA must be much more transparent in its standards work and act according to that transparency."[48] His words seem to be as close to an acknowledgment of responsibility as the famously secretive agency would ever give, but they were not enough to stop future encryption designers from mistrusting the NSA.[49]

Dual_EC was forever tainted. After additional scrutiny from the cybersecurity community and bad press, in 2016 Juniper entirely removed the flawed pseudorandom number generator from its ScreenOS systems. At long last, the 2008 backdoor was finally closed for good, and the spy-versus-spy game over this particular bit of code concluded. Though other code manipulation engagements surely continued, this backdoor saga—which had begun so covertly and unfolded inch by inch for years—ended with an abrupt public finale. Despite all the struggle and drama, there was no clear winner.[50]

4

Strategic Espionage

FOR YEARS, THE EMAILS ARRIVED IN A TORRENT. They landed in the inboxes of executives and engineers, of human resources staff and high-ranking government officials. They appeared to come from bosses, colleagues, accountants, friends, and potential business partners. They stretched across wide swaths of Western society, reaching organizations in virtually every strategically important sector of commerce, technology, and national defense. They often contained an email attachment or a link. None of the messages were real. All of them were dangerous.

While the precise launch date of China's cyber espionage campaign is uncertain, it probably began in earnest not long after 2000. It has only grown in the decades since. Spear-phishing—the practice of sending socially engineered emails in order to dupe a target into surrendering vital information or opening malicious code—was and is a common Chinese tactic. China's hackers, spread across organizations like the People's Liberation Army and the Ministry of State Security, used the technique again and again because it worked so well. From the comfort of their homes and offices, they could blast out thousands of emails, some more carefully crafted than others, and wait to see what catch of the day came back.

Although no single book chapter can do justice to the full expanse of China's multi-decade strategic espionage campaign, it is essential to present both the depth and breadth of China's operations. The Chinese were able to go deep, thoroughly penetrating some targeted organizations, stealing some of their most valuable secrets and gaining economic and geopolitical advantages as a result. At the same time, the hackers were able to go broad, hitting thousands of targets, many of which had direct relevance to the Chinese Communist Party's strategic priorities. Then-FBI Director James Comey said in 2014 that the Chinese were "just prolific. Their strategy seems to be: 'We'll just be everywhere all the time—and there's no way they can stop us.'"[1]

China had good reasons to undertake such an aggressive and multi-faceted espionage campaign. It had lagged behind the United States for decades in both business and geopolitical competition. Its commercial innovations were inferior. Its military, though large, lacked the technologies that gave the United States a global advantage. Its authoritarian political leaders worried about how the openness of the internet might empower dissenters and free expression. By spying on such a vast scale, the Chinese government could gain an economic advantage over Western companies, match American military capabilities, and better keep a stranglehold on power within its borders.

The Chinese hackers aimed not just to gain secrets of tactical and operational value, but to reshape the strategic relationship with the United States in their favor. The speed, scale, and scope of their efforts were of a different magnitude than the traditional espionage that predated the digital age. In large part, this is because digital information is much more portable than paper. For example, before Daniel Ellsberg, the Vietnam War whistleblower, could leak the Pentagon Papers, he and his family and friends spent more than a year photocopying the seven thousand pages, one at a time, racking up thousands of dollars in fees as they went.[2] By contrast, once computer hackers gain access, they can often vacuum up and freely move similar volumes of information in hours, if not minutes.

The impact of these operations is enormous. Economically, the value of the trade secrets the Chinese pilfered is likely in the hundreds of billions of dollars.[3] Former NSA Director Keith Alexander was fond of saying that the Chinese operations enabled the "greatest transfer of wealth in history."[4] Militarily, the Chinese have developed and deployed several weapons systems disconcertingly similar to those of the United States' counterparts, likely aided by the theft of designs and plans. Even worse, the capacity of United States military equipment to stand up to Chinese cyber attacks has been thrown into doubt. The Defense Science Board reports that, due to foreign hacking, "the cyber threat is serious and . . . the United States cannot be confident that our critical Information Technology (IT) systems will work under attack from a sophisticated and well-resourced opponent utilizing cyber capabilities in combination with all their military and intelligence capabilities."[5]

China launched such an aggressive campaign for a reason: it does not have the home-field advantage that the Five Eyes enjoy. Though the country has more than a billion people, it is far less optimally placed on the world's data flows and its technology companies do not command the world's data in the way that Google and Facebook do. Passive collection and corporate access serve the regime well within its borders, but if the government wants to learn more about what is happening on the other side of the Great Firewall, it has to hack those targets proactively. Spear-phishing is often the easiest way in. For that reason and others, the flood of fake messages began.

Operation Aurora

Throughout the summer and fall of 2009, hackers affiliated with the Chinese government sent their malicious emails and instant messages to targets all over the world, including in the United States. When targets opened the messages and clicked the link inside, their browsers brought them to a website hosted in Taiwan. That website contained a software exploit that the browser dutifully downloaded and executed. This is a method of delivering malicious code that cybersecurity researchers call a drive-by download.

The exploit took advantage of an unpatched vulnerability in Internet Explorer, the dominant browser at the time. This malicious code downloaded still more malicious code from the Taiwanese website, disguising it as an image to avoid raising suspicion. The additional malicious code, now established on the targeted computer, reached out to the hackers' command-and-control servers, also located in Taiwan, for further instructions. By this point, after just a single click of the wrong link by the user, the Chinese hackers were in.

This spear-phishing and drive-by download effort was part of a broader intrusion initiative known as Operation Aurora, a name the hackers appear to have used themselves. Operation Aurora stretched throughout American society, targeting thirty-four major companies, including Google, Microsoft, Juniper, and other firms.[6] All told, when Operation Aurora became public in 2010, it was one of the most intrusive cyber espionage campaigns ever discovered.

The hackers had at least three objectives for Operation Aurora. The first was to spy on Chinese dissidents using American technology.

After its investigation, Google wrote that "we have evidence to suggest that a primary goal of the attackers was accessing the Gmail accounts of Chinese human rights activists." Google's security systems seem to have been mostly successful in thwarting this Chinese effort, limiting their access to just two accounts of dissidents, and even for these accounts revealing only the subject lines of the emails rather than the full content.[7] The *Financial Times* reported the hacking of two accounts belonging to Ai Weiwei, one of the most noteworthy internal critics of China, especially on issues of human rights and democracy.[8]

Google responded forcefully to this intrusion. It made public some details of how it had been breached— an unusual move at the time. It condemned the Chinese action and warned, based on its investigation, that Operation Aurora might be part of a broader government effort to target dozens of notable dissidents all over the world. Most significantly, Google said it was no longer willing to work with the Chinese government on censoring search results inside China, effectively ending its business inside the country at the time.[9] For Sergey Brin, the Google cofounder whose family came as refugees from the Soviet Union, the issue of free expression clinched his decision: "Having seen the hardships that my family endured—both while there and trying to leave—I certainly am particularly sensitive to the stifling of individual liberties."[10]

But the Chinese hackers were out to do more than just repress dissent. Their second objective was to undermine the home-field advantage that so greatly benefited the United States. They wanted to know which targets in China the United States was surveilling through Google's systems. After hacking their way in, the Chinese operators began querying names on the company's internal "legal-discovery" portal. This portal managed the requests for information that law enforcement made to Google for information pertaining to ongoing investigations; it was probably separate from the PRISM system used by the NSA. With access to the legal-discovery system, the Chinese could see a list that former top Justice Department official John Carlin, who led the government's effort to prosecute the hackers, described as a "who's who" of the spies, hackers, and criminals known to the United States.[11] By hacking Google, China could check to see if the United States was using American technology companies to watch the activities of suspected Chinese intelligence officers and their assets.

A third motive for the Chinese operation against American technology firms was that the hackers wanted access to those companies' secrets—starting with their source code. Code is itself a valuable form of intellectual property, often highly coveted by foreign governments and their favored state-owned enterprises. The source code of the companies Operation Aurora targeted would have been of enormous value to their Chinese competitors trying to gain an edge in the global marketplace.

But knowing the secrets of the source code benefits more than just rival product development. Having actual code to study makes it easier to find software vulnerabilities and write software exploits to take advantage of them. Discovering and exploiting software vulnerabilities is vitally important to cyber operations. Without these exploits, including the one Operation Aurora's perpetrators used against Internet Explorer, cyber espionage and attack become a lot harder. Having hacked popular American companies, the Chinese were better positioned to write exploits and hack the companies' customers around the world.

Also prized as corporate secrets are signing certificates, those cryptographically complex markers that verify that a particular piece of code came from a known source, such as Google, and can thus be trusted. Advanced cyber operations like Stuxnet, described in Chapter 6, have stolen signing certificates in order to impersonate the code of other companies and avoid detection. Based on searches the Chinese hackers were running once they gained access to Google's network, it appears they were attempting a similar trick, though it is not clear that they were successful.[12]

One last temptation might have motivated the hackers: with access to a company's secrets, especially source code and software development systems, they could manipulate its products. As the last chapter showed, sometimes these illegitimate modifications can be made subtly enough to avoid detection. This is not easy, since employees of the company continuously review and edit the code, but the Juniper case shows that it has occurred at least twice. If hackers can get their source code changes to stick, the capabilities they enable will persist into the final binary code versions that the company ships out to customers all over the world. There is no evidence that the Chinese used their access to change any American companies' source code during Operation Aurora, but it is impossible to know.[13]

Unit 61398

One of the remarkable things about modern cyber operations is how observable they can be, given the right visibility. Governments can track what other governments are doing, as the next chapter will show. By the beginning of 2013, the United States intelligence community had uncovered key components of Chinese hacking. But American policymakers faced a quandary: how much should they say? The government could reveal what it knew about the hackers' motivations, techniques, and targets. Doing so would potentially improve the cybersecurity of American businesses and make it harder for the Chinese to operate, but it would also alert the Chinese that the United States intelligence agencies were tracking their hackers. For years, US officials thus said little in public about Chinese operations, just as the CIA and KGB largely stayed out of public view during the Cold War. Counterintelligence is best kept to the shadows.

The cybersecurity industry is more open. Private-sector companies, many of which employ people who previously served in the intelligence community, also track foreign hackers and defend their clients against intrusions. Unlike the intelligence community, these companies have some incentive to be public about what they know, especially if they can garner media attention. As a result, published reports from the private-sector cybersecurity community are among the best and most detailed sources of analysis of what government hackers are doing in their expensive and top-secret programs.

These private-sector cybersecurity researchers earned high praise from General Paul Nakasone, head of the NSA and director of Cyber Command. "They have global presence and the ability to collect an enormous amount of information," he said in 2019. "They have strong analytic capabilities. The products they produce often rival what we see being done by the intelligence community."[14] While some things remain out of view, the dynamic is striking; imagine if, during the Cold War, the private sector had seen an opportunity to profit by finding clandestine nuclear weapons programs and exposing them for the world to see.

The beginning of high-profile private-sector reporting on government-backed cyber operations can be traced back to a precise date: February 19, 2013. That was the day that a firm called Mandiant released its detailed account of the activity of a Chinese hacking group it named Advanced Persistent Threat 1, or APT1.

While other private-sector companies had published reports on foreign hackers before, Mandiant's revelations provided much more detail and received widespread media attention, including a front-page story in the *New York Times*. In one fell swoop, the company put geopolitically motivated hacking in a spotlight, to which it would return again and again in years to follow.

Most significantly, Mandiant began its sixty-page report by identifying the group's military origins and sponsors. The company, having watched the hackers for years, concluded that they came from Unit 61398, a part of the Second Bureau of the Third Department of the People's Liberation Army (PLA) of China. The report even included pictures of the building the Chinese hackers used as their base of operations.[15] It was a watershed moment, one of the first times the public learned the identities of foreign hackers.

APT1's ambition was staggering. While Operation Aurora showed the depth to which one group of Chinese hackers could go, the APT1 report revealed the breadth of Unit 61398's efforts. It showed how they had, in the previous seven years, penetrated at least 141 of Mandiant's clients. To achieve this, the hackers had maintained a frenetic pace, sometimes breaching as many as seventeen new organizations in a single month.[16] But APT1's hackers did not move away from their victims quickly. Once they gained access, they often lurked for months or years, averaging almost one year before they left or were kicked out—a figure that, Mandiant carefully noted, was likely to be an underestimate.[17] In one case, the hackers maintained their access to a target for more than four years.

The victims were primarily Western companies, organizations, and government agencies. English proficiency was a requirement for the hackers in Unit 61398, Mandiant reported, and 115 of the 141 breached targets were located in the United States. APT1 claimed victims in twenty industries, including information technology, legal services, manufacturing, telecommunications, and aerospace, as well as in government agencies and nonprofit organizations. But APT1 was not hacking at random; Mandiant noted that the intrusions were weighted heavily to some of the strategic priorities listed in the Chinese government's then-current five-year plan, a clear sign of the geopolitical aims that underpinned the hacking campaign.[18]

APT1's hackers chose targets for their secrets. During their long operations, they gathered enormous quantities of information from the organizations they compromised. They took product designs, test results, manuals, simulations, manufacturing processes, business plans, negotiating positions, pricing information, corporate merger files, plans for joint ventures, policy documents, meeting minutes, emails from senior executives, and user passwords—basically anything that might be useful to the Chinese state.[19] In some cases, APT1 gathered terabytes of data from its victims, vacuuming up entire repositories of private files.

In most cases, APT1 followed a simple pattern, one that hackers of all stripes use over and over again. After some basic reconnaissance, hackers established an initial presence in the target network, often by spear-phishing. Some recipients of these emails were aware of spear-phishing risks and responded to the lure asking if it was safe to open the attachment or click the link. The APT1 hackers wrote back and reassured them that it was.

Once inside the target network, they established a mechanism to communicate with their malicious code. To avoid detection by network defenders, they often tried to disguise the instructions to their malicious code and the data they received from it as ordinary web traffic. Once this command-and-control mechanism was set up, they moved laterally within the penetrated network, stealing employee passwords and getting access to still more computers and servers and the information they contained. They also took steps to make it hard for defenders to root them out, such as gaining access to company Virtual Private Networks and installing malicious software throughout the networks they compromised. APT1's objective was years of uninterrupted spying on its targets, all in service of China's geopolitical goals.[20]

Some of the targeted firms did large amounts of business in China, including deals announced with great fanfare. For example, on July 24, 2007, the CEO of Westinghouse Electric Company entered China's Great Hall of the People in Beijing ready to sign a multi-billion-dollar agreement committing his company to a deal with Chinese state-owned enterprises.[21] At the time, Westinghouse was the world's leading nuclear power firm, responsible for half the globe's nuclear power plants. Its AP1000 nuclear reactor was a well-known model that the company had spent fifteen years designing; in China, Westinghouse would build four of them. The two sides had negotiated for more than two years and the July agreement represented a significant milestone: while some provisions would be left for later discussion, the major parts of the deal were done.

But even as the partnership unfolded, APT1 began hacking the company. On numerous occasions, they targeted Westinghouse's computers and servers. Among other things, they stole information on the design and construction of the AP1000 nuclear plant, sparing the Chinese company the effort of doing its own research and development. As Westinghouse continued to negotiate with its Chinese counterparts on the contract and on other potential business in 2010, APT1's hackers gained access to the internal deliberations, better positioning the Chinese in the talks. All told, APT1 pilfered around seven hundred thousand pages of emails and other documents from

Westinghouse.[22] In 2017, in part due to increased Chinese competition and in part due to other factors, Westinghouse declared bankruptcy, ceding market leadership for the construction of nuclear power plants to Chinese firms.[23]

APT1's intrusions accompanied many other Chinese joint ventures, negotiations, and litigations. SolarWorld, a company that makes photovoltaic products such as roof panels, provides another example. In 2012, SolarWorld petitioned the United States Department of Commerce because Chinese competitors receiving unfair subsidies from their government were able to undercut its pricing in the United States. After preliminary Commerce decisions ruled against the Chinese firms, APT1's hackers penetrated SolarWorld, stealing thousands of executive emails, proprietary financial information, intellectual property related to the manufacture of solar panels, attorney-client communications, and private filings submitted to the United States government. In short, the hackers worked to give the Chinese companies an unwarranted competitive edge against their American counterpart, both in the ongoing legal dispute and in the marketplace.[24]

A similar story played out with US Steel, the legendary American company formed by J.P. Morgan. The company, which was the first ever to reach a billion-dollar valuation, struggled against Chinese competition strengthened by Chinese government subsidies. In 2010, US Steel began fighting Chinese trade practices, alleging that its Chinese competitors received unfair subsidies, a claim that was later found to be credible. In response, APT1 hackers sent a barrage of forty-nine spear-phishing emails laced with malicious code to various employees, eventually gaining access to vulnerable computers and servers within the company and accessing its internal files.[25]

Even unions found themselves on APT1's target list. United Steelworkers, a union representing around one million active and retired members, fiercely opposes Chinese trade practices that help Chinese steel products undercut American ones. Beginning in 2010, APT1's hackers carried out an extensive campaign against the group, gaining access to internal emails and files that reflected the union leaders' debate about strategy. At key moments when the union's anti-China activity increased, such as during World Trade Organization proceedings or Congressional lobbying efforts, APT1's hackers gathered information about its plans and activities. As the union prepared to argue against increasing reliance on Chinese goods, the Chinese government and firms used hacking to anticipate the union's claims and advance their own arguments instead.[26]

Years after these operations began, and more than a year after Mandiant's seminal report, the US government was ready to hit back. After lengthy internal debates and proceedings, the Department of Justice indicted five members of APT1.[27] Its investigation confirmed much of Mandiant's reporting regarding the activities of PLA Unit 61398. To add to the drama, American officials made giant, wild-west-style "wanted" posters with the faces and names of the five indicted hackers. Officials challenged the Chinese government to back up its thin denials of responsibility.

But the Chinese hackers were out of reach. They and their compatriots could continue to hack with abandon, safely ensconced within China and protected by the state. While the United States made a habit of indicting foreign hackers after the APT1 case, most of them easily evaded arrest. Many indictments seemed like no more than detailed press releases, noteworthy for how much information they contained but ultimately insufficient as a tool of statecraft. One case, however, was an early exception, and it revealed yet another aspect to the Chinese hacking campaign.

Hacking for Military Advantage

In 2012, it seems, the NSA's signals intelligence apparatus picked up a series of emails among three Chinese nationals. Two of them were military hackers in China. The third was a late-forties businessman in Canada named Su Bin, who supervised the British Columbia office of an aviation company called Lode-Tech. Lode-Tech's business was to track global aerospace technology developments for its clients; Su Bin's mission was to track American military aerospace developments for China. He used his knowledge of the industry, aviation, and English to guide the Chinese hackers toward the most valuable targets.

It appears the NSA gave Su Bin's emails to the FBI, which assigned agents to the case.[28] The FBI investigation found that Su Bin and his military counterparts had been spying on United States airplane developments for years, beginning in 2009.[29] Their method of operation was simple. Su Bin would figure out which companies were working on aircraft projects of importance. He would then inform the Chinese hackers, who would use spear-phishing to gain access to executives' emails and companies' networks. The hackers would copy large lists of files from within the compromised corporate networks, and Su Bin would carefully study these lists and determine which files were important. Using this technique, the hackers accessed massive amounts of information. In one case, the printed list of just the file names—not even of the files themselves—stretched to six thousand pages of text.

Su Bin knew what to look for: the secret designs of some of the United States' most important military aircraft. One of the targets in his sights was the C-17, Boeing's giant cargo plane that the US Air Force uses in a wide variety of missions. Su Bin went through the thousands of file names the hackers provided to find the ones shedding the most light on the C-17's design, maintenance, and operational requirements. He directed the hackers to thousands of pages of secrets that were of enormous benefit to China in its own development of a similar cargo plane.

After one breach, Su Bin combed through a 137-page list of files to find the two thousand files most useful to China. The effect was immense. John Carlin, the senior Justice Department official who managed the case, later wrote that "thanks to Su Bin, the Chinese were able to develop, build, and deploy their own copy, in barely a third of the time it had taken the United States to design, test, and build the original C-17." Su Bin himself bragged about his efforts, claiming to have taken a total of 630,000 files related to the C-17. "We safely, smoothly accomplished the entrusted mission in one year," he wrote, "making important contributions to our national defense scientific research development and receiving unanimous favorable comments."[30] Su Bin's self-congratulation aside, China's success was undeniable. At a November 2014 air show, China's military parked its C-17 knockoff, the Xi'an Y-20, right next to the American original. It was a stunning visual symbol of what hacking can do.

The C-17 was not the only target. Su Bin and his hacker colleagues also set their sights on other powerful planes in the American arsenal. This included the F-22, a fighter jet optimized for air-to-air dogfighting, as well as the F-35, the Joint Strike Fighter that was the most expensive airplane project in history. Once more, Carlin and others made clear the value of this sort of espionage: "The thefts were critical to helping the Chinese understand—and copy—America's most advanced fighter plane."[31] With each hack by Su Bin's team, China was working to close the technological gap and undermine American military supremacy. The total cost of the team's effort was only one million dollars. Given the multibillion-dollar price tag of the systems in play, it returned much more than that in value.

The Chinese wanted to shift the ground beneath the Americans' feet, avoiding detection and quietly stealing valuable information. Secrecy was essential. Su Bin and his team devised elaborate protocols to obscure their operations. They disguised the data before they copied it out of the defense contractor systems to avoid setting off internal alarms. To throw any investigators off the scent, they set up a series of servers around the world through which they routed the files. Each time they exfiltrated data, they moved it through three different foreign countries, always choosing at least one that was not an ally of the United States, so that intelligence investigations would be hindered. The stolen secrets' last digital stop was Hong Kong or Macau, where Chinese officers picked up the digital files in person and brought them back to mainland China.[32]

Su Bin's case is remarkable because, unlike most Chinese hackers, he was living in Canada and thus within the reach of Five Eyes' law enforcement. He was arrested in 2014 and eventually extradited. In 2016, he pled guilty and was sentenced to forty-six months in prison in the United States. It was a success for the United States Justice Department, as it marked one of those rare cases in which a hacker working for a foreign military was held responsible and faced legal consequences. Talking to a *Washington Post* reporter, Carlin basked in the victory: "There are some who say, 'You'll never catch anyone.' . . . Well, we have caught someone."[33]

Yet, the exceptional outcome of the Su Bin case also highlights the many, many other Chinese hackers and spies who have accessed American military secrets and evaded justice. Based on leaked documents and other reporting, it is possible to assemble a partial list of successful Chinese operations of this sort. Even with many operations likely out of sight, a survey of the available information showcases an extensive Chinese hacking campaign that reaches into nearly every part of the American military enterprise.

Drawing on leaked classified documents, the *Washington Post* reported that Chinese hackers stole key files relating to missile defense including "the advanced Patriot missile system, . . . an Army system for shooting down ballistic missiles, . . . and the Navy's Aegis ballistic-missile defense system." The hackers also gathered information on planes, helicopters, and ships, including "the F/A-18 fighter jet, the V-22 Osprey, the Black Hawk helicopter and the Navy's new Littoral Combat Ship, which is designed to patrol waters close to shore."[34] These were the weapons on which the United States would rely in a fight with China, and their vulnerabilities were now exposed for China to study.[35]

Internal NSA documents provide still more insight. They reveal the existence of more than a dozen distinct Chinese hacking groups that sought to learn not just about the technology of the United States military but also about its operational plans. Many hacking efforts were made against Pacific Command, the part of the United States military that would be directly involved in any war with China. Chinese hackers also extensively targeted senior Defense Department officials, with some success, likely seeking to understand their priorities in Asia and their contingency plans for a military conflict.[36]

The NSA documents also provide an overall accounting of the extent of the Chinese campaign up to 2012—an onslaught that, with a few exceptions, also seems to have continued since then. The NSA concluded that the Chinese had caused at least thirty thousand "hacking incidents" in the Department of Defense, at least five hundred of which counted as "significant intrusions." They copied around fifty terabytes of data, equivalent to around five times the amount of information in the books of the Library of Congress. They gained access to tens of thousands of military users' passwords and tens of thousands of personnel records, including those of generals and other senior leaders; in cases where officials reused their work passwords for personal email accounts, the hackers could have had even more access. As ever, the Chinese sought to understand and possibly copy key military technologies, especially planes and space-based capabilities. The hackers also focused on discovering the logistical operations that enabled the United States military to function, such as aerial refueling missions in the Pacific.[37]

It seemed that the Chinese, in line with their military doctrine, were working to thwart the United States' ability to mobilize for war. Chinese hackers breached a large number of the contractors and civilian organizations serving the US military's Transportation Command, which is responsible for getting troops and weapons in position for battle. In just one fourteen-month period, the hackers made more than twenty successful intrusions into Transportation Command partners. Time and time again, the Chinese hackers used spear-phishing to gain access to these targets.[38] For their part, the US government and hacked organizations were slow to respond, often failing to detect the breaches and, even when they did, failing to notify intelligence and law enforcement officers.[39] It was a failure of cybersecurity and coordination that the Chinese were only too happy to exploit again and again.

Spying On Everyone

One final set of intrusions, showing both the breadth and the depth of the Chinese strategic espionage campaign, was directed against targets with gigantic databases. Perhaps the most notable example was a breach of the Office of Personnel Management, or OPM—the part of the United States government that stores large amounts of information on current and former employees. The same group of Chinese hackers penetrated OPM's systems in the spring of 2015, taking advantage of the office's poor cybersecurity practices.[40] Though the exact method of entry is not known, it seems likely that the Chinese used their tried-and-true technique of spear-phishing to acquire the passwords of an OPM contractor. From there, they went on to access vast amounts of stored data.

Once inside, the Chinese set their sights on the information of most importance to them: the personnel records of government employees. Included in these files were not just Americans' social security numbers and other personal identifiers, but also their answers to questions on a form known as SF-86, a legendarily complex questionnaire that pries deeply into employees' personal lives. Government investigators determining employees' eligibility for security clearances use the form to collect information on such personal matters as debts, divorces, affairs, medical treatments, foreign travel, job history, salary history, addresses, family members, and more.

The Chinese wanted to know all this information, too. They got their wish by breaching OPM, acquiring intimate details on almost twenty million Americans, including everyone for whom OPM had processed a background check in the previous fifteen years, as well as some friends and spouses of government employees. For good measure, the Chinese also vacuumed up biometric information, including more than 5.6 million sets of fingerprints of government employees.[41] The United States government had gone to the trouble of gathering and organizing all this private data on Americans but had not secured it nearly well enough. The Chinese took easy advantage.

It is hard to know what happened to the data once it made its way to China but, safe to say, from the American vantage point, it was nothing good. In the words of former FBI Director James Comey, it was "a very big deal from a national security perspective and from a counterintelligence perspective. It's a treasure trove of information about everybody who has worked for, tried to work for, or works for the United States government." What worried Comey in particular was the amount of detail the files gave foreign spies to exploit: "Just imagine you are an intelligence service and you had that data."[42]

A savvy intelligence service could do a lot with this trove of pilfered information. Most obviously, spies could identify American government workers with clearances who might be susceptible to blackmail for their affairs or other activities. The security clearance files would also reveal those American federal workers in particular economic straits or perhaps experiencing the kind of stress that has in the past caused individuals to betray their country by selling secrets.

Maybe most significantly, the data could be used to identify American spies abroad. The base of one of the largest CIA stations in the world is the American embassy in Beijing. Since State Department employees were included in the OPM database but CIA employees were not, Americans who were posted in Beijing as "diplomats" but did not appear in the trove probably were of great interest to the Chinese intelligence services. Likewise, the biometric data made it harder for those in the database to operate under an alias. After the breach, one senior intelligence official quoted in the *New York Times* bemoaned this fact: "I am assuming there will be people we simply can't send to China."[43] Then-Director of National Intelligence James Clapper offered his own grim remark: "You've got to salute the Chinese for what they did." The comment highlighted that such data breaches are endemic to modern international competition. "If we had the opportunity to do the same thing," Clapper added, "we'd probably do it."[44]

Perhaps what was most remarkable about the Chinese intrusion into OPM, however, was that it was only one part of a much larger effort to assemble information on tens of millions of Americans. At the time of the breach, one senior United States government official told the *Washington Post* that the Chinese had a "strategic plan" to carry out this kind of massive data collection through hacking.[45] It was another sign of the times: in the era of cyber operations, it is possible to scoop up immense quantities of data, including information on millions of individuals who have no connection to international espionage, and then sift the haul for the insights that lie within.

Other Chinese operations showcase the extent of this ambition. From at least early December 2014 to the end of January 2015, a group of what appear to have been Chinese hackers gained access to critical databases within the health insurance company Anthem, the second-largest insurer in the United States. The hackers gained access to information on almost eighty million Americans, including their social security numbers, addresses, phone numbers, emails, income, and job history.[46] In May 2014, Chinese hackers targeted Premera Blue Cross, a major healthcare provider, and gained access to its database of eleven million customers. The company did not discover the breach until January 2015. In addition to the usual haul of personally identifiable information, the hackers also gained access to patients' clinical records and medical histories.[47] In February 2015, the FBI privately warned companies about ongoing Chinese efforts to compromise government and commercial networks.[48]

The biggest prize of all was perhaps the least flashy: the data from credit monitoring bureaus. To help financial institutions approve or reject loans and credit cards, these companies keep tabs on virtually all adult Americans. In 2015, Equifax, one of the largest monitoring firms, alerted the FBI and CIA because it believed employees had given reams of proprietary data to the Chinese.[49] In May 2017, the firm suffered a devastating hack, which it did not discover until July. The hackers accessed private data that Equifax stored on more than 145 million Americans, including intimate details of their financial histories.[50]

While the attribution to Chinese hackers is not conclusive, there is strong suggestion that the hack originated with a state interested in gathering large amounts of data on Americans, rather than with a non-state criminal actor. Even more than two years after the breach, there is no indication the data has appeared on criminal forums or for sale online. The secrets, like the files from so many Chinese operations that came before, simply vanished.[51]

5

Counterintelligence

IN 1934, HIROSHI ŌSHIMA, then a colonel in the Japanese Army, became the military attaché to Adolf Hitler's government in Berlin. He rose quickly, aided by his near-perfect German, formal military style, and affinity with the senior members of the Nazi party. Within four years he earned the rank of lieutenant general and was named Japan's ambassador to Germany. When the Japanese government briefly called him back home, the Nazis insisted that he return, which he did in early 1941. Their demand reflected the fact that he was, as one historian puts it, "more Nazi than the Nazis."[1]

Ōshima's military training had taught him to keep meticulous notes and write detailed reports. His access to the high command of the Nazi regime, including as a personal confidant of Hitler himself, allowed him to fill his files with uncommon levels of observation and analysis. He became an unparalleled source of insight for his Japanese superiors on what was happening in Germany.

Whenever Ōshima drafted a message with an update on Nazi leadership activities and intentions, Japanese staff in Berlin radioed it back to Tokyo. To guard against interception, they encrypted the messages with a cipher known to the Allies as PURPLE, which depended on modified Enigma machines to work. Much of the Japanese high command considered it unbreakable.

These Japanese leaders were wrong. Just as the Allies considered it imperative to break the Nazis' Enigma encryption, they also made it a priority to crack PURPLE. After a great deal of hard mathematical work and the discovery of several important vulnerabilities in the cryptographic design, the code-breakers succeeded.[2] This enabled them to decrypt and read Ōshima's dispatches, which numbered in the hundreds. Even if he was not on the Allies' side—indeed, *because* he was not on the Allies' side—he was positioned as well as any human asset could be. The Allies so prized his insights into German leadership and decision-making that General George Marshall, the chief of staff of the Army, identified him as "our main basis of information regarding Hitler's intentions in Europe."[3] Ōshima, a defender of the Axis Powers and a warrior-diplomat to his core, died in 1975. He almost certainly had no knowledge of the role he unwittingly played in the Allies' victory in the European theater.[4]

This is the power of counterintelligence. While the discipline is often seen as defensive, the Ōshima case and others like it offer reminders that the most powerful counterintelligence missions are proactive. Traditional spying focuses on stealing political, military, and economic secrets, but counterintelligence goes further, penetrating an adversary's intelligence service to find out what it knows and how it knows it. The American spymaster Allen Dulles, who headed the Central Intelligence Agency in the early years of the Cold War, ordered his officers to compromise the sources, methods, people, and codes of foreign intelligence services—and that mission continues.[5] Achieving it requires intrusive and aggressive collection. It also necessitates spying broadly, since sometimes the best source of information on a foreign intelligence service is in another state entirely.

Just as cyber operations increase the power of other kinds of covert action, they supercharge counterintelligence efforts. It makes sense: robbers steal from banks because that is where the money is, and spies steal from other spies' computers because that is where the secrets are. Sometimes the best way to repel or mislead an adversary is to spy first and spy better. Paul Nakasone, director of the NSA and commander of Cyber Command, acknowledged as much in 2019. "If we find ourselves defending inside our own networks," he said, "we have lost the initiative and the advantage."[6]

Advanced cyber operations targeting a foreign intelligence service can reveal the plans and intentions of an adversary's spies. They can uncover the other side's sources and methods, rendering those hacking techniques ineffective and easy to detect all over the world. Maybe most significantly, hackers can exploit the hard-won access and insight that another intelligence agency spent years of painstaking effort to gain for itself. This sort of collection can sometimes go undetected and be operative for years, yielding reams of valuable intelligence—and the target, like Ōshima, might never know.

Hacking the Hackers

As discussed in Chapter 4, the Chinese aimed an immense number of hacking efforts at a wide range of American targets in the late 2000s. United States intelligence agencies eventually code-named the campaign BYZANTINE HADES. Within this series of intrusions, the agencies also identified several subgroupings likely corresponding to different teams of hackers, one of which they named BYZANTINE CANDOR. The Chinese hackers in this subgroup focused primarily on breaking into the United States Department of Defense, while also spying on economic transactions of geopolitical interest, such as oil deals.[7]

BYZANTINE CANDOR proved to be an effective hacking group. Like so many others, it usually employed spear-phishing as its method of entry. When the target, often a United States government official, opened the message, the hackers' malicious code would deploy and grant the hackers remote access to the target's system. The hackers would then move throughout the target network, sometimes using additional malicious code or stolen passwords to gain access to more machines. They would then find secrets of interest and send them back to China.

The hackers took precautions to mask their identities. They first hacked the computers of innocent third parties. These computers, which cybersecurity researchers call hop points, had little intelligence value but were easy to compromise. Once the hackers had control of the hop points, they routed their operations through them, obscuring the source of the activity. In just one eight-week period in the summer of 2009, the Chinese hackers sent their malicious communications through more than 350 of these hop points spread all over the world, but primarily in the United States.[8]

The Chinese hackers also took steps to hide the instructions they sent to their malicious code on infected computers. In one neat trick, the group used automated posts on obscure Facebook pages to send commands to and from machines all over the world. Once it landed on a target, the malicious code posted a prearranged message—which looked like indecipherable nonsense—on a specific Facebook page. The Chinese hackers then read the message and replied to it with their own seemingly nonsensical reply, which their malicious code knew how to translate into commands. Unless someone knew to look at these specific pages in advance and could tell what each message meant, it was nearly impossible to observe or stop the malicious code's remote control.

Faced with such hard-to-spot threats, NSA analysts realized they had to be proactive. They recognized that the basic forms of cyber defense that took place within the United States' own computer networks—including software updating, antivirus scanning, and network security monitoring—were necessary but insufficient against sophisticated hackers. To defend against nimbler adversaries, it was also necessary to take the initiative. Defenders sometimes had to venture out from their own networks into a more active posture. For better cybersecurity, the NSA realized, it was best to hack the hackers.

The NSA Threat Operations Center, an organization tasked with helping to defend American military networks, decided to look for opportunities to do just that. The group reached out to the elite offensive unit within the NSA then known as Tailored Access Operations, or TAO. TAO's specialty is hacking foreign targets, especially the ones that are hardest to breach. The request from the NSA's network defenders was straightforward: could TAO hack the hackers who had hacked the Department of Defense? And by doing so, could they find intelligence that would make it easier for the cyber defenders to block future intrusions?

TAO's answer was yes. In their subsequent effort, called AR-ROWECLIPSE, the NSA's hackers began with the hop points the Chinese used to hide their identity. Most of the computers hacked by the Chinese were within the United States and owned by Americans, and targeting them would raise legal complexities for the NSA. But some of the machines were located overseas, and TAO targeted these foreign hop points with success. The unit stealthily placed its malicious code on these machines, right alongside the Chinese code.

From this intermediate vantage point, the team at TAO sat back and observed as a wealth of useful information passed by. They watched as the Chinese conducted vulnerability scans and looked for new targets. They spotted Chinese misdirection efforts using email account masquerades and spear-phishing in action. The Chinese hackers were sloppy at times, demonstrating a lack of discipline and operational security. From the same hop points they used for espionage efforts, they sometimes logged into personal email accounts, checked stock portfolios, and watched pornography. TAO quietly kept tabs on them all the while.

Once again, the situation highlights the absurd cat-and-cat-and-mouse game endemic to modern cyber operations. The Chinese had hacked computers from which they hacked American targets. In their own operation, the NSA found and hacked those same computers to spy on the Chinese effort. The regular people who owned the computers likely had no idea anything out of the ordinary was happening.

But TAO was not done. By targeting a wide range of hop points, the unit could determine the IP addresses from which the Chinese communicated with those points. Yet the Chinese changed their IP addresses regularly, trying to disguise even their communications with their own hop points. These constant changes in virtual location made them harder to identify and target, despite TAO's advanced hacking tools. The Chinese hackers' computers thus seemed tantalizingly out of reach, to the NSA's great frustration. Another round of proactive measures would be necessary to gain a counterintelligence edge.

TAO decided to hack the internet service provider that furnished the Chinese operators with connectivity. This was a large-scale operation, since the provider likely served many thousands of customers. TAO was in pursuit of the Chinese hackers who used the provider to communicate with the hop points. By compromising the provider's giant internet routers, as well as its customer and billing records, TAO got a clear picture of which IP addresses the provider assigned to which computers at which times. The NSA unit could then link specific Chinese espionage activities to individual user and customer accounts. This move exposed new sources of evidence on the hackers and pointed to a clear conclusion: the hackers behind BYZANTINE CANDOR hailed from the Third Department of the Chinese PLA.

By now, TAO had the upper hand in this operation. The unit had observed the PLA's espionage activities, had hacked the organization that provided them with internet connections, and had substantiated who was carrying out the Chinese efforts. Even as the PLA generated new hop points, TAO had such good access and insight into the PLA's efforts that it could identify the new computers fairly easily. But why stop there? Instead of observing from hop points and watching from the PLA's internet provider, TAO could go further. The NSA's hackers could, at long last, target the actual computers owned by the hackers in this part of the PLA.

TAO employed something called a man-in-the-middle operation. This requires access to the target's internet traffic, access that TAO's hacking efforts had gained with their penetration of China's hacking infrastructure. From this privileged vantage point, the NSA's hackers could intercept and sometimes manipulate the PLA's data as it moved from its source to its destination and back again.[9] Using this access, TAO appears to have added some secret malicious code to the PLA's normal internet traffic, hacking the computers from which the Chinese carried out their operations.

With this trick, TAO reached five computers tied to known PLA hacking accounts, as well as additional computers not linked to any previously known hacking activity. TAO found a large amount of information on the computers, but much of it was relatively useless for counterintelligence purposes. They stumbled upon old family photos and pet pictures that the PLA hackers had saved to their machines. Other pieces of data, such as images of the PLA officers in uniform, were more interesting, though not directly related to the NSA's cyber defense effort.

Toward the end of October 2009, TAO caught a big break. The unit managed to hack the computer associated with the operational leader of this particular PLA hacking effort. The hack gave the NSA's unit much greater insight into the PLA's operation and the people who were carrying it out. TAO conducted a series of additional hacking operations against the PLA's machines. This included efforts against the home computer of at least one of the Chinese hackers. After many months of work, the NSA's counterintelligence effort had at last thoroughly penetrated its counterpart.

The payoff was big. Through this proactive operation, TAO gained insight into the PLA's activities against the United States government, defense contractors, foreign governments, and more. TAO could see where the PLA had been and gained access to the data of Chinese hacking victims. American analysts were also able to determine which targets the PLA was considering hacking next, since the PLA had stockpiled biographical information on these individuals, including White House officials. Maybe best of all, TAO's hack revealed information on Chinese hacking tools, including the exploits the PLA used to gain access to victim machines.[10] The NSA integrated this intelligence into its effort to defend American networks, including into a program known as TUTELAGE that attempted to learn of and block adversaries' hacking efforts before they made entry to their target networks.[11]

With BYZANTINE CANDOR, the NSA's boldness had paid off. The agency had leapt out of a defensive posture and seized the initiative. The intelligence gained from this and similar efforts proved to be useful in defending the United States against future PLA operations. When the PLA launched a subsequent intrusion attempt, the United States was able to block it. At least for this round, the Americans had won.

This was just one battle, however. Even though the NSA blocked some intrusion attempts that would have succeeded had it not been for the counterintelligence mission, many other Chinese efforts still got through. As with the Su Bin arrest, one case was not enough to stem the relentless tide of Chinese espionage. Modern states succeed in their cyber espionage efforts not just through ingenuity and creativity, but through persistence and aggressiveness. No one intelligence or counterintelligence effort is decisive by itself. The struggle for geopolitical advantage remains broad and never-ending. It can be hard to keep track of all the secret operations, and to know who is doing what and how. But the NSA nonetheless must try.

Tracking the Hackers

It is fairly common for multiple signals intelligence agencies to hack the same computers and networks. What is of interest to one state is often of interest to another. Perhaps the most notable example is an unnamed research institute in the Middle East that the Russian cybersecurity company Kaspersky Lab called "The Magnet of Threats." Six different major groups hacked the institute's systems: two

English-speaking groups (likely corresponding to the NSA and GCHQ), two Russian groups associated with different intelligence agencies, a French intelligence agency, and a Spanish-speaking group of hackers.[12] If any of these hacking groups had realized what was going on, they would likely have spotted the opportunity to spy not just on their target, but also on the others spying on the same target.

This is where information of the sort gathered in TAO's operation against the PLA can prove very helpful. Analysts can use detailed knowledge of an adversary's tools and procedures not just to protect government systems, but also to detect that adversary's hacking efforts against other targets. When the NSA hacks a foreign computer network, it can try to determine who else has done the same by looking at the digital fingerprints the other hackers left behind. In the same way that an offline criminal develops a signature modus operandi over time, so too do hackers. The NSA focuses on telltale clues, such as file names hackers use in their code or changes they make to the configuration of computers they compromise. The information gained from counterintelligence capabilities can aid awareness of what adversaries are up to not just in American networks but all over the world.

To spot and seize these kinds of counterintelligence opportunities, the NSA has its Territorial Dispute program, which agency employees often abbreviate to TeDi. By assembling information the NSA has gathered about a wide range of significant hacking groups all over the world, the TeDi effort builds a "signature" for each group, identifying its distinguishing elements. These signatures can include telltale file names, snippets of code, or habitual behaviors.[13] Using two to five indicators per actor, the NSA is able to differentiate among its adversaries; each group has a unique combination of indicators making up an unintentional calling card.

Using TeDi, the NSA was tracking at least forty-five hacking groups as of 2013. Initially, the program focused just on Russian and Chinese hackers. Before long, however, the effort expanded to include hacking groups from all major states conducting cyber operations. This included states that did not tend to receive much media attention, such as South Korea.[14] In some cases, the NSA appears to have identified particular foreign hacking groups several years before those hackers attracted much scrutiny from the private sector or academia.

The NSA instructs its analysts on what to do if they encounter a specific hacking group on a machine that the agency has also hacked. The instructions depend on which adversary is found. Sometimes, the signature suggests that the hacking is by a friendly group, perhaps a Five Eyes ally. In those cases, manuals tell the analysts to get assistance from managers and not to interfere with the allied agencies. In other cases, TeDi files flag particular signatures corresponding to unknown malicious code and warn analysts to exercise caution; interacting with the code poses a risk of alerting foreign adversaries to the NSA's presence. In still other cases, the agency's manuals inform its analysts that particular malicious code represents "dangerous malware" and that they should "seek help ASAP."[15]

Sometimes, the discovery of a piece of foreign malicious code about which little is known can lead to the discovery of a new threat actor. In November 2009, the Canadian signals intelligence agency CSEC hacked targets inside Iran and found something odd. Using a Five Eyes tool for detecting anomalies on hacked computers, they noticed the presence of another hacking group on the Iranian systems. The unknown group's other targets included the Ministry of Foreign Affairs, the University of Science and Technology, and the Atomic Energy Organization of Iran. The hacking did not fit the profile of any threat actor the Canadians had seen before. Based on its behavior, the analysts concluded the people involved were likely another state's signals intelligence agency, not profit-motivated criminals.

The Canadians wanted to learn more about these unknown spies. Analysts began to develop signatures for the hackers and to track their activities across the internet. To do this, they married the indicators of the group's activity with the broad net of the Five Eyes' passive collection apparatus. They were able to see the hop points from which the hackers operated, and, due to the hackers' poor operational security, log into those systems themselves. This increased collection of information revealed that, in addition to their interest in Iranian targets, the unknown hackers also spied on computers in North Africa, in French-speaking media organizations, in former French colonies, and in European supranational organizations.

The analysts discovered that the group's hackers referred to their project as Babar, the name of a beloved French children's book character. Perhaps in an attempt at misdirection, the hackers used English in their communications, but the Canadians noticed many phrases that native speakers would not use. More collection and analysis led to the conclusion that this effort was a previously unknown hacking group from the French government.[16] Counterintelligence capabilities had uncovered a new actor.

An operation carried out by a group of undercover American spies in Beijing worked similarly. The United States effort began by targeting the Wi-Fi networks of the Indian, Singaporean, Pakistani, Colombian, and Mongolian embassies. In the Indian network, analysts noticed something odd: activity by Chinese hackers. By tracking that activity, the American spies discovered that the Chinese government had compromised key computers within the Indian embassy.

With this illicit access, the Chinese hackers copied an average of ten sensitive diplomatic documents per day, addressing a variety of timely topics. The Americans recognized the opportunity to piggy-back on the Chinese collection to gain intelligence they otherwise would not have on India's geopolitical strategy. Meanwhile, the improved understanding of Chinese espionage helped them find China's hackers in several other locations.[17]

The Five Eyes want to deploy their counterintelligence capabilities in this way, to track known threats and to discover new ones. They do not, however, want to have others deploying the same sort of counterintelligence capabilities against them. A key goal of the TeDi program, therefore, is to protect the Five Eyes' own operations by identifying anyone else present on computers the NSA has hacked. One former intelligence official said it was TeDi's objective to be alert to those who "could steal or figure out what we were doing. It was to avoid being detected."[18] Counterintelligence is a two-way street.

Fourth-Party Collection

Two men face each other. One is downtrodden and defeated, the other tall and triumphant. "I broke you and I beat you," the victor says. The slumped man pleads his case, attempting to make a deal for territory he holds and believes still has value. "If you would just take this lease," he begins, desperate for an opening. But he is about to learn that the land is worthless.

The victor spells out how he has triumphed, gesticulating dramatically for emphasis: "Here, if you have a milkshake, and I have a milkshake, and I have a straw—there it is, that's a straw, you see?" He is holding up a menacing finger. "And my straw reaches *across* the room, and starts to drink your milkshake . . ." The conclusion he yells into the face of the beaten man leaves no mistake about the capacity of the strong and powerful to take from the weak and un-suspecting: "I . . . drink . . . your . . . milkshake!"

The scene is not from some international negotiation gone wrong. It is from Paul Thomas Anderson's classic *There Will Be Blood*. The "milkshakes" are oil wells, the focus of the characters' desperate com-petition. The film vividly depicts the ferocity of turn-of-the-century petroleum prospectors in Southern California. Exploiting the vacuum of law and order, one driller can extract assets that another thinks are safe and valuable.

For an NSA briefer preparing a highly classified talk on the agen-cy's counterintelligence operations, Anderson's scene provided in-spiration. The cover image for the presentation is an extra-long straw silently pilfering the contents of a soda-fountain glass. The famous "milkshake" quote is splashed across the title slide, just above the classification labels that mark the document as top-secret.[19]

In the competition among intelligence agencies, the precious re-source is information. Previous chapters have shown how spies use cyber operations to gain better intelligence on their targets. This chapter has so far focused on how agencies track one another, im-proving their own defenses against adversaries. But as intrusive as TAO's effort against the PLA and Canada's effort against France were, neither was designed to drink an adversary's milkshake. Still more is possible.

The NSA presentation with the milkshake cover explains what is known as fourth-party collection.[20] This term builds on some older concepts. First-party collection is information collected by the agency itself. Second-party collection is intelligence gathered and shared by another Five Eyes member. Third-party collection is in-formation obtained by an intelligence agency outside the Five Eyes and shared with the NSA. Fourth-party collection is the realm of illicit milkshake-drinking: it involves knowing that one state has intelligence on another state and helping oneself to it.

The NSA distinguishes between various types of fourth-party collection.[21] The first type is what the agency calls passive acquisition. As the name suggests, this type of intelligence gathering does not rely on directly hacking the target. Instead, the NSA uses its passive collection capabilities, as described in Chapter 1, to quietly get what it wants. Perhaps, for example, the Chinese intelligence agencies regularly hack Russia. The NSA can tap the internet infrastructure that routes data between China and Russia. As the intelligence pilfered by the Chinese passes by the NSA's wiretaps, the agency can try to make a copy and understand it. If successful, the NSA not only gains insight into Chinese collection capabilities but also learns the secrets gathered from Russia. The agency can sustain this unobtrusive form of passive collection for long periods of time; in this hypothetical example, neither China nor Russia knows of the NSA's subtle eavesdropping.[22]

This method does not always suffice, however. Sometimes an adversary's intelligence-gathering infrastructure does not connect over cables and data hubs accessible to the NSA. Other times, adversaries encrypt the communications they use for intelligence collection in ways the NSA cannot decipher, foiling even the NSA's special efforts to decrypt the command-and-control instructions of foreign malicious code.[23] Still other times, the NSA simply desires a more direct presence on the adversary's hacking infrastructure, perhaps to enable other collection operations of its own.

In circumstances like these, the agency uses the second type of fourth-party collection, which it calls active acquisition. Here, the NSA hacks into and gathers information directly from the adversary's digital infrastructure and hop points, snooping over the virtual shoulders of foreign hackers as they work. From this more direct vantage point, an intelligence agency can get a detailed view of its counterpart's activities—again, both observing the tools it uses and learning the secrets it gathers from its targets.

The NSA deployed active acquisition techniques against a China-based group it called BYZANTINE RAPTOR. The agency began by gathering information about a computer used by these Chinese hackers to issue commands to their malicious code around the world. Armed with what it learned from initial reconnaissance, the in-house intrusion team at TAO hacked the machines through which the Chinese sent instructions to their malicious code. Using this active acquisition technique, TAO developed the capacity to collect intelligence on the Chinese operation in a quiet and sustainable way.

During its reconnaissance, the NSA noticed that one of the targets was the United Nations' computer network. The Chinese hackers regularly found documents and other files of interest on United Nations computers and copied them back to China. BYZANTINE RAPTOR's compromised command-and-control infrastructure served as a way station and coordination hub for a great deal of this espionage, enabling the NSA to get its own copies of many documents swiped by the Chinese.

This was a great help to the agency given that, as Chapter 1 showed, the United Nations is a top target. Whenever the American operators got new documents from their spying on the Chinese who were spying on the United Nations, they sent them to the NSA's data repository for storage. They also tipped off the NSA analysts tasked with reporting on the relevant international developments. Based on the fourth-party collection of files originally pilfered by the Chinese, the analysts generated at least three notable intelligence reports, all relating to significant, high-profile, ongoing events.[24]

In the BYZANTINE CANDOR case mentioned above, TAO used its access to the PLA's hop points to eventually make its way upstream toward the Chinese network. The reverse is also possible: TAO could have worked downstream from those points to the networks the Chinese had hacked. The NSA calls these processes victim sharing and victim stealing, and they constitute the third type of fourth-party collection. They let the NSA find and hack new targets of mutual interest. Sometimes, the agency can go further to take control of foreign intelligence services' hacking tools. Even more aggressively, it can remove those tools and replace them with its own tools.

The state on which the NSA piggybacks need not be an adversary. Sometimes it can even be an ally, as another example from East Asia demonstrates. North Korea, a high-priority intelligence target of the United States, is also a high-priority intelligence target of American ally South Korea. The NSA, in seeking to gather information about the northern country, tries to determine what the southern one knows, and how its agencies know it. While there are diplomatic channels and other means of officially swapping intelligence between the United States and South Korea, the two governments do not share every secret.

At one point, South Korean signals intelligence appeared to have better insights into its northern neighbor than the United States had. One person involved in the NSA's effort to target North Korea noted that the American agency's access to the famously isolated state at the time was "next to nothing." To remedy this, the NSA used its espionage capabilities to target South Korea's intelligence-gathering efforts. The agency found that South Korean spies had managed to get their malicious code onto the computers of North Korean officials. The NSA discovered the hop points used by the South Koreans to move this data, and gained access to those machines. Spying on South Korea's spying on North Korea thus yielded a range of documents that would have been harder to access otherwise.

The NSA then used the intelligence collected from South Korea as a guide to hacking North Korean networks. The agency penetrated the North Korean systems in part out of paranoia: some in the NSA worried that the South Koreans would discover the NSA was piggybacking on their intelligence gathering efforts and act on that knowledge, perhaps by misleading the Americans with false information.[25] Such distrust and competition are endemic to the duplicitous world of counterintelligence, even among allies.[26]

In the case of the Koreas, the story went one level deeper still: much of the intelligence acquired by the NSA via fourth-party collection against South Korea described North Korea's own hacking efforts. One person involved in the operation called this fifth-party collection. If fourth-party collection has the ferocity of *There Will Be Blood*, then fifth-party collection has the complexity of *Inception*: it involves American spies spying on South Korean spies spying on North Korean spies spying on other countries. As ever, counterintelligence is messy.

PART TWO

ATTACK

6

Strategic Sabotage

STUXNET WAS A WATERSHED, an indication of what states can do with hacking when they are extremely ambitious. The episode underscores what it takes, in terms of operational skill, preparation, and opportunity, to sabotage a specific target—to inflict physical damage—with cyber capabilities. Yet, even with its massive resources, Stuxnet reveals the limits of such operations.

Stuxnet was a destructive computer worm hatched by innovative hackers in US and Israeli intelligence, designed to set Iran's nuclear centrifuges to dangerously high speeds. The malicious code escaped the confines of Iran's nuclear facilities, however, and spread all over the world. Incredibly, its origins might have escaped scrutiny if not for the combination of a continually restarting computer in Iran, a small antivirus firm in Belarus, and eventually a team of talented researchers working at major cybersecurity companies. When all was said and done, the operation was a mixed success for the United States and Israel, but a boon for those seeking to understand how advanced cyber operations work. With good reason, the attack quickly became the most widely discussed hack among both cyber-security researchers and scholars of international relations.

And, remarkably, the story didn't end there. Stuxnet was not the only tool of sabotage deployed against Iran. A larger cyber campaign against Iranian economic interests also unfolded in 2012—one that has largely escaped public view and enjoys far less popular cachet. In some respects, this largely overlooked operation holds more mysteries. Known only as Wiper, it too shows the power of targeted sabotage in the digital age.

A Worm Is Born

The problem facing George W. Bush's administration was obvious but intractable: Iran was moving ever closer to obtaining nuclear weapons. The United States was bogged down in war in Afghanistan and in Iraq, where Iran was growing in influence and an insurgency was fracturing near-term prospects for peace. The White House had sought to bring pressure on Iran from the international community, but building support for an aggressive sanctions program was difficult, especially since America's global relationships had soured after the Iraq invasion. Israel was pressing Bush to do more, with the strong implication that it might act if the United States did not. This was no idle threat; in September 2007, the Israelis had launched a stealthy unilateral air raid against a Syrian nuclear facility.[1]

The president needed a new strategy. Doing nothing was unwise, as Iran continued its slow march toward greater nuclear capability. A full-on invasion was unthinkable. Iran was alert to traditional types of sabotage.[2] Diplomacy seemed to be faltering, at least in the minds of senior officials in the Bush White House. Air strikes might work for a while but would be a massive provocation, potentially leading to new Iranian acts of terror or a spiraling conflict. In any case, bombs could not stop Iran's underground nuclear program forever. Israel grew more anxious by the day, reportedly asking Bush for assistance with an attack.[3] The president said no, but knew he could not hold Israel off forever. More than anything, Bush needed time.

The US government's technical experts came up with a new option, which would eventually become known as Stuxnet. It was a targeted sabotage operation against the centrifuges at Natanz, Iran's leading nuclear facility. These centrifuges were upright silver cylinders, taller than a person and several inches wide. Centrifuge rotors spin at rapid and carefully calibrated speeds to separate different isotopes of uranium from one another, a process known as enrichment. Iran had restarted its enrichment program in 2006, and it was an essential step on the path to nuclear weapons. Mahmoud Ahmadinejad, Iran's president at the time, made no attempt to conceal his desire for more centrifuges. In one tour of the Iranian nuclear facility, he spoke of plans to build and operate fifty thousand of them.[4]

The United States wanted to derail that ambition, and saw a way to do so through sabotage. There is nothing more frustrating for engineers than fickle systems suffering random and unexplained failures. By wreaking silent havoc on the centrifuges, the saboteurs could destroy vital equipment and cause the Iranian engineers to slow their efforts, distrust their own scientific advisors, and doubt their capacity to build a nuclear weapon. If all went as hoped, Iran would take systems offline while looking for the problem, amplifying Stuxnet's equipment damage into an extended delay. If no one knew the true cause of the centrifuge failures, the delay and uncertainty would create more opportunity for the United States' strategy of pressure and diplomacy to work.

Another strategic benefit was that the United States could work with Israel's excellent cyber operations units on the covert mission. The joint effort was a way of showing commitment to an ally and offering up a solution to the Iran problem that did not involve another war in the Middle East. With these benefits in mind, President Bush signed off on the program. The United States government gave it the code name Olympic Games, reportedly a reference to the international partnership between the United States, Israel, and European allies.[5]

The orchestration of the sabotage operation was impressive. One of the first orders of business was to develop a detailed understanding of the Iranian nuclear facilities' configuration. In conventional physical attacks using weapons like cruise missiles, operators can fire at different types of targets without changing the weapon itself. By contrast, the cyber attack team needed to tailor its weapon to the specifications of the systems it wanted to destroy. This required in-depth reconnaissance of the Iranian nuclear facility to figure out how the centrifuges worked—and how they could break.

To carry out this reconnaissance, it is reported that the attackers had the benefit of a mole inside Natanz. The mole, recruited by Dutch intelligence, provided the attackers critical insights on how the Iranian program was designed. In addition, it also seems likely that the United States used a custom piece of malicious code that cybersecurity researchers would later name Fanny to spy on Natanz; if the United States did not use Fanny for this purpose, it almost certainly used a piece of malicious code that worked similarly.[6] The story behind Fanny is still not entirely clear, as it was not discovered until 2015, long after Stuxnet.[7] It appears, however, that the United States built one version of the code in July 2008 and put it into use not long after that.

The first part of the digital reconnaissance mission was simple to outline but hard to do: get inside Natanz. Because the computers that controlled the centrifuges were not connected to the internet, the hackers could not reach them directly; in the parlance of cybersecurity researchers, these systems were "air gapped" from the internet. To defeat this protection, Fanny's creators designed the code as a worm, meaning that it could spread itself from computer to computer on its own, without any real-time direction from its creators.

Fanny was able to spread autonomously thanks to some previously unknown vulnerabilities in key components of Windows. One of the vulnerabilities related to how Windows handled portable USB drives. By taking advantage of this weakness, Fanny could hide itself on such a device, and when a user plugged that drive into a new computer, Fanny would infect the computer even if that computer did not automatically run files from external devices. Once on board the newly infected machine, Fanny could spread itself to other machines. Before long, exponential growth would dictate that the worm reached a large number of targets, from which the hackers could gather information via a disguised command-and-control system. Eventually, someone carried Fanny across the air gap, enabling the worm's creators to gather information on the targets of their planned attack; it is unknown if human intelligence sources played a role in this infection.[8] Without this extensive reconnaissance, the Stuxnet attack would have been impossible.

Even with a more detailed understanding of how the Iranians configured their centrifuges, the attackers had substantial work to do before they could launch their sabotage effort. Among their tasks was writing and testing the code to make sure it would have the desired effect on the Iranian targets. In this effort, the United States got help from an unlikely source: the old Libyan nuclear program.

Libya had ended its nuclear program in 2003, at which time the United States acquired its centrifuges. These came from the same network of suppliers as Iran's. Using the Libyan centrifuges and others in a series of proof-of-concept operations in secret labs in the United States, the Americans destroyed a number of them with ever-improving iterations of cyber attack code. Israel seems to have done the same with its own copies of Iranian centrifuges, setting up a replica facility in a remote desert location that mimicked Natanz exactly.[9] With the success of these tests—including one that produced centrifuge fragments later shown to President Bush—the operation moved ahead.[10] When the presidency transitioned from George Bush to Barack Obama, Obama saw the value of Olympic Games and ordered that the operation be accelerated.[11]

The Stuxnet attack code that gradually took shape during this period was a worm, just like Fanny. Early versions appear to have been able to spread only via USB drives, and may have initially been placed into Natanz by the mole. Later versions had much more power to spread themselves from one computer and network to the next, eventually deploying no fewer than eight different propagation mechanisms.[12] Infecting a broad range of computers, especially within contractors for Iran's nuclear program, increased the odds that Stuxnet would cross the air gap and reach the centrifuges. Five contractors appear to have been the initial targets, the patient zeroes who unleashed the wider infection.[13] Sure enough, Stuxnet eventually made its way into Natanz.

Stuxnet's creators programmed different versions of the code to talk to one another like gossiping teenagers. When a new version of Stuxnet infected a computer that had been previously infected by an earlier version, the two copies of the worm compared notes and combined their information. Versions landing on internet-connected computers sent their information back to Stuxnet's creators in messages disguised to look like visits to innocuous soccer websites.[14] Thus, the list of machines the operation had infected across Iran was constantly updated, and the data it had collected steadily accumulated. The worm had a strange sort of hive mind.

No doubt, this talk of newfangled cyber sabotage, secret infections, and hive minds would have worried any lawyer. In national security, at least in the West, lawyers are ever-present, and the Stuxnet operation was no exception. At key moments, these attorneys raised concerns about unintended consequences—and rightly so. While the Stuxnet code tried to stay mostly contained within a fairly narrow set of targets, its worm-like nature made it far harder to control than other sophisticated cyber operations tools.[15]

Throughout the development and testing process, Stuxnet's creators added a series of target verification checks, using information acquired from earlier reconnaissance. They made it so Stuxnet would cease creating new infections after a certain date, several years away, in June 2012, and the code would launch its most destructive payload only if it was sure it was in Natanz.[16] There were so many of these self-restraints that former White House cybersecurity czar Richard Clarke remarked that it looked like a team of Washington lawyers had written the code.[17]

The Stuxnet payload, once launched, was unprecedented. While there were numerous variants of Stuxnet over the years, two stand out. One variant that dates to 2007 manipulated the amount of uranium hexafluoride gas that flowed out of the centrifuges. By manipulating the valves that controlled the release of gas, Stuxnet could adjust the pressure inside the centrifuge. The code increased the pressure to levels five times above where they should have been for normal enrichment, prompting the gas to transition to a solid state of matter. This in turn caused the centrifuges to fail.

Manipulating the system in this way required enormous knowledge of nuclear engineering and deep reconnaissance of the Iranian systems. The attackers understood the weaknesses of the centrifuges, how Iranian engineers had compensated for those weaknesses, and how the overall system could be subtly manipulated. One investigator marveled at the intricacies of the attack code and the detailed understanding of Natanz they revealed. The attackers, he wrote, "may as well know the favorite pizza toppings of the local head of engineering."[18]

Stuxnet's creators could have launched a devastating strike that would have destroyed many centrifuges at once. But doing so would have let Iran know it was under attack. Seemingly, Stuxnet's creators in both the Bush and Obama administrations wanted to hide, subtly slow the program, and frustrate the Iranians. One person involved in the program told a *New York Times* reporter that "the intent was that the failures should make them feel they were stupid, which is what happened."[19]

To do this, Stuxnet deployed a devious trick. In essence, the code took command of the interface that let Iranian nuclear scientists monitor their centrifuges in action. Stuxnet could dictate what information the Iranians saw, showing information that was wholly false. When the time came to attack, Stuxnet hid its manipulation of the gas pressure by playing back a recording of normal functioning on a loop.[20] It told the Iranians what they expected to see: that all was fine. Meanwhile, undetected, the prized centrifuges began to destroy themselves from within.

For reasons that are unknown, a more aggressive version of Stuxnet superseded the pressure manipulation attack. In the new version, which appeared in 2009, the attack code manipulated the speed at which the rotors at the core of each centrifuge spun, a key variable in the enrichment process. Stuxnet undid the Iranian commands and substituted in a set of new ones. The worm's creators had designed the new commands during the extensive development and testing phase, enabling Stuxnet to disable key safety and control mechanisms. At certain times, the code ordered the rotors to accelerate to very high speeds, 84,600 rotations per minute, and then to slow to a languid pace, only 120 rotations per minute. The changes placed tremendous stress on the fragile components, causing erratic failures, all without any pattern that the Iranians could discern. Changing rotor speed was simpler and potentially more detectable than manipulating pressure, but it appears the Iranians still did not figure out that they were under attack.[21]

The operation seemed to work. Stuxnet evidently destroyed more than a thousand centrifuges, although analysts debate the exact number. The delays the Iranians suffered in nuclear enrichment put them somewhere between one and three years behind their expected pace.[22] They struggled to figure out what was causing the unexplained failures at Natanz. Reports suggested that officials fired engineers, either for incompetence or treason, as they flailed about trying to get things back on track.[23] It seemed that they would never learn the truth about what was really going on—until one day they did.

Discovery

Stuxnet would not be the story it is without a young Belarusian cybersecurity researcher named Sergey Ulasen who worked for Virus-BlokAda, a small company. In June 2010, one of the company's clients in Iran was having an issue with a Windows computer: it would continually crash and restart, seemingly without any cause.

This was not good, at least not for Stuxnet's creators. Ulasen's client was not in Natanz, but elsewhere in Iran. It was not an intended target, but Stuxnet had wound up on its systems anyway. Once it was there, the worm was inadvertently interfering with the computer, despite knowing, thanks to its target verification mechanisms, not to launch its full attack routine. Stuxnet, with its aggressive propagation tricks, had spread too far. Worse, because of its worm-like nature, the code would only continue to spread.

Over time, it infected more than a hundred thousand computers around the world, primarily in Iran, but in more than a hundred other countries as well.[24] For their part, some US government officials, up to and including Vice President Joe Biden, privately blamed their Israeli allies. They contended that the Israeli changes to the code had increased the aggressiveness of the infection mechanism.[25] After-action analyses differ on who was to blame.[26] It might be no one; simple bad luck can ruin even the best-planned operations.

Ulasen did not know any of this. He was sure at first that the cause of the restarts was something mundane. Misconfiguration of the operating system can cause erratic crashes, as can conflicts between two installed software programs. It was only when Ulasen learned that the problem was happening to other computers on the client's network that he thought something more was amiss. When he realized that it was affecting computers that had fresh new installations of Windows, presumably free from configuration errors and software conflicts, he grew even more interested. Most of all, he was baffled that all malicious code-detection systems indicated that the affected systems were clean of infections.

Ulasen was at a friend's wedding reception in the Belarusian countryside one Saturday night when this pattern of facts became clear. As well-dressed and increasingly intoxicated revelers paraded by, he stayed in the corner of the party, glued to his phone. When the party shifted to the woods, he remained on the case, remotely teasing out the facts with the help of a friend in Iran. Neither he nor the friend realized their project would eventually become the most famous cyber attack investigation in history.

Ulasen and his colleagues dug in more deeply, uncovering many of Stuxnet's secrets and its impressive technical accomplishments. They noticed the way it exploited previously unknown software vulnerabilities to spread from computer to computer, a propagation mechanism that was unusual. They discovered its elaborate attempts to hide itself inside other software processes running on Windows, a sign that the worm's creators had enormous technical skill and wanted to avoid detection. They were struck by how the Stuxnet code drew on stolen signing certificates, a mechanism used to ensure that code run by the operating system is legitimate. That the attackers could steal and deploy such certificates suggested they had access to significant resources and placed high priority on operational security. But, for all of these insights, it became clear that Stuxnet was too big and complex for VirusBlokAda to fully understand and combat on its own. The company needed help.

Ulasen reached out to Microsoft. He tried to tell the firm what he had found but received no reply. He contacted Realtek, the company whose digital certificate Stuxnet had illicitly used, and was met with similar silence. It was only after he and his colleagues began posting analysis online that the cybersecurity community started to take notice.[27] In July 2010, the well-respected journalist Brian Krebs wrote a small story about one of the exploits at the core of the worm.[28] After that, Microsoft started examining the malicious code, as did other cybersecurity companies.[29]

One of those companies was Symantec, a large American firm. Unlike VirusBlokAda, Symantec had the resources to do a major investigation into the code, which it called Stuxnet, a word made up by combining some of the attackers' file names. While the company's researchers were at first skeptical that Stuxnet would be significant, they came to realize it was a colossal piece of malicious software, about fifty times larger than was typical.[30] In time, they deduced that the code's creators wanted to sabotage industrial control systems, but they did not fully understand which systems were at risk and in what way. Even Symantec needed more specialized help. The firm posted a report to its website, sharing what it knew and hinting at all the mysteries of Stuxnet that remained.[31]

The person who provided the next round of insights would become another well-known character in the cybersecurity world: Ralph Langner. Langner, with his stylish attire and outspoken nature, was also one of the world's experts on industrial control systems. He ran an international cybersecurity firm that focused exclusively on keeping those systems safe. Unlike Symantec's researchers, he knew there was a neat trick that would help piece together what Stuxnet was trying to do.

Langner's trick was to take a copy of the worm and put it in a virtual environment that simulated an industrial control system. By subtly and painstakingly altering this environment time and again to simulate different systems and configurations, he was able to watch how Stuxnet's behavior varied in different circumstances. In this indirect way, and after much investigation by his firm, Langner eventually learned what he thought was the worm's ultimate objective: a particular kind of industrial control system arranged in a very specific configuration. Langner realized that it was the most advanced cyber capability the world had ever seen, but it aimed at just one specific target.

Yet Langner and his researchers still had to figure out what that target was. There was no doubt that it was a target of geopolitical significance, and one that the attackers wanted to strike in secret. Because of this, the researchers worried that Stuxnet's perpetrators might try to thwart publication of their findings or kill Stuxnet's investigators. At a tense moment in the investigation, one analyst wrote to others, "If I turn up dead and I committed suicide on Monday, I just want to tell you guys, I'm not suicidal." Another half-joked about being the target of motorcycle assassins, a method Israel had employed to kill Iranian nuclear scientists.[32]

Technical analysis alone was unable to determine the target. To find the answer they were seeking, Langner and his team had to consider strategic dimensions, as well. Eventually, after weeks of fruitless investigation, Langner started thinking in more depth about the geopolitical implications of the Stuxnet code. In a night of web searching, he read about Bushehr, an Iranian nuclear site that had been under development but had suffered delays in operation.

The next day, he announced his theory to stunned colleagues: "This is about taking out Iran's nuclear program."[33] They were skeptical, but Langner's instincts were spot-on. Even though he got some of the details wrong—namely, believing that Stuxnet targeted Bushehr, not Natanz—his further investigation proved he had the big picture right. To confirm his hypothesis that the worm aimed to disrupt centrifuges, he called a well-placed friend. The friend told him only that everything about the subject was classified, but Langner took his non-denial as encouragement.[34]

Langner decided that Stuxnet was too important to sit in obscurity. In September 2010, he wrote two online posts that laid out what he knew about how Stuxnet worked. In them, he called the operation a "directed sabotage" attack, one that was "the hack of the century."[35] Langner had finally assembled and published a majority of the pieces of the Stuxnet puzzle, the physical attack he and others had long feared. Like so many scholars of cyber attacks before and after him, Langner framed this bold and aggressive sabotage operation that was never supposed to see the light of day in stark terms. He told his readers: "Welcome to cyberwar."[36]

Wiper

As Stuxnet was emerging into public view in 2011 and 2012, tensions between the United States, Israel, and Iran continued to rise. Renewed rumors swirled about an imminent Israeli air strike against Iran. Many analysts feared Iranian escalation, perhaps in retaliation for the cyber attack on its enrichment facility. Meanwhile, the Obama administration and its allies increased the economic sanctions designed to cripple the regime. In this high-stakes geopolitical struggle, no one was sure what the next move would be.

On April 23, 2012, the computers in Iran's Oil Ministry stopped working. This was not the first time this kind of malfunction had happened. Since December 2011, less damaging shutdowns of this sort had occurred during the last ten days of each month.[37] The cause was not immediately apparent. By March, Iranian network defenders may have figured out that they were under attack, but they were unable to stop the hostile operation from continuing or make much headway into how it worked.

Unfortunately for Iran, the April attack was much more serious than the ones that had preceded it. Though the damage is hard to assess with any precision, some reports claimed widespread and significant digital destruction. It seems the Iranians also took additional systems offline to limit the damage. One Oil Ministry official told the *New York Times* that the ministry had "disconnected all oil facilities, operations, and even oil rigs from the Internet to prevent this virus from spreading."[38]

For the second time, a sophisticated cyber attack was ripping through Iran. Iranian government officials recognized that the country was once more suffering the effects of a significant foreign sabotage operation, and even though, as with Stuxnet, the attackers did not claim credit, they had some pretty good guesses about who was responsible. A spokesman close to the Supreme Leader of Iran condemned the attack and projected a resilient image. "This is again an attempt to wage soft war by the West," he proclaimed defiantly, "and does not have any impact on our operations."[39]

The attack quickly earned the name Wiper because of what it did to the data on Iranian hard drives. While it did not impact Iran's oil production, the attack wiped key computers in many parts of the country's oil infrastructure. This included the National Iranian Oil Processing and Distribution Company, the National Offshore Oil Company, the National Iranian Gas Company, and a range of organizations under the umbrella of the National Iranian Oil Company. Six major oil terminals, a key part of the country's infrastructure, went offline. Among them was one terminal that transferred 80 percent of Iran's crude exports, totaling more than one million barrels of oil per day. Quasi-official Iranian news outlets confirmed the extent of the damage as the attack unfolded, suggesting that, despite some Iranian claims, things were not entirely under control.[40]

Yet, as bad as the damage was, there was little trace of the attack code itself. One of the most remarkable things about Wiper was how thorough it was—both in destroying its target and also, after the job was done, destroying itself. The Russian cybersecurity company Kaspersky Lab launched a major investigation but came up nearly empty, noting that Wiper had removed almost every piece of evidence on most of the computers it targeted. The company's investigators could not find a single sample of the code. But with careful investigative work, they pieced together an understanding of how Wiper worked.

Kaspersky found that the operation was complex. Just before the attack was about to begin, a mysterious piece of code within Wiper activated. The code triggered another file that appears to have had a random name, one that was different on each computer it infected. Once started, these pieces of code deleted themselves and then overwrote the deleted files with garbage data, further obscuring the trail of evidence. It seems that, above all, the overarching goal of Wiper was to hide how the code worked, or even that it existed at all. As with Stuxnet, its creators seemed to desire devastating but erratic and inexplicable failures that would hurt Iranian operations and undermine confidence but not suggest foreign interference.

In its attack, the code seemed also to prioritize efficiency. Its designers knew that fully deleting and overwriting all the files on a large hard drive would take a substantial period of time, and such an attack might be interrupted before it could be completed. To maximize the amount of harm the attack could do, Wiper's creators carefully plotted how Wiper moved through the target computer's files.

The first priority was destroying documents, programs, and files key to the functioning of Windows. Wiper eliminated these files first because they were more likely than others to be of importance to the target. Next, the code targeted entire folders likely to hold valuable data, such as the Documents folder, just to make sure it had not missed anything in the first destructive pass. When it found important files, it deleted them from the hard drive and then overwrote them with meaningless information to inhibit recovery.[41] Lastly, Wiper tried to purge entire sectors of the hard drive, seemingly trying to do as much damage as it could before the computer crashed or defenders could intervene.

In its construction, Wiper bore remarkable technical similarities to Stuxnet and to other pieces of malicious code known as Flame, Gauss, and Duqu, each of which had been deployed elsewhere in the Middle East. The strong similarities among them indicate that they shared the same architects. Rather than reimplement important functionality in different ways, the creators of this family of malicious code seemed to have shared components.[42]

Why launch Wiper at all? There is an intuitive answer that easily fits the evidence: to damage Iran's economy. Wiper could well have been a complement to the biting sanctions the Obama administration was putting into place. It may have been launched by the United States or Israel or both. Regardless, the code seems to have been an attempt to strike directly at the heart of Iranian oil production, sabotaging the lifeblood of the Iranian regime without leaving a trace.

The Power To Thwart

During the Cold War, Thomas Schelling and a chorus of other international relations theorists extolled a theory of warfare that focused on bargaining. What mattered, they said, was "the power to hurt"—to coerce an adversary into bending at least partially to one's will to avoid the imposition of further costs.[43] This concept of war involves sending clear and credible signals to an adversary about the pain to come if they do not behave as desired.

Stuxnet was different. It was not an attempt to inflict visible harm or to signal the prospect of more to come. Instead, it was an attempt to shape the situation, to buy time and undermine confidence, key pillars of the United States' strategy for dealing with Iran. No worm could delay the Iranian nuclear program forever, but Stuxnet could give the United States a better chance of overall success. As the worm tore apart Iranian centrifuges and slowed their enrichment progress, the noose of economic sanctions tightened, aided in part by Wiper's sabotage.

As a result, Stuxnet's creators craved secrecy. Without it, the effectiveness of the nuclear sabotage effort would diminish. If the Iranians knew that the cause of the random centrifuge failures was not their own incompetence or traitorous scientists but foreign interference, they could proceed full steam ahead. But if the Iranians continued to doubt their own abilities and take systems offline for inspection and maintenance, then the United States would have more time to negotiate a deal for peace.

In the most favorable interpretation, Stuxnet provided not just time but leverage. A *New York Times* analysis after the Iran deal's signing concluded that the United States' power to thwart Iran's ambitions mattered. The analysis noted that, for as much as the Obama administration praised diplomacy and economic sanctions, equally important were the "covert actions that repeatedly, if briefly, set back the nuclear program and convinced Iranian elites that its secrecy had been compromised."[44] Whether this was an overall success depends in part on one's view of the deal itself; the Trump administration later withdrew from the agreement.

That the worm came to light at all is perhaps the most striking part of the entire saga. An ad hoc group of cybersecurity professionals that most people had never heard of uncovered a classified operation ordered at the highest levels of the American government. The United States carried out Stuxnet in quiet partnership with an ally, tested it in extreme secrecy and at great expense, delivered it to another country's secret nuclear facility on the other side of the world, and then watched as its details eventually emerged for all to see. While bad luck had previously ruined covert missions and intelligence operations, this was more than misfortune. The Stuxnet outcome hinted at a pattern that would become increasingly apparent as time went on: states had tremendous power in cyber operations, but nonstate actors including researchers and journalists were increasingly important, as well.

Indeed, it was journalism that made Stuxnet famous. In the summer of 2011, *Wired*'s Kim Zetter wrote an in-depth profile of the affair, which she later turned into a book-length history of the worm.[45] In the summer of 2012, *New York Times* reporter David Sanger wrote a book confirming what many had suspected—that the United States and Israel had carried out the attack—and adding new details about its authorization and implementation.[46]

These accounts paint a consistent picture: Stuxnet and Wiper were mostly technical successes and likely also short-term geopolitical victories. But Iran's leadership had learned firsthand what cyber operations could do, and adjusted their own ambitions accordingly. Even as nuclear diplomacy was starting to develop, Iran prepared to join the digital fray.

7

Targeted Disruption

LINES OF EMPTY GASOLINE TRUCKS STRETCHED FOR MILES. Employees lost access to their corporate emails and to their phones and had to shuttle documents via interoffice mail. Fax machines eventually offered a faster method, but only after the information technology staff figured out where to go to buy them. In lieu of computers, many workers took up typewriters, pens, and paper. Unable to process payments, corporate leadership decided to give the oil away for free while systems were offline. It was quite a blow for Aramco—the most valuable company in the world, owner of the globe's largest oil fields, and producer of 10 percent of the planet's annual oil output.[1]

The most significant fact about Aramco is that the leadership of Saudi Arabia owns every single share of the business. Even more inextricably than other oil companies, Aramco is tied to geopolitics. To its government owners, the firm's reserves and power over the price of oil are significant levers of statecraft, and the Saudi royal family has employed them at various points in history. To outside observers, Aramco's sprawling network of facilities and its worldwide brand are symbols of Saudi Arabia's strength and global ambitions.

To a group of Iranian hackers looking to strike a blow against the desert kingdom in retaliation for its work with the Obama administration on sanctions against the Islamic Republic, it was the perfect target.[2] In August 2012, they launched their devastating attack.

Whereas Stuxnet and Wiper sought to be silent and stealthy, Iran's operations aspired to be loud and disruptive. While the attack did not rise to the violence of traditional conflict, it demonstrated the Iranian hackers' capability to disrupt the core business of a global company.[3] Attacks like this brought cyber operations, which had long been buried in the shadow world of espionage and covert sabotage, more fully into view. With these capabilities, Iranians signaled positions and intentions, though in the end they showed the limits of using hacking to signal in hopes of changing adversary behavior.

Shamoon

The operation against Aramco was Iran's first major cyber attack.[4] It seems to have begun with a spear-phishing email, as so many attacks do. At some point, perhaps in mid-2012, an Aramco employee using an internet-connected machine opened an email and clicked on a malicious link or file, unwittingly granting Iranian hackers a foothold in the company's network.[5] From this initial point of compromise, the hackers worked to expand their presence by spreading malicious code to other computers and servers. They used a computer within the company's network as a proxy of sorts, issuing instructions to it and having it relay those instructions to other machines across the firm.

Once it got onto a target computer, the hackers' code loaded itself to a folder it labeled Shamoon, which quickly became investigators' name for both the code and the operation. Shamoon's code consisted of three components. The first of these copied itself to various places on the computer and the Aramco network. It also configured itself to run in the future whenever the targeted computer started up. This is a fairly common technique for achieving what cybersecurity experts call persistence: the capacity to remain on a targeted system despite actions taken by users, such as rebooting the machine or trying to delete malicious code. With this foothold established, the Shamoon code deployed its other two components: one to wipe files from the target system, and one to let the attackers know how the operation was proceeding.

Once the Shamoon attackers activated the wiping component, it deleted an existing part of the computer system known as a disk driver, which helps manage the reading and writing of files on the hard drive. It then replaced that disk driver with its own prepared copy. This copy appeared to be legitimate to the computer's operating system and avoided raising suspicion. The wiping code then looked for folders containing important files, such as documents, downloads, pictures, music, and videos—basically, everything a user might value. Having found these folders, the wiping code proceeded to overwrite their contents. This was more powerful than simply deleting the data, as it made recovering the original contents harder.

With this done, the code turned its attention to wiping a key component known as the master boot record. This central repository of vital information on a computer's hard drive contains information about how to store files and what the computer should do when it starts up. Without that guidance, it is nearly impossible for the machine to function normally. This impediment to normal functioning was exactly what the hackers desired. Shamoon was not as sophisticated as the Wiper attack against Iran's oil industry, but it didn't have to be.

Researchers called the third component of the malicious code Reporter. For each targeted computer, Reporter collected data on the computer's IP address and the number of files overwritten during the attack. Just as air commanders during World War II and later conflicts assessed bomb damage after air strikes to better understand their effects, the Iranian attackers sought to discover how much harm their operation did. Reporter gave them those insights in nearly real time, and with a level of precision beyond anything imagined by traditional military commanders.[6]

With the Shamoon code positioned throughout the company, the attackers were ready to go. On the morning of August 15, 2012, the operation began. Across vast swaths of the Aramco network, the code began to overwrite files on Windows computers. The attack rendered more than thirty-five thousand machines inoperable, the vast majority of the computers in the company and far more than any previous cyber attack had managed to strike. On some of the computer screens, it displayed the image of a burning American flag, presumably condemning the alliance between the United States and Saudi Arabia.[7] There was no doubt that a bold and damaging attack was underway.

The attackers also posted a message. Styling themselves the "Cutting Sword of Justice"—a group no one had ever heard of—they took square aim at Saudi regional policy. They said they acted because they were "fed up of crimes and atrocities taking place in various countries around the world, especially in the neighboring countries such as Syria, Bahrain, Yemen, Lebanon, Egypt" and more. To them, the culpability of the Saudi royal family was clear, as was the link to Aramco's profits. "One of the main supporters of this disasters is Al-Saud corrupt regime that sponsors such oppressive measures by using Muslims oil resources," they wrote. "This is a warning to the tyrants of this country and other countries that support such criminal disasters with injustice and oppression."[8] The attack was a protest, and a destructive one at that.

The attackers timed their operation well. They chose to strike during the Ramadan holidays and in the scorching summer heat, when about half the information technology and cybersecurity staff was on vacation. Those Aramco employees who were on the job scrambled to contain the damage. While Shamoon does not appear to have targeted or damaged the company's physical oil production or distribution systems, it caused major disruptions to company operations, including the rampant technology shutdowns and halts in payment processing. Workers hastened to physically disconnect key data centers and other parts of the company from the internet and from one another, fearful of what attacks and damage might still come. Incident response units rushed to figure out how the attack worked and who might be responsible.[9]

For Aramco's CEO, Khalid Al-Falih, the lesson from the experience was clear: even if Aramco did not have the major online profile that Apple or Google did, every modern company at some level was a technology company at risk of being crippled by cyber attack. "Never underestimate how dependent you are on your information technology and systems," he said. "It's become like oxygen. You think you can live without it but you can't."[10]

As Aramco struggled to respond, the attackers twisted the knife. They posted another message online, mocking the company for its lack of communication during the crisis. This message showed that the Iranians had taken the time to do thorough reconnaissance of the network: it included log-in information for key routers and revealed Al-Falih's email address and password. It also publicly identified Aramco's various cybersecurity vendors, and ridiculed the company's use of default passwords for some of its important systems. The message concluded by reveling in the achievement: "We think and truly believe that our mission is done."[11]

The attackers were proud of the lasting harm they had inflicted. Shamoon had decimated Aramco's computing infrastructure. Under crushing pressure to get operations running normally again, the company hired a massive incident response team at great expense. The firm also needed new hard drives in a hurry to replace the ones Shamoon had corrupted. Here, the firm's ample resources came in handy. Deploying its fleet of private airplanes, it flew employees to the factories that built the drives, mostly in Asia. Once there, the employees outbid all other potential buyers to get the fifty thousand new drives the company required. This cost many millions of dollars, while raising prices and slowing shipments for other customers, but ensured that Aramco got its computing capacity back as fast as possible.

It took five months and untold sums of money for the firm to fully recover.[12] Meanwhile, even as the identity of the Aramco perpetrators was subject to at least some debate in cybersecurity circles, Iranian hackers were preparing a cyber attack against their next target: American businesses.

Operation Ababil

The financial industry in the United States is perhaps the closest analog to the oil industry in Saudi Arabia: it is both a symbol of American geopolitical might and a means of projecting and increasing that power. The United States had long worried about what an attack on the sector might look like; in particular, it worried about threats that could undermine consumer confidence in financial institutions. With memories still fresh of how the 2008 global financial crisis had weakened trust and caused a credit crunch, American government officials worried that a cyber attack might shake the faith of consumers and businesses all over the world.

In September 2012, Iran made this fear more than hypothetical. The attackers called their effort Operation Ababil. To carry it out, they deployed a technique that others had used for more than a decade: a distributed denial-of-service attack. The operational concept behind this kind of attack is simple. In the ordinary course of online interactions, internet servers process requests and commands from computers all over the world, but if large volumes of meaningless requests and commands overwhelm those servers, the machines either crash or fail to handle the legitimate requests. A deluge of useless information prevents systems from functioning.

Denial-of-service attacks first came to public prominence in 2000. In February of that year, a fifteen-year-old Canadian named Michael Calce—much better known by his online nickname, Mafiaboy—used the technique to knock Yahoo (then the largest search engine), eBay, CNN, Amazon, and others offline. Mafiaboy's attacks gained wide attention when a joint investigation by the FBI and the Royal Canadian Mounted Police resulted in his arrest and guilty plea.[13]

As the technical sophistication and frequency of denial-of-service attacks grew after Mafiaboy's escapades, a technique that teenagers tried out for kicks morphed into a tool deployed by government-aligned hackers. Saboteurs all over the world developed new methods of crafting data to confuse or slow internet servers. In 2007, hackers sympathetic to the Russian government launched a series of denial-of-service efforts against Estonia. The attack disrupted citizens' access to the websites of government agencies, banks, broadcasters and more; this interference was especially damaging in Estonia, one of the most technologically savvy countries on Earth.[14]

In the summer of 2008, a similar team of Russian attackers hit Georgia during a period of increased tension. This group of operations included denial-of-service attacks against the website of President Mikheil Saakashvili, as well as other Georgian targets. Some of the operations seemed to coincide with preplanned Russian military activities, marking the first public instance of cyber and conventional forces working together.[15]

The key to any denial-of-service attack is throwing enough of the right kinds of meaningless data at the targeted system to gum up its works. Attackers often compromise large numbers of computers which they then use to bombard the target. Cybersecurity researchers call these computers bots, and a group of them working together at an attacker's direction is known as a botnet.

The Iranians started assembling their botnet around December 2011. Their hackers started by scanning the internet to identify computers and servers that used content management software like WordPress, a system most commonly used for updating websites. In particular, the hackers looked for computers running this software that had not applied security updates. Without these patches, the content management software could function as a point of entry for the hackers. The Iranian hackers gained access to thousands of computers and servers spread all over the world using this technique.

Unbeknownst to their owners and operators, the computers and servers were now under Iranian control. Having gained access to these machines, the hackers installed their own software, enabling them to use the computers to send information to specific targets. To manage this botnet, the hackers remotely leased servers from companies within the United States and elsewhere that they set up for command-and-control purposes. These allowed the hackers to perform reconnaissance on their targets and issue orders for the botnet to attack.

The hackers attacked American corporations sporadically throughout the first half of 2012, but the major action did not begin until September. On September 18, an online group appeared on *Pastebin,* a website where anyone can post information. The group called itself the Cyber Fighters of Izz ad-din Al Qassam, apparently honoring an early-twentieth-century Syrian preacher who had resisted British and French rule and later became a militant opponent of Zionism. Its members proclaimed their intent to attack the United States in retaliation for a video promoted by a controversial pastor that mocked and criticized Islam. The video, *Innocence of Muslims,* fueled protests around the world that resulted in fifty deaths and may have contributed to the terrorist attack on the United States diplomatic compound in Benghazi, Libya, that killed the US ambassador to Libya and three other Americans. The Cyber Fighters announced that their digital protest would focus on two targets: Bank of America and the New York Stock Exchange.[16] The next day, the group publicly added Chase Bank to the target list.[17]

The attackers then began a phase of attacks that lasted several weeks. At various times throughout the day, the targeted American banks started to see a flood of unanticipated internet traffic from computers all over the world. This was an exemplar of cyber operations at their most basic: there was no attempt to pilfer secret data, wipe hard drives, manipulate bank funds, or even place malicious code inside the target network. The goal was simply to overwhelm the institutions to the point that they could not transact business with customers online.

Researchers measure the strength of denial-of-service attacks by examining how much data the attackers hurl at the target each second. The Mafiaboy attacks in 2000 succeeded by launching less than eight hundred megabits of data per second at their targets. Iran, by contrast, managed to transmit sixty-five gigabits per second, a massive eighty-fold increase made possible in part by the rapid growth of the internet during that period and by Iran's more sophisticated abilities. At times, a United States indictment would later note, the Iranian operation grew even more powerful, reaching 140 gigabits per second, or three times the entire operating capacity of one targeted bank.[18]

This much data was bound to have an impact on the banks' networks. For substantial periods of time throughout September and early October 2012, their websites creaked under the heavy load of the data that Iranian attackers continually threw at their servers. As the banks and other financial institutions scrambled to improve their network capacity and strengthen their defenses, their customers sometimes lost access to their online banking platforms. On October 8, the attackers promised that the attacks would continue as long as the video insulting Muslims remained online.[19]

United States government officials debated, at very senior levels, how to react. At the core of the discussion was a key question: What were these attacks, really? Though they were comparatively sophisticated for denial-of-service attacks, they were much less harmful than deeply penetrating espionage operations. Seeming more like acts of vandalism, the disruption attacks were far less destructive than the attack on Aramco, which caused lasting damage and required the purchase of thousands of pieces of replacement equipment. But the perpetrator mattered, too; the United States intelligence community determined fairly quickly that Iran was responsible.[20] If these incidents were a contest of wills between states, perhaps they required a more forceful response.

On October 11, 2012, Secretary of Defense Leon Panetta gave a major speech on cyber operations. His long-planned comments did not specifically address the current, ongoing attacks, but did call out Iran for the previous operation against Aramco, describing it as "the most destructive attack the private sector has seen to date." As part of the push for cybersecurity legislation and improved defensive standards, Panetta alluded to the many possible dangers of cyber attacks. He invoked the idea of a "cyber Pearl Harbor" and warned of damaging strikes on critical infrastructure. He promised that the Department of Defense would do its best to defend against and hunt down attackers of significance.[21] But soon enough, it became clear that Iran's attacks on the banks did not meet this significance threshold, even as the banks' costs for defense and remediation ran to tens of millions of dollars.[22] The Obama administration, after enormous internal debate, declined to pursue an aggressive response.

The attackers responded to Panetta just a few days later. They labeled his speech a distraction and posted what appeared to be a crude phallic symbol next to his name. More significantly, they announced that their attack would continue because the anti-Islamic video was still online.[23] The first phase of their operation continued for another week, and subsided only with the arrival of the Islamic holiday Eid al-Adha. For good measure, the Iranians threw in another round of insults at Secretary of Defense Panetta before falling silent.[24] This could be construed as signaling, though it seemed mostly to convey anger rather than credible and calculated threats.

The attacks resumed in December and lasted into January 2013, but seemed to have less impact. The hackers took to posting weekly updates identifying targets and claiming successes, but they did not attract much media attention and the financial companies got better at protecting themselves.[25] The hackers reiterated that YouTube must remove particular copies of anti-Muslim videos for the attacks to stop, but their demand had little impact beyond getting one posting taken down.[26] As 2013 went on, the Iranian attacks seemed less disruptive to the well-defended financial targets and less alarming to the American public, who perceived little harm.

Throughout the operation, the attackers disavowed allegations of Iranian government ties, denied any connection to the Aramco attack, and argued that their sole objective was the removal of insults against Muslims—all claims that the American intelligence community assessed as false.[27] In reality, the attackers worked with the Iranian government, with the knowledge and apparent support of senior leaders, and the attacks appeared to be retaliation for what the United States and its allies had done to Iran's nuclear program. Whether the same hackers conducted the denial-of-service attacks and the Aramco attack remains unclear, but intelligence assessments linked both operations to the Iranian regime's push to build their own cyber capability, a billion-dollar effort motivated by the Stuxnet and Wiper attacks and aided in part by Iran's close study of those operations.[28]

Most significantly, as Operation Ababil was winding down, an American intelligence report predicted that Iran would continue to employ cyber operations in the future. In the judgment of the report's authors, Iran would not launch attacks within the United States and United Kingdom with the kind of lasting destructive effects the Aramco attack had produced. They qualified that assessment, however, by noting that ongoing events might change the Iranians' calculus.[29] That caveat proved to be a smart one.

Sands Casino

Sheldon Adelson is one of the richest people in the world, with a fortune currently well above $30 billion. He amassed that wealth through his global casino business, Las Vegas Sands, with major hubs in the United States, Singapore, and Macau.[30] Adelson uses his money primarily to fund two favorite causes. First, he is one of the top political donors in the United States, giving hundreds of millions of dollars to Republican candidates.[31] Second, he is a vociferous defender of Israel, a country in which he controls three news outlets and personally socializes with the conservative prime minister, Benjamin Netanyahu.[32]

In October 2013, when tensions between Israel and Iran were running high, Adelson spoke on a panel in New York. He used the opportunity to cast doubt on the potential for a diplomatic bargain to end the ongoing nuclear crisis. "What are we going to negotiate about?" Adelson asked rhetorically. He imagined how the discussions with Iran should go: "What I would say is, 'Listen. You see that desert out there? I want to show you something.'" The United States should then incinerate the area while the Iranians were watching, he continued, setting off a bomb. The detonation wouldn't "hurt a soul. Maybe a couple of rattlesnakes and scorpions or whatever." But it would send a clear message to Iran as it considered the future of its nuclear program: "You want to be wiped out? Go ahead and take a tough position."[33] Adelson was advocating for old-school signaling.

Iran did not take Adelson's words lightly. Its supreme leader, Ali Khamenei, returned fire two weeks later, saying that the United States "should slap these prating people in the mouth and crush their mouths."[34] Not long after that, Iran began devising a way to hit back with more than just rhetoric. Any physical strike against Adelson or his properties would risk escalation and have to overcome large amounts of on-site security. Iran needed another option, one that was potent and destructive but plausibly deniable and beneath the threshold of traditional armed conflict. Hacking fit the bill.

Investigators later noticed that a significant uptick in Iranian activities against Adelson's company began about one month after his appearance on the panel. Whether through careful reconnaissance or blind chance, Iranian hackers zeroed in on Sands Bethlehem, a small casino of Adelson's in Pennsylvania. It had approximately three thousand slot machines and its own separate computer network. On at least three different occasions in January 2014, several Iranian hacking teams deployed software in a brute-force effort to access Sands Bethlehem's Virtual Private Networks through employees' password-protected accounts. The software's approach was to keep guessing passwords until one worked. Casino staff noticed these hacking attempts but did nothing much about them. They added some additional security measures and watched as their defenses held for the time being.

On February 1, the Iranians tried a different tactic. They found a vulnerability in a server that the casino's Bethlehem-based information technology employees used only for software development and testing. Using this server as an entry point, the hackers were able to get inside the Pennsylvania network and deploy a widely used tool called Mimikatz to collect employees' passwords as they went about their work. These passwords also granted access to other computers on the Bethlehem network, but did not work outside of Pennsylvania on the global Sands network.

Within a week or so of gaining access to the network, the Iranians caught a break when an executive from Sands headquarters made a work trip to the Bethlehem casino. Using an on-site computer, he logged into his home network, thereby exposing his password to the hackers. This password, unlike all the others they had pilfered, could get the hackers into the company's main systems in Las Vegas. It was the bridge the Iranians needed to get where they wanted to go.

Once in the main Las Vegas Sands network, the Iranians set up their attack. In an operation similar to the one against Aramco, they targeted Sands' data and the integrity of the company's computers. They prepared customized malicious code that would wipe data from Sands' systems, then overwrite the computers' hard drives with random patterns of ones and zeroes, impeding recovery. The goal was to do as much damage as possible, or so it seemed.

On the morning of Monday, February 10, the attackers were ready. They activated the malicious code to devastating effect. It crippled thousands of computers and servers within the Sands network, including three-quarters of the ones in Las Vegas. Incident response teams worked quickly to save what they could from the digital attack. Sands technicians, once they figured out what was happening, ran from room to room, unplugging computers before the attack could reach them.[35] The Sands leadership decided to disconnect wide swaths of the corporate infrastructure, fearful of what might come next—especially given that the hackers were gathering large amounts of Sands private files, hinting at an espionage operation connected to the more obvious and destructive attack.

Even as the attack's potency became clear, the Sands team realized they had been lucky in at least one sense. The Iranians' wiping code had severed key links between the Sands networks in the United States and those overseas. The code had inadvertently prevented itself from spreading to the foreign parts of the Sands empire and wreaking havoc there. Most of the damage, as bad as it was, remained localized in the United States. A better-orchestrated attack plan, more informed by pre-attack reconnaissance, would have wrought still more destruction.

The day after the initial strike, the hackers kept up the assault. This time, they made their message unambiguously clear. They gained access to Sands' websites, which another company hosted online, and replaced the normal messages and images with some of their own. Alongside a picture of Adelson and Prime Minister Netanyahu together, they posted a map of Sands casinos with flames on it. Also posted was a warning: "Encouraging the use of Weapons of Mass Destruction, UNDER ANY CONDITION, is a Crime." The message was signed by the "Anti WMD Team." Another taunt addressed Adelson directly: "Don't let your tongue cut your throat."[36]

Next, the attackers showed that they had, in fact, been able to pilfer sensitive data from the company. They shared some employee information, including social security numbers. After Sands leadership publicly downplayed the attack, the hackers posted an eleven-minute video on YouTube that first showed Adelson's comments about attacking Iran and then revealed that the hackers had copied thousands of folders of internal company files, including many passwords for information technology systems. It was clear that the incident responders' effort to thwart the ongoing espionage operation had been, at least in part, too late. All in all, Sands later estimated the damage at around $40 million, making it one of the most significant cyber attacks then on record.[37]

Signals Full of Sound and Fury

The events that many in the United States had long feared had come to pass, at least in miniature. With the Iranian attacks on American financial institutions and on Sands, a foreign government's hackers had launched two successful cyber attacks against United States targets. With the earlier attack against Saudi Arabia, a United States ally had been damaged. Each of these attacks had interfered with key business functions of well-known companies and caused tens of millions of dollars in damages. Disruptive cyber attacks were no longer a speculative threat, but an actual policy matter.

While Stuxnet and Wiper tried to shape the environment, these public-facing attacks were about signaling. But they just were not very effective as signals, failing for three reasons. First, the message was hardly nuanced: Iran was displeased with geopolitical actions and statements. Conveying this displeasure revealed no new information about Iran's geopolitical views and ambitions. Long before Shamoon, every observer knew that Iran and Saudi Arabia were regional adversaries. Before Operation Ababil, it was no secret that Iran was greatly aggrieved by Stuxnet. Similarly, the mutual enmity between Iran and Sheldon Adelson was widely known, even if Adelson did escalate the rhetoric with his call for a nuclear test in the Iranian desert. Signals are an attempt to change behavior by revealing credible information about one's priorities; the Iranian operations fell well short of this bar.

Second, signals are more meaningful if a state commits to them. At best, the attacks showed that Iran was developing cyber operations capabilities, but the Iranians undermined the credibility of their cyber operations as a tool of statecraft when the attackers' mouthpieces denied ties to the Iranian regime. Even if very few observers believed these disavowals, they weakened the force of the threat. Whereas military mobilization and other forms of traditional signaling are credible because they imply clear and lasting commitment, the public denials made the Iranian efforts seem like one-off operations. The Aramco attackers' claim that their mission was complete also undercut any impression that this was a concerted attempt to bargain for a new geopolitical status quo. In this sense, the attacks were impulsive; Keith Alexander, the director of the NSA during the Iranian attacks, later said that Iran was an unpredictable adversary because it did not calculate in its hacking operations but rather "will act emotionally."[38]

Third, a key element of nuanced geopolitical signaling is having the capacity to inflict carefully measured amounts of violence, with the threat of more to come. The Iranian attacks all failed in this regard. In each case, the particular cyber capability was mostly spent as soon as the attack was launched. In the cases of Aramco and Sands, the Iranians burned much of their access and capability with the attack, and in the denial-of-service campaigns, the additional harm that could be inflicted was minimal. Even when the Iranians inflicted less damage than they might have, as in the Sands attack, the limitation did not come across as deliberate signaling but seemed much more likely to be an error on the part of the attackers.

Absent any capacity to escalate further or credibly suggest additional power to hurt American interests, the attacks were disruptive but insufficient to change American or Saudi behavior. The Sands attack was at the time the most devastating cyber attack on United States soil, but former NSA and CIA director Michael Hayden said that even it would not require a major government response. "If this would have come across my desk when I was in government, I would have just put it in the outbox," he said, implying that, because Sands was not a government entity, an attack on Sands need not be treated as an attack on America.[39] Similarly, Saudi Arabia does not appear to have meaningfully retaliated, though its relationship with

Iran has worsened for a variety of reasons. Nor does Adelson appear in any way to have warmed up to the Iranian regime or wavered in his public support for Israel.

Even as the Iranian attacks failed as a tool of signaling, they revealed a great deal about the continuing evolution of cyber operations. They marked the opening of a new chapter in the developing story of cyber attacks, one in which states beyond top-tier powers like the United States or Russia began deploying these new kinds of capabilities for their own use. More significantly, the Iranian attacks introduced the new phenomenon of cyber attacks designed to be noticed, even if these early examples were not terribly effective as signals. They showed that attacks of this sort could cause damage and yet not prompt retaliation. Another foreign state might take the Iranian example and up the ante still further, increasing its potency to try to send more specific, credible, and calibrated signals. And before 2014 was over, one did.

8

Coercion

"I NEVER THOUGHT I'D BE HERE BRIEFING ON A BAD SETH ROGEN MOVIE, sir," an Obama aide said to the president. It was a preamble to an intelligence discussion in the White House. Obama asked how he knew the film in question, *The Interview*, was a bad one. The aide had a ready comeback: "Sir, it's a Seth Rogen movie."[1]

While *WarGames* kickstarted President Reagan's interest in cybersecurity and *There Will Be Blood* served as an inspiration of sorts for some of the NSA's counterintelligence efforts, *The Interview* caused an actual cyber attack all by itself. The film was a buddy comedy featuring Rogen and costar James Franco playing a pair of media personalities aiding a CIA-orchestrated assassination of Kim Jong-un.

There was no way that the movie could be anything but provocative. Its title was originally *Kill Kim Jong-un* and its original final scene featured the explosion of the leader's face. Placing the film in a real country gave the movie an "edge," according to the production team. Amy Pascal, the cochair of Sony Pictures Entertainment, loved the screenplay. Test audiences found the film appealing.[2]

The government of North Korea saw things a little differently. After *The Interview's* trailer was released in June 2014, North Korea's foreign minister put out a harsh statement condemning the United States government. North Korean officials perceived the film as an aggressive act meant to insult their leader, one that came from the White House. They said the movie was the result of the United States "bribing a rogue movie maker" rather than an independent act of free expression or satire. To produce a film "insulting and assassinating the supreme leadership" was "terrorism" and a "war action," and the regime would meet it with a "strong and merciless countermeasure."[3]

Nevertheless, production continued apace. Sony executives apparently talked to United States officials after the North Korean saber-rattling, but neither side seemed overly concerned about the possibility of North Korean escalation.[4] Rogen weighed in with a snarky comment on Twitter: "People don't usually wanna kill me for one of my movies until after they've paid 12 bucks for it."[5] Though some parts of the film, such as the final scene, ended up softer than the filmmakers had originally envisioned, in the fall of 2014 it seemed on schedule for its grand debut in theaters on one of the biggest box-office dates of the year: Christmas Day.

While *The Interview* got little attention within the United States policymaking community, it is fair to assume that the movie was a major priority for North Korea throughout the last half of 2014. The film presented a challenge of coercion, a theoretical construct of great renown during the Cold War. More specifically, it was a type of coercion known as compellence, in which one side causes its adversary to change course. Could the North Koreans force an American movie company (acting, according to their version of reality, at the behest of the United States government) to back down? What costs could it impose to make Sony recognize that the problem was serious, and what additional harms could it threaten to compel a change in behavior?

Coercion is one of the bedrock goals of foreign policy, as it offers the possibility of attaining desirable outcomes without full-scale conflict. It is signaling in its purest form. Whereas Iran was limited to retaliating for past behavior and actions it did not like, North Korea had an opportunity, in advance of *The Interview's* release, to force Sony to change its mind.

To do so, North Korea turned to its arsenal of cyber capabilities. The regime had come a long way since 2009, when a United States National Intelligence Estimate had largely disparaged its hacking efforts.[6] In 2011, North Korean hackers had targeted a range of South Korean critical infrastructure, media, and financial targets, though they made no attempt to steal money. The next year, they had hacked a different South Korean media organization, and just a year after that they had executed a wiping attack against computers in South Korean banks and news outlets.[7] The attacks showed remarkable technological capability for a country where 40 percent of the population is malnourished.[8]

Now, a year after the notable attacks in South Korea, North Korea had a major American film studio in its sights. The resulting effort would become one of the most hyped—though poorly-examined—cyber operations in history and one that would foreshadow the increasing use of leaks as a strategic tool. In carrying out the operation, the North Koreans provided an excellent example of the allure of cyber coercion but also of its stark limits.[9]

The Attack

On September 24, 2014, an employee at Sony Pictures Entertainment received an email that appeared to be from a person named Nathan Gonsalez. Gonsalez's email address was bluehotrain@hotmail.com. Inside the email was a link that, when clicked, appeared to open a video file relating to the advertising of another business. Included in the file's name were the words "video" and "Adobe Flash"—presumably there to mislead an employee into thinking this was a media clip that would play in the Flash software commonly used at the time. Curiously, the email was signed not with the name Nathan Gonsalez, but with the name of an executive at another business.

Like so many others, this email was not at all what it appeared to be. It was not from Nathan Gonsalez or the other business executive. Bluehotrain@hotmail.com was not a normal internet user's email address. The purported video of another business's advertisements was in fact something much more dangerous. The attachment was an executable file designed to load malicious code onto the employee's computer. Once on a recipient's computer, the malicious code executed the North Korean hackers' first preset instruction: connect to five IP addresses specified in the code. These IP addresses were under the control of the hackers, and included one located in China. Once the malicious code reached out for further commands, the computers at the addresses sent out instructions on what to do next. The code checked in at least seven times between September 24 and October 6.

The North Koreans used this code to expand inside the Sony network from a foothold to a much wider presence. The malicious code could map the network's directories of files, make copies of information in the targeted computers' memory, deploy malicious code to the Sony network, and wait silently for further instructions.[10] In short, the malicious code had a full complement of features, allowing the hackers to control its activities in Sony's network from afar.

Because the North Koreans later did so much damage to Sony's network, destroying vital evidence in the process, it is hard to construct a blow-by-blow account of what happened next. There is no doubt, however, that the hackers spent a great deal of time in the fall of 2014 traversing Sony's systems. They gathered large amounts of information on the inner workings of the network, accessed key servers and file storage drives, and performed the reconnaissance necessary to enable their eventual attack. One analyst later concluded that, after the hackers found their initial access point, it was "highly likely that they had gained unfettered access to the entire network prior to the attack"—all without Sony noticing their intrusion.[11] The hackers also used this access to gather up vast troves of information that Sony wanted to keep confidential, including private emails and managerial documents.

On November 21, two months after their initial spear-phishing success, the North Koreans were ready to act more aggressively. They sent an email to five top Sony executives claiming to represent a group called "God'sApstls." In that message, they issued a warning in broken English: "We've got great damage by Sony Pictures. The compensation for it, monetary compensation we want. Pay the damage, or Sony Pictures will be bombarded as a whole. You know us very well. We never wait long. You'd better behave wisely."[12] One senior executive who was sent the message either chose to ignore it or failed to see it in his overflowing inbox. Another intended recipient never got it because of her spam filter.[13] At least one recipient did see it and forwarded the email to the FBI, according to Sony.[14]

Given its unspecified threat and ambiguous meaning, the email was apparently dismissed or overlooked. The hackers, however, continued to escalate.

On November 22 or 23, the North Korean operators delivered a piece of malicious code known as Destover across the Sony network. This step marked the end of the espionage phase of their mission, during which they had gathered all sorts of internal private information from Sony Pictures. Now, after Sony executives failed to acknowledge their threat, it was time to attack. Destover was the tool that made it possible.

The hackers set up the attack in Sony's network in a structured and regimented fashion. Destover's architects designed it to avoid some of the cybersecurity protections commonly deployed on Windows machines. When hackers loaded it onto a target machine and activated the malicious payload, the code would run through a preset sequence of events to do as much damage as possible. The hackers deployed several copies of the Destover code at once, orienting each toward a different part of the target computer. Together, these copies executed the combined attack.

The first copy aimed at the master boot record—the same central repository of vital information on a computer's hard drive that Iranian hackers had targeted in the Shamoon attack. What worked in Saudi Arabia worked against Sony, too. For each targeted machine, the Destover code iterated through the hard drives connected to the computer and tried to identify and overwrite the master boot record on each.

With the master boot record corrupted, the data was present but mostly inaccessible, though computer forensic techniques could have recovered it and helped restore operations. To thwart this recovery, the next copy of Destover aimed not at the master boot record but at the data itself. For each hard drive connected to the target computer, Destover examined every file it could find, iterating through all the folders on the system. If it found what looked like a data file that might be valuable to the user, Destover overwrote it with other information to make it harder to recover. It then tried to delete the file from the hard drive entirely. Along the way, this copy of Destover also deleted files that were not data files, such as software programs, doing still more damage.

The third part of the attack sequence did not do any damage at all. Instead, this copy of Destover served up a web page, an image, and a sound file of the hackers' choosing. This show had little operational effect on the target systems but was meant to deliver a clear message about who was responsible and why, with a direct warning that more damage could follow.[15] Once the Destover code executed this step, it would be obvious to all that a massive cyber attack was underway. In this sense, the attack on Sony was more similar to the Iranian operations than it was to Stuxnet and Wiper. The North Koreans wanted everyone to know.

On November 24, the Monday before Thanksgiving, the attack began. The three instances of the Destover code worked in parallel on machines all across the Sony network. Computers and servers stopped working. Employees saw the image of a skeleton under the banner "Hacked By #GOP"—the abbreviation of the hackers' self-styled name, Guardians of Peace. Under this banner came a new message: "We've already warned you, and this is just a beginning. We continue till our request be met. We've obtained all your internal data including your secrets and top secrets. If you don't obey us, we'll release data shown below to the world. Determine what will you do till November the 24th, 11:00 PM (GMT)." Below this text were five links, each to a repository of internal Sony information and files.

Among the thirty-five hundred employees on the Sony campus in California, the message quickly earned the nickname "the screen of death."[16] More accurately, though, the image was a smokescreen of sorts, distracting the target while the other copies of Destover wreaked havoc on their computers. Some Sony employees managed to thwart the hackers' destructive computer code and save their machines by quickly unplugging them. The majority, though, did not know what to do when they saw the gruesome picture. While they consulted with coworkers or sounded the alarm internally, Destover wiped their files away.

The total damage was tremendous. One estimate suggested that the Sony studio lost 70 percent of its computing power in the attack.[17] Key servers went down. The company scrambled to take even more systems offline in an attempt to limit the damage. The shops on the campus switched to cash-only. Word spread quickly among the workforce: disconnect everything possible from the corporate network. As a result, employees could not do their jobs nearly as well. One Sony employee told a reporter that it was as if the company had been transported more than a decade into the past, before the internet was ubiquitous in offices.[18] Like Aramco and Sands Casino before it, Sony quickly discovered how important computers were to its everyday business.

The firm did its best to try to keep things working. Employees relied on personal email accounts and hand-delivered files and scripts.[19] Someone found 190 old BlackBerrys in a basement and gave them to executives and key employees.[20] The accounting department tried to find old machines so that it could pay staff on time.[21] Executives set up a command center in the studio's Gene Kelly building, named for the famed actor and dancer, but were unsure what to do. From there, they sent out messages to employees on paper, urging resilience.

Sony's leaders worried that the hackers would do still more damage. In particular, they were anxious about the hackers' stated 11:00 PM deadline on November 24. But that hour came and went without further destruction or communications. Top executives prepared a message to be delivered on paper to employees as they arrived on November 25. Despite the unusual circumstances, it read like standard corporate-speak: "We want to thank you for all your hard work, innovative thinking and positive attitudes as we work to resolve the system disruption that we are experiencing."[22] With the attack seemingly over, leadership cautioned that it might take until after the Thanksgiving holiday to get things back on track.[23]

The Leaks

On November 25, copies of Sony's unreleased movies began appearing online. The hackers posted *Annie,* a remake of the famous musical, and the biopic *Mr. Turner,* both of which were scheduled for release in December. *Still Alice* and *To Write Love on Her Arms* also cropped up on multiple file-sharing websites. So did *Fury,* starring Brad Pitt, which had only recently debuted in theaters. Sony executives scrambled to get the illegal copies taken down, but in some cases it was too late. More than 1.2 million people illegally obtained *Fury* in just the first five days after the hackers put it online, and hundreds of thousands more pirated the other films.[24] The surprise appearance of these five movies gave Sony's management fresh cause for alarm. The cyber operation against the studio was not over, but merely entering a new phase.

Things got much worse. On the morning of Saturday, November 28, several journalists received unusual emails. Among them was Kevin Roose, a senior editor at the media startup *Fusion.*[25] The sender claimed to be the "boss" of the group that had hacked Sony. The message referenced the leaked movies that were still online and then offered a tantalizing prize: access to a trove of internal Sony files. They claimed it was "tens of terabytes in size"—a tremendous hoard.[26] They told Roose that links to some of the files were hosted on *Pastebin,* a favored site of hackers, and accessible with a password alluding to a hoped-for demise of Sony Pictures Entertainment: diespe123.

Roose said later that when the email first arrived, he was sure it was spam. Nonetheless, he opened it "on a whim."[27] He found that, remarkably, the sender delivered the goods. Roose now had access to twenty-six repositories of private data from within the Sony movie studio. Roose emailed Sony's communications department seeking comment on the leak. They did not get back to him.[28]

Predictably, Roose and other journalists then began writing stories. Roose's first piece, published on December 1, focused on the sort of spreadsheet that every company wants to keep private: a list of salaries. The sheet showed a striking pay gap between men and women at the company, underscored by the fact that, of the seventeen executives making more than one million dollars per year, sixteen were men (of whom fourteen were white) and only one was a woman.[29] The next day, Roose revealed that the leak included personal information, including social security numbers and birth dates, for more than thirty-eight hundred Sony employees.[30] Soon, a series of identity theft attempts suggested that criminals were beginning to use this data.[31]

Roose wrote that other pilfered files included information on fired Sony employees, including the cost of their severance pay. The trove featured detailed performance reviews for many employees at the company, including managers' judgments on, for example, whether they were "flight risks."[32] There was even a cache of leaked files relating to the salaries of thirty thousand employees at Deloitte, the accounting firm; evidently a Sony employee had previously worked there and had departed with the files in hand. The North Koreans' wide net swept them up, like so much else.[33]

Sony now had employee relationship crises and public relations crises on top of its data and network crises. Its employees, most of whom had nothing to do with *The Interview*, found themselves in a foreign government's line of fire. The skeleton image on computer screens the week before and the massive disruption to business had seemed absurd but disconnected from individuals. Only after the release of private information did the consequences feel personal. As one employee put it to Roose, "Last week when we came into the offices, we were like, is this a joke? It got real when the Social Security numbers got released."[34] People quickly grew frustrated with a perceived lack of communication from corporate executives and the futility of the credit-monitoring services Sony had provided.[35] Some took matters into their own hands, emailing Roose and other journalists to see if their personal data was in the files posted online. Without exception, it was.[36]

On December 5, the North Koreans ramped up the pressure. In an email to many Sony employees, they ordered recipients to register their personal objection to their employer's actions, but the North Koreans did not specify what this objectionable activity was. The email contained a clear threat, warning each employee that a signature was required "if you don't want to suffer damage. If you don't [sign], not only you but your family will be in danger."[37] Given the volume of personal employee information, including home addresses, already made available, this threat was not as far-fetched as it might otherwise have seemed. As the situation escalated, the North Korean news agency issued a thin denial, saying the government was not responsible for the operation but praising it as a "righteous deed."[38]

The following Monday, December 8, the hackers served up the clearest indication yet of their motives. In a message posted online, they wrote that "We have already given our clear demand to the management team of SONY, however, they have refused to accept. . . . We are sending you our warning again. . . . Stop immediately showing the movie of terrorism which can break the regional peace and cause the War! You, SONY & FBI, cannot find us. . . . The destiny of SONY is totally up to the wise reaction & measure of SONY."[39] While many employees and analysts had already assumed that the hack was related to *The Interview*, this message appeared to provide clear confirmation that the ultimate goal of the operation was not to damage Sony but to coerce it into canceling the particular film that offended North Korea so much.

The December 8 message was overshadowed by the avalanche of new files that accompanied it. Included in this wave were thousands of Sony contracts, showing what the firm had paid for all sorts of services, and financial forecasts for upcoming movies. There were also dozens of scripts of upcoming films and dozens of the market analyses that went into decisions to green-light new movies, plus studies of leading Hollywood stars' popularity and detailed contact information and aliases for many famous actors and actresses. Documents related to ongoing litigation and other legally sensitive matters also appeared in this latest trove.[40]

These files were not the juiciest part of the leak, however. That distinction went to the emails of Amy Pascal. As the cochair of Sony Pictures Entertainment, Pascal was one of the most powerful people in Hollywood. She was responsible for major decisions to produce some films and pass on others. Everyone in Hollywood seemed to know her, thanks in part to her indefatigable efforts to keep in touch with a wide range of stars, producers, and executives—most frequently by email.

During their several-months-long reconnaissance of Sony's networks, the hackers had copied approximately five thousand of Pascal's messages. Now, they had dumped them online. The opinions of Pascal and some of her colleagues—often expressed in blunt, irreverent, or rushed ways, with the expectation that messages would be received in confidence—were exposed for all to see. For all those who wondered what happened behind the closed doors of a Hollywood movie studio, the airing of Pascal's messages was a salacious gift.

The unvarnished emails were revealing and often unkind. In the midst of heated negotiations over a Steve Jobs biopic with a screenplay by famed writer Aaron Sorkin, producer Scott Rudin called movie star Angelina Jolie a "minimally talented spoiled brat" with a "rampaging spoiled ego." Pascal labeled Leonardo DiCaprio's behavior "despicable." Other Hollywood machinations leaked out into view, including Pascal's attempts to get the fierce and often profane Rudin to help fend off a fight over acclaimed director David Fincher.[41] Another email exchange between the two featured racially charged comments, as they joked that Pascal might ask President Barack Obama, whom she was about to see at a fundraiser, if he liked *Django Unchained, 12 Years a Slave,* or *The Butler*—all films with African-American stars.[42]

Other leaked emails included messages between Pascal and her husband, Bernard Weinraub, formerly a *New York Times* journalist. These stirred controversy because, in addition to revealing conversations between husband and wife, they suggested that Weinraub had been given an advance look at a piece about Pascal by *New York Times* columnist Maureen Dowd.[43] Both the *Times* and Weinraub denied that the piece had actually been shared before publication, and there is no evidence to the contrary. Still, the messages provided tantalizing hints of the hidden lives of media moguls.[44]

Major news outlets and their reporters could not resist these kinds of stories. Names like Jolie, Sorkin, and Fincher could generate clicks all on their own, but the addition of closed-door negotiations, acrimony between executives, and overly cozy relations between Hollywood and the press boosted readership to new levels. Web-based media outlets like *Gawker* and *BuzzFeed* feasted on the Pascal emails, quoting them at length and using them as sources of color for their entertainment reporting.[45] More staid outlets such as the *New York Times, Wall Street Journal,* and *Los Angeles Times* joined the fray, covering the story in detail from the earliest leaks through Pascal's ouster in February.[46]

Some critics pushed back hard against this sort of media coverage. Aaron Sorkin wrote in the opinion section of the *New York Times* that "every news outlet that did the bidding of the Guardians of Peace is morally treasonous and spectacularly dishonorable." Borrowing a basketball metaphor, he wrote that the hackers "just had to lob the ball; they knew our media would crash the boards and slam it in."[47] Others, including the *New York Times* public editor, Margaret Sullivan, countered that the Sony emails contained "legitimate news" content.[48]

Debates over journalistic ethics aside, the hackers had stumbled across something powerful. Their operation against Sony was an attack, first and foremost, and one that dealt a severe blow to the company's computing infrastructure. But the part that got the most lasting public attention was the parade of stories that came from the hackers' data dumps. Even several years later, the *New York Times* and others would still focus on what the email leak and dismissal of Pascal meant to the industry and to her.[49] It was as if Sony were a piñata, and the real event came only after the blow, when its innards poured out for all to see.

To Release or Not To Release?

On December 16, with *The Interview*'s planned Christmas Day nationwide release just over a week away, the North Koreans continued to raise the stakes. "Soon all the world will see what an awful movie Sony Pictures Entertainment has made," they wrote as they dumped the emails of Sony's CEO, Michael Lynton. "The world will be full of fear." Most strikingly, they threatened terrorism and violence at theaters that showed the movie: "Remember the 11th of September 2001. We recommend you to keep yourself distant from the places at that time. (If your house is nearby, you'd better leave.)"[50]

The reaction to the physical threat was enormous. Costars Rogen and Franco canceled all media appearances.[51] Sony nixed *The Interview*'s New York premiere. The day after the hackers' threats, December 17, the major movie theater chains in the United States decided not to show the film due to concerns about safety and Sony's wavering commitment.[52] The National Association of Theatre Owners, a trade group representing independent cinema operators, issued a statement on behalf of its members advising that some might put off showing the movie. With theater owners balking, Sony canceled the holiday debut and considered distributing the movie only through video-on-demand services.[53] After further deliberation, however, it decided against distribution of the movie altogether, and publicly announced it had "no further release plans."[54]

In a message sent privately to Sony executives on December 18 but obtained by *CNN,* the North Koreans called the company's decision "very wise." At the same time, they added new demands: "Now we want you never let the movie released, distributed or leaked in any form of, for instance, DVD or piracy. . . . And we want everything related to the movie, including its trailers, as well as its full version down from any website hosting them immediately." In short, they wanted Sony to make it as though *The Interview* had never existed. The hackers reminded Sony management that "we still have your private and sensitive data." Yet they pledged to "ensure the security of your data unless you make additional trouble."[55] It was as clear as a coercive threat could get, though it paled in comparison to the threat of physical harm that had come two days before.

By this point, it was also reasonably clear that the North Korea government had carried out the operation. On December 19, the FBI weighed in, stating that its investigation had concluded as much.[56] While the notion of North Korean culpability met with some skepticism at the beginning, particularly from media outlets and cybersecurity firms seeking attention, the evidence soon became clear.[57] In January, the *New York Times* reported that the NSA had hacked the North Korean networks for intelligence purposes and had additional sources inside the country, giving the United States great insight into North Korean operations.[58]

After the FBI's announcement of North Korea's responsibility, President Obama weighed in. In his end-of-year news conference, he panned Sony's decision, though he said he understood its concerns. "I think they made a mistake," he said. "We cannot have a society in which some dictator someplace can start imposing censorship here in the United States. Because if somebody is able to intimidate folks out of releasing a satirical movie, imagine what they start doing when they see a documentary that they don't like or news reports that they don't like." Even worse, he continued, would be the chilling effect if "producers and distributors and others started engaging in self-censorship because they don't want to offend the sensibilities of somebody whose sensibilities probably need to be offended."[59]

Criticizing North Korea's action and Sony's response was one of the few cards Obama could play. No matter how important the idea of freedom of speech was, everyone knew the United States was not going to war in the Korean peninsula over *The Interview*. While the United States could and did impose more sanctions, no one thought that a bit more economic pressure on the most isolated country on Earth would change its thinking. Likewise, while the United States eventually indicted the North Korean hackers, any expectation that they would be extradited to face trial was laughable. Presidential naming and shaming was the only real option left.

Michael Lynton, the top Sony Pictures executive, responded directly to Obama's criticism. "I don't know exactly whether he understands the sequence of events that led up to the movie not being shown in the movie theaters," Lynton said. "Therefore I would disagree with the notion that it was a mistake." He went on to suggest that Sony still wanted to show *The Interview*. "We have not given in. And we have not backed down. We have always had every desire to have the American public see this movie." But with distributors scared by the threat of North Korean cyber attacks and terrorism, the studio also had limited options.[60]

Nevertheless, for the filmmakers of *The Interview*, Obama's comments seemed like the turning point, the moment when the cavalry arrived. Lynton reached a deal with Google—no stranger to foreign cyber attacks—to help distribute the film online. A few hundred independent theaters agreed to show it on Christmas Day and be-yond. Seemingly overnight, a ridiculous comedy starring Seth Rogen and James Franco became a symbol of free speech and resis-tance to foreign interference, available for the low online rental price of $5.99. Within a month, the movie had become the best-selling online release ever, garnering more than $40 million. It sold out in theaters and streamed widely on Netflix. The turn of events was stunning.[61]

North Korea's government raged at this outcome. It blasted *The Interview* as a "dishonest and reactionary movie hurting the dignity of the supreme leadership of the DPRK [North Korea] and agitating terrorism." It called Obama "the chief culprit who forced the Sony Pictures Entertainment to indiscriminately distribute the movie." For good measure, it included obviously racist language, saying that "Obama always goes reckless in words and deeds like a monkey in a tropical forest."[62] In the end, for all its bluster, the North Korean gov-ernment must have recognized that its attempts to thwart *The Inter-view* ultimately boosted the film's commercial success.

The Failure of Cyber Coercion

From its first announcement, *The Interview* placed North Korea in a bind. The regime felt an imperative to stop the film. When its initial threats did not cause Sony to change its behavior, it turned to coercion via cyber operations. The decision made sense—in fact, it is hard to imagine a more perfect opportunity for signaling via cyber operation. Five points suggest as much.

First, the North Korean government was highly motivated to compel Sony to cancel the movie. *The Interview* insulted North Korea's leader, whose power depended in part on projecting a deity-like image. While American presidents and other democratic leaders accept that relentless criticism and unflattering portrayals come with leading a free society, Kim Jong-un certainly did not. It was thus an obvious North Korean national priority to bury *The Interview*.

Second, North Korea could communicate clearly and credibly. Sony knew, at least abstractly, the danger it courted when it gave *The Interview* the green light. The North Korean government expressed its displeasure and warned of serious consequences months before the movie was scheduled for release. While Sony doubted these initial threats, it knew with certainty by the time the cyber operation unfolded in the fall that the hackers were serious. The North Koreans were able to share their views directly by emailing Sony executives through thinly disguised personas or posting their missives online.

Third, North Korean hackers could do real harm to Sony. By so thoroughly penetrating the company's network, they gained the capacity to steal information and destroy computer systems. Their reconnaissance collected at least thirty-eight million files from Sony's network, including plenty of juicy tidbits, corporate secrets, and personnel details. The North Koreans' access was so extensive and their attack code so powerful that they could launch a devastating opening blow.

Fourth, after decimating Sony's computing infrastructure, the North Koreans could still credibly threaten to do more harm. The latent power to hurt was obvious. The cascade of file dumps suggested that the North Koreans would not hesitate to escalate the damage to Sony if its executives did not comply. Nor would this power to hurt diminish anytime soon; the files were in North Korean hands, and nothing could bring them back. North Korea held the cards and everyone knew it.

Fifth, as much as *The Interview* meant to North Korea, for Sony it was just one film among many. The silly comedy was expected to do decently at the box office, not to be a blockbuster with any real staying power. Sony's initial decision to cancel *The Interview* suggested as much. Other studios realized this, too. As the showdown continued, Fox backed out of another edgy film set in North Korea, which had been set to star Steve Carell and begin production in March.[63]

Yet, even in such ideal conditions, signaling via cyber operations came up short. Despite the high importance of the film to North Korea, the clear communication of that importance, the punishment for noncompliance, the obvious threat of more digital punishment, and the fairly low stakes for Sony, North Korea was not able to get what it wanted. Indeed, it was only when the North Koreans threatened physical harm, rather than digital destruction, that the film truly seemed in jeopardy. In the end, *The Interview* transformed from a movie likely to have a short shelf life into a cause célèbre for democracy and freedom of speech. And the North Koreans had to come to terms with the fact that, despite all their perceived advantages, their cyber coercion attempt had failed.

9

Testing and Demonstration

IN THE PARADE OF IMAGINED CYBER ATTACKS, the blackout has always been the grand marshal. The prospect of a country plunged into darkness has resonated far and wide. Its specter is summoned in sensationalized reporting and blockbuster films. Time and time again, scholars and officials have warned of the damage a blackout could do. Some say an attack on the power grid would cost hundreds of billions of dollars. Others worry about all the critical national security systems that depend on the civilian supply of electricity.[1] Insurance documents calculate the tens of millions of people who would be left in the dark, while big-name journalists write books—thin on evidence—with titles like *Lights Out*.[2] Cyber attacks are intrinsically difficult to portray visually, so it is the dangerous darkness of night that has become the defining image of cyber war.

Indeed, tests have shown that cyber operations could in fact destroy the key components of the industrial control systems that comprise the electric grid. In 2007, the United States government conducted a notable public demonstration of such an attack. The Department of Energy vividly showed how a mere twenty-one lines of the right computer code could cause the physical destruction of a diesel power generator. By rapidly opening and closing the system's breakers, the code forced the generator out of sync and exerted tremendous stress on its physical components; to use a common analogy, it was akin to the stress placed on a car's transmission when a driver shifts into reverse while the car is speeding forward. In the dramatic video, the power generator starts to smoke and shake before finally succumbing to the effects of the cyber attack. Eventually, components break and fly off at high speeds, some landing many feet away.[3]

This is the backdrop of dread against which the long-anticipated blackout finally did arrive—and ironically, did not garner nearly as much attention as one might expect. The power outage occurred in Ukraine, a country that was embroiled in a growing conflict with Russia and important for American strategic interests, but far from the US public's consciousness. It happened just two days before Christmas in 2015, when much of the news media had moved into holiday mode. Many reporters, too, were focused on the 2016 US presidential primary elections starting in February. But the fundamental reason for the muted media coverage was that, contrary to what sensationalized predictions had primed the world to fear, the blackout was neither permanent nor overwhelming. It plunged hundreds of thousands of people into darkness for six hours, but did not devastate cities or starve populations as some had warned an all-out cyber attack could.

A year later, nearly to the day, hackers hit the Ukrainian power grid again. Once more, key parts of the country went without electricity. Again, the case received only a smattering of headlines, having been sidelined by another holiday week and the swirling controversies of the Trump administration's ongoing transition. The conventional wisdom seemed to have shifted: if the long-anticipated cyber Pearl Harbor had come, it had taken the form of Russian election interference (the subject of Chapter 10), not power grid sabotage related to a territorial dispute in Eastern Europe.

With the benefit of hindsight, and thanks to the work of some diligent investigators, the story takes on more importance. Three big lessons have emerged from the blackouts in Ukraine. First, this case counters the claim that cyber operations are the new nuclear operations, capable of destroying societies in a single blow with a weapon fired from afar. Even allowing that future blackouts might be more destructive, the force of cyber capabilities will remain well short of what nuclear weapons can do. Ukraine provides more evidence that the common analogy simply does not hold up.

Second, the blackouts rebut the notion that cyber operations are akin to conventional operations, in which states deploy widely understood capabilities in ways other states know how to interpret. Because the attackers in Ukraine showed a restraint or impotency that did not lend itself to easy explanation, observers could variously view the blackouts as a signal, a test, or a failure. Even in the context of the irregular conflict in Ukraine, in which Russia has used a wide range of military and intelligence capabilities to advance its interests, it is not apparent what particular purpose the blackouts served. In general, the goals of hacking operations are less clear than many scholars and policymakers assume, and they are obscured still further by technical complexity. Even when the real-world effect is obvious, signaling intentions with cyber capabilities is still difficult.

Third, the blackouts show that operational art and practice matter. Orchestrating the attacks required months of preparation, reconnaissance, and code development—all processes where even minor mistakes can have substantial effects. Understanding these steps and what they might mean requires a similar level of operational exposition. Exploring the nuances of the attacks requires telling the story in full.

The First Blackout

Ukraine has twenty-four regions, each served by a different power company. In 2015, Russian hackers sent socially engineered emails to system administrators and information technology staff at three of these utilities. Attached to the emails was a Microsoft Office file with malicious code tucked inside. When the email recipients opened the document, their computers prompted them to enable a macro, an Office feature that automates tasks and can execute certain kinds of computer code. Hackers had used the macro trick for decades, but it still proved an effective means of gaining access.

Once the users turned on macros, a piece of malicious code known as BlackEnergy3 installed itself to their computer hard drives. The code served as an initial foothold for the Russian hackers. It opened up a communication channel through which they could issue commands from afar and deliver still more malicious code to run on the infected machine. At this point, the hackers were able to begin their operations inside the targeted Ukrainian power companies' computer networks.[4]

The power companies had wisely adopted a strategy of network segmentation and multiple layers of defense so that a single carelessly clicked link or duped user could not expose the whole electricity supply to hackers. To protect their most critical systems, the companies isolated the computers that managed the electric grid from the ones that handled other corporate functions. System administrators placed a firewall between the two network segments to keep intruders out. This meant that the hackers, having gained access to the corporate side of key Ukrainian critical infrastructure networks, still had a lot of work to do before they could pivot to the operational side with the systems they wanted to attack.

Hackers frequently encounter this sort of roadblock, especially when operating against more sophisticated targets. Sometimes, to get around security protections, signals intelligence agencies deploy an exploit aimed at a vulnerability in the firewall's software. The exploit takes advantage of a weakness in the vendor's code and grants the hackers unauthorized access. Leaked documents show that the NSA and other agencies regularly catalog the vulnerabilities they find in systems all over the world in case the day comes that they need to exploit one to clear such an obstacle.[5]

The hackers in Ukraine chose another approach. They spent months doing reconnaissance on the corporate side of the Ukrainian power companies' networks. They mapped out which computers connected to which other computers, how the targeted company stored its sensitive information, and which users managed the flow of power. In their reconnaissance, the hackers gained access to vital machines known as Windows domain controllers. In a typical network, the domain controller is centrally important because it manages the user accounts for everyone on the network; it holds the keys to the digital kingdom. Once the hackers had successfully compromised these machines, they gained access to the usernames and passwords of vital individuals.

The firewall guarding the operational parts of the network did not block all connections to the Ukrainian power system. It enabled some remote connections so that certain corporate employees could manage critical parts of the electric grid. Users with the right permissions could establish an encrypted link to issue commands or otherwise configure the operation of the power systems. For the hackers, the employee-access mechanism offered a simple way in. Rather than defeat the defenses the Ukrainian companies had set up, the hackers just needed to impersonate the right people. Logging in as those employees gave the hackers access to the operational side of the network and all that it controlled.

The operational side of the network contained machines used for technical work known as supervisory control and data acquisition (SCADA). SCADA systems directly manage components of critical infrastructure all over the world. A hacker with the opportunity and skill to manipulate such a system could do substantial damage. The United States and Israel proved this to the world with the Stuxnet attack, and now Russian hackers were preparing to try their hand at it in Ukraine.

When the hackers made their way to the Ukrainian grid's operational network, they gained the access they needed to control the SCADA systems responsible for managing power in the targeted areas. For amateur hackers, this would have been a cause for celebration and impulsive action—they could now try turning off the power. The blackout to which many hackers had aspired for years was within tantalizing reach. But the Ukrainian grid's hackers did not act on any impulse to strike right away. Instead, they continued to perform careful reconnaissance. For each of the three companies they hacked, they studied how the firm arranged its electricity distribution network. They then developed a multistep plan for launching their operation, with each part carefully prepared and readied for action long before the first light went out. When the time was right, a five-pronged attack would unfold.[6]

One prong manipulated the breakers that controlled the power. The hackers did not need to devise custom malicious code for this, as the Stuxnet creators had. They could, with their stolen credentials, simply log in as operators and issue commands to the industrial control systems directly. When the attack did come, this mechanism provided a stunning visual, captured by a panicked Ukrainian engineer on his iPhone. The video shows a mouse cursor on a computer screen operating outside of his control, clicking away to open one breaker after another. In power system parlance, an open breaker stops the flow of power, while a closed breaker bridges a gap and permits electricity to flow. By opening enough breakers, the hackers were able to cause a blackout.[7]

Another prong targeted the backup power system. This is most commonly called the UPS, short for uninterruptible power supply, but the hackers' attack made this a misnomer. These devices play a key role in a crisis, providing backup electricity to the company if the power goes out so that the company's operators can more quickly bring things back online. The hackers reconfigured them so that this would not happen. Once the power was down, the companies would be in the dark, as well. The effect of this move was twofold. It disrupted the power operators' ability to respond, and also scored a psychological victory, making the utilities seem so inept that they could not keep even their own lights on.

The third prong was even more devious and innovative. The hackers knew that the effects of their malicious commands would not last for long; the power system's operators would surely work quickly to close breakers and bring the grid back online. But many of the power substations, the hackers also realized, relied on a vital piece of hardware known as a serial-to-Ethernet converter. This converter took commands from one set of computer systems and processed them so that other systems on the power grid could interpret them. The hackers devised a way to replace the code that made the converters work, turning the converters into useless bricks at a decisive moment.

This attack thwarted what should have been straightforward moves by power operators to restore normal functioning. No longer able to rely on automated systems, they had to travel physically to each power substation and make configuration changes.[8] In many cases, the power company also had to buy new converters and integrate them into their systems. Robert M. Lee, a well-known expert on industrial control system security and leading investigator of the Ukraine blackout, summed it up succinctly: "In essence, they blew the bridges."[9] It was an aggressive and technically savvy operation without historical precedent.

The fourth prong of the operation, continuing the themes of disruption and psychological impact, was a telephone denial-of-service attack. The hackers knew that, once the power went out for hundreds of thousands of Ukrainians, citizens would promptly call their power companies. The practical and emotional toll of the attack would rise if their calls could not get through. The power companies would be cut off from customer updates on what was working and what was not, and customers would be made to feel helpless, unable to trust their country's critical infrastructure and lacking any sense of when they would have power again. To swamp the phone lines, the hackers prepared to launch a flood of nonsense calls of their own. These calls, which appear to have originated in Moscow, were meant to stop legitimate customers from connecting.[10]

The fifth and final prong was the most direct. Named KillDisk, it was malicious code that aimed directly at the master boot record, that critical component of computers' hard drives that enables proper startup and functioning. This was an approach that both Iran and North Korea had used to great effect in their hard drive-wiping operations. At key moments, the hackers of the Ukrainian utilities could use their KillDisk code to further impede the functioning of the power company's computers. As well as hampering the response to the on-going blackout, this code would deal a psychological blow to power operators accustomed to being in full control of their systems.

With these five prongs of attack prepared, the hackers gained enormous freedom of action. Their preparation, coupled with the Ukrainian power companies' failures to detect the intrusions, allowed them to seize the initiative and control the pace of events. The attack would unfold on their terms, at a time and a place of their choosing. It was exactly what so many had predicted for so long: a latent and lurking threat aimed directly at a country's critical infrastructure.

At 3:30 PM local time on December 23, 2015, the hackers began their attack. Like a conductor in front of a well-rehearsed orchestra, they began releasing their prepared instruments of destruction one by one. They flipped open breakers, disrupting the normal flow of electricity managed by the Prykarpattyaoblenergo power company. They watched as the misconfigured backup power supply caused the operators themselves to lose electricity, impeding recovery. They rendered the key serial-to-Ethernet converters unable to process new commands. They overwhelmed the power companies with meaningless phone calls, severing communications between the utilities and their customers. And they deployed KillDisk as needed, manually activating it here and there to wipe key machines and in some cases setting it up for timed release, so that its digital payload would detonate in the middle of operators' efforts to respond to the ongoing attack.

All told, these five steps combined to cross the Rubicon that analysts had long discussed: a cyber attack had caused a large-scale public utility failure. The blackout lasted one to six hours, depending on the area. Hundreds of thousands of residents went without power as technicians raced to switch systems to manual operations and bring them back online. It took upwards of a year to restore normal operations.[11] By that time, the hackers were ready to strike again.

The Second Blackout

On December 17, 2016, the lights went out again. This time, the blackout occurred in Kiev, the capital of Ukraine. The power at the Ukrenergo substation failed and one-fifth of the city of almost three million people lost power; this single substation ordinarily supplied two hundred megawatts of electricity, more than the combined output of all the sites knocked offline in 2015.[12] When forensic investigators later reviewed what had happened, they found the case to be quite similar to the 2015 blackout on the surface, but intriguingly and revealingly different upon closer examination. These differences are almost always ignored in geopolitical analyses—a fatal error.

The operational security of the 2016 hackers' effort was simply much better than in the 2015 attack. As a result, many components of their operation remain hidden. Most notably, how they contrived to deliver their malicious code to the target is still not public knowledge. Spear-phishing is an obvious guess, given its general effectiveness and its use in 2015, but no direct evidence confirms this hypothesis. Even after sustained investigations by some of the world's foremost industrial control systems experts, the whole story cannot be told.

The most significant fact, however, is known: the 2016 hackers used malicious code that was extraordinarily automated, modular, and powerful. In short, the operation was much more sophisticated than the one that preceded it.[13] Even as the hackers appear to have made some notable mistakes, they demonstrated in-depth understanding of how to target and disrupt advanced power systems; it may be that they targeted the Ukrenergo power substation specifically based on how automated it was.[14] When investigators began disentangling the threads of the 2016 operation to understand how it worked in practice, what they found was striking in its ambition and potency.

In the 2015 operation, malicious code gave the hackers access to the targeted network. Since it enabled the acquisition of employee credentials, the code helped them manipulate the power control systems. Other pieces of malicious code, such as the illicit firmware updates, were useful in prolonging the power outage and impeding recovery efforts. Doing the actual manipulation of the grid, however, were human hackers, armed as they were with the employees' passwords.

The 2016 operation was different. This time, the hackers' code could do much more damage all on its own. It was the first known piece of malicious code that was specifically designed to manipulate power grids. Noting the number of uses within the code of the word "crash" and its ability to override key industrial control system processes, researchers at Dragos, a leading industrial control system security company, named it CRASHOVERRIDE.

To make CRASHOVERRIDE so powerful, clearly its creators had studied previous attempts at targeting industrial control systems. The most infamous of these attempts was Stuxnet. As Chapter 6 showed, Stuxnet's architects exhibited a deep understanding of the Iranians' industrial processes for uranium enrichment. They understood how the centrifuges worked and how illicit computer code could manipulate these processes and cause them to fail. They also understood the importance of testing the code on similar or replica machinery and refining it to have a tailored and well-defined effect against the intended target. CRASHOVERRIDE's creators internalized all of these lessons, even if they could not execute them all perfectly.

Two other pieces of malicious code seem to have inspired CRASHOVERRIDE. The first, Havex, was purely an espionage tool. According to some estimates, the Havex operators, believed to be of Russian origin, used it to spy on more than two thousand industrial sites all over the world. Once on a target network, Havex preyed on a widely used protocol known as Open Platform Communications (OPC), which enables industrial components of all types to share information with one another. Cleverly, the Havex hackers used OPC to gather intelligence on potential targets. Havex itself was not an attack, but it collected information to enable attacks.[15] Tucked within CRASHOVERRIDE was a similar capability to use OPC to map target networks.

The other inspiration for CRASHOVERRIDE was malicious code known as BlackEnergy2. This was the precursor to BlackEnergy3, the code that contributed to the 2015 blackout by establishing that first foothold in a power company's administrative systems. Among other capabilities, BlackEnergy2 could spy on the interfaces that operators of critical infrastructure frequently use to control their systems. Some BlackEnergy2 hackers exploited these interfaces' potential to gather information about the networks they served. While the interfaces offered only slight capacity to do lasting physical damage, they served important roles within the network and were thus excellent sources of information on its functioning. The interfaces sometimes connected both to industrial control systems that were potential targets and to the internet, enabling easier access for hackers.[16] CRASHOVERRIDE likewise targeted them effectively.

Unlike its Havex and BlackEnergy2 forefathers, however, CRASHOVERRIDE was not oriented toward gathering information. Indeed, key functions that would have been useful for espionage purposes were missing from the code. There was no significant built-in capacity to copy data from the target network, for example, and exfiltrate it back to headquarters for review. Instead, the software featured several modules working together to serve a different and unambiguous purpose: attack.

The first component was a launcher—code loaded onto the target machine as preparation for the attack. After a one- or two-hour delay (depending on the version), it activated a second component, the data wiper, to overwrite critical data in a vital portion of the target computer. The data wiper also erased any configuration files it could find for industrial control systems. The code focused on destroying the files that automate the functioning of power substations, in some cases preventing Ukrainian workers from being able to remotely monitor the state of various substations and breakers. For good measure, the data wiper erased other Windows files in an attempt to make the computer system unusable.

The next set of modules presented the hackers with a variety of ways to find and damage target devices. Three modules used industrial control systems protocols to change the status of the systems from "on" to "off." To launch an attack, the hackers only had to provide data about the target system and some additional instructions; the automated attack modules took it from there. Another module required even less from the hackers. It could identify and manipulate system switches all on its own.

It is here that the analysis of CRASHOVERRIDE gets particularly confusing. Still other capabilities in the code provided hackers with different attack options, some of which are not well understood by investigators. Parts of the CRASHOVERRIDE code suggest that the attackers had at least one more trick, though not one they used successfully in 2016. To understand this trick, it is first necessary to understand a key part of the electric grid known as a protective relay. These critical devices are meant to prevent physical damage to power system components, preferring to disconnect systems and stop the flow of power rather than risk harm to critical equipment. When protective relays across the system fail to coordinate in managing faults and irregularities, major blackouts can occur, such as the 2003 blackout in New York—but even these blackouts are preferable to the physical destruction of power grid components that can occur when protective relays are disabled or removed.

CRASHOVERRIDE's final trick was thus to try to disable the relays. Exactly why is unclear, though analysts at Dragos offered one alarming explanation: that the aforementioned manipulation of the breakers that caused the blackout was in fact meant to be only the first step in a far more destructive attack, one that never came to fruition. The data wiper component would have served as a second phase, blinding the Ukrainians from monitoring how their system was performing. This would have perhaps caused the third phase, the quiet disabling of protective relays, to remain unnoticed. If the Ukrainians had rushed to restore manual operations at this point, as they did in 2015, they might have inadvertently surged electricity throughout the system. Without functioning relays, this surge would have potentially caused physical damage to key components of the power grid. In essence, the initial blackout might have been bait for a far more destructive attack to follow.[17]

There is also a possibility, also uncovered by Dragos, that the attackers intended to disable the protective relays for a different purpose: to cause an "islanding event." In this kind of attack, they would have used CRASHOVERRIDE to toggle switches to continuously and automatically open and close a substation's breakers, activating other safety mechanisms that would have disconnected substations and stopped the flow of power.[18] But, if the attackers were aiming for a large-scale attack through either a power surge or an islanding event, they failed. There were errors in the parts of CRASHOVERRIDE that tried to disable the protective relays. Even if the attackers had not made those mistakes, it is not clear if the attack would have worked as Dragos thinks the attackers imagined it would, since other safeguards may have thwarted physical damage.

In the end, the Ukrainians did indeed switch to manual operations to bring the power back online, but the protective relays remained in place and no major lasting damage was done. The outage was thus short-lived. Still, it was the second time in a year that computer hackers had plunged Ukrainian citizens into darkness. Even after investigations revealed how it had been done, two questions remained: who and why?

Just A Test?

Even though the 2015 and 2016 operations were quite different from one another, investigators concluded with high confidence that the same group of hackers carried out both. Or, if there were two groups of hackers, it was highly likely that they were tightly linked. The investigators drew on computer forensic evidence as well as other, confidential sources to draw this high-confidence conclusion.[19]

Investigators also linked the 2015 and 2016 attacks to a group of hackers most commonly known as Sandworm. The group had earned this nickname due to the allusions within its malicious code to the classic science fiction novel *Dune*, in which the sandworm is a species; it is not known why the group included these references. The cybersecurity community had been tracking the Sandworm hackers for several years before the blackouts. Like police investigating a string of bank robberies, they carefully noted the overlaps in tradecraft, tools, and technique from one hack to the next.

In the years prior to the blackouts, researchers had watched as Sandworm hacked a large number of targets in Ukraine and around the world. Along the way, the hackers maintained a high operational tempo and an aggressive posture, but sometimes made revealing mistakes. FireEye, a leading threat intelligence company, noted that Sandworm's interest in industrial control systems was hardly limited to Ukraine; some analysts suspected the group of using BlackEnergy2 to spy on many sites within the United States in 2014, though it had never launched an attack.[20] The common conclusion was that Sandworm was linked at least indirectly to the Russian military intelligence agency, the GRU.[21]

But although the *who* was reasonably clear, the *why* remained something of a mystery. What caused the hackers to turn off the power when and where they did? Russian belligerence toward Ukraine was well-established by 2015, especially after the Russian takeover of Crimea in 2014 and the conflict between the two countries. Yet, even in this wartime context, it remained unclear how short blackouts in parts of Ukraine far from the front lines served Russian interests.

Geopolitical context is vital in developing even a provisional interpretation. Much of the tension between Russia and Ukraine focused on the provision of electricity. After Russia took control of Crimea, pro-Russian forces began to nationalize Ukrainian-owned energy companies, causing great consternation in Ukraine. In response, the Ukrainian government debated nationalizing energy companies in Ukraine owned by Russian oligarchs. There had also been a power outage affecting two million residents in Crimea, caused by Ukrainian activists who physically damaged power systems and interfered with repairs.[22]

The 2015 blackout occurred in the midst of all this, although the timing of events muddies the analysis of cause and effect, as the hackers of the Ukrainian power companies had embarked on their initial intelligence gathering before the Ukrainians' physical attack on Crimean substations. It is natural to assume that the cyber attack served as a warning in the context of escalating tensions. It may have been a warning not to interfere with the business interests of the oligarchs, or alternatively a retaliation for the physical damage to the power substations. Robert Lee, the industrial control systems expert, said that, if this explanation holds, it "is very mafioso in terms of like, oh, you think you can take away the power [in Crimea]? Well I can take away the power from you."[23] But there is no conclusive evidence that this is the case; unlike in the Sony hack, the hackers did not post any demands or clarifying messages online.

Any answer to the question of *why* would have to account for one important and vexing fact: strong evidence suggests that the hackers restrained themselves in some substantial ways. In the 2015 blackout, even though the attackers had spent months doing reconnaissance and developing a plan of attack, they did not translate this effort into maximum damage. The hackers either missed or ignored opportunities to do greater harm, such as by targeting other parts of the power grid. Given their overall level of skill and preparation, it seems more likely that they chose to hold back.

The 2016 blackout is more complicated. The hackers perhaps could have deployed the CRASHOVERRIDE malicious code against many locations in Ukraine at once.[24] Doing so would have dramatically increased the risk of a more lasting and expensive outage. Instead, the attackers chose only to target a single substation in Kiev. The failure to successfully target protective relays is also unexplained. In short, the hackers built a tool for scalable attack against highly automated systems, but then deployed it in such a way that took very little advantage of its possibility for scale and broader impact. It is possible that this was due not to self-restraint but to error; the attackers may have expected that CRASHOVERRIDE would have disabled the protective relays and caused physical damage when technicians tried to bring systems back online. If this is right—and it is very hard to know for sure—the Ukrainians dodged a significant blow.

Even if it was meant to be more powerful than it turned out to be, it is plausible that the 2016 attack was some kind of test. Perhaps the deployment of CRASHOVERRIDE in Ukraine provided the hackers a chance to see how the code worked in practice so they could refine it for future use. This is an explanation favored by Lee, who said the attack "looked more like a proof of concept or a test run than a final outcome."[25] Some media speculation suggested that Ukraine may have been nothing more than a live testbed for Russian hackers, avoiding the need to build replica facilities of their ultimate targets. The test explanation seemed also to explain other, less high-profile attacks on Ukraine, such as those against government offices, where Russian hackers deployed some but not all of their capabilities.[26]

Indeed, CRASHOVERRIDE's modularity and flexibility suggests that the code would be effective as an attack tool against a wide range of industrial control systems all over the world. With some minor changes, it could function as an attack tool against the North American power grid, although American operators, if they studied what happened in Ukraine, would presumably be better able to defend themselves. After reviewing the code, Lee thought it was clearly designed for broader application. "The way it's built and designed and run makes it look like it was meant to be used multiple times. And not just in Ukraine."[27]

It is also possible that the test itself was supposed to send a kind of message by demonstration. To some degree, all public weapons tests are at least implicit signals of a sort, and it might be argued that—given how difficult offensive cyber operations are—a demonstration of this capability is particularly meaningful. It could be that CRASHOVERRIDE, coupled with the extensive Russian espionage against American industrial control systems, was meant to show that Russia had developed advanced blackout-causing cyber attack capabilities and was not afraid to use them; this message would have been even more threatening had the code successfully disabled the protective relays and done more lasting damage. In this sense, perhaps CRASHOVERRIDE was an attempt to intimidate the United States. Maybe the Russians were trying to match the high-profile media leak in fall 2016 indicating that the United States had prepared its own cyber capabilities against Russian critical infrastructure.[28] But this, too, is speculation.

While the attacks may have tried to send a message, there seems to be no consensus on what exactly that message is, making it hard to interpret the case with confidence. The message might have pertained only to regional tensions in Ukraine, or it might speak to broader geopolitical issues or to the development of generalized Russian cyber attack capability. The two blackouts, each with their different methodologies and potencies, could also each carry different intended messages. As ever, despite the legions of international relations scholars working to unpack the ways in which policymakers maneuver to send and interpret credible signals with conventional and nuclear capabilities, little of the literature applies well to the vague messages transmitted and received with technically complex cyber capabilities. Worse still, few policymakers seem prepared to sort through the technical details to determine what restraint was accidental and what was intentional. As a result, if the intent of the 2015 and 2016 blackouts was to send a clear and unambiguous warning, then it seems the operations did not succeed.

Thus, like the Iranian and North Korean attacks of earlier years, the Ukrainian blackouts ought to give pause to anyone who expects states to use cyber capabilities for signaling purposes. In one sense, the 2015 and 2016 cases could represent the realization of a scenario long imagined: that a state might try to use cyber attacks on critical infrastructure to threaten an adversary and compel a change in its behavior. For decades, cyber-caused blackouts showed up only in fiction and in speculative scholarship. Some scenarios suggested that China might use a blackout to signal strength during a crisis in the South China Sea, for example, while others worried that Russia would cause one as a sign of increasing aggression against the United States.[29] In each of those hypothetical cases, the severity of the blackout ranged from moderate to extreme, but the intent behind it was always unambiguous. Yet, after decades of waiting, when the first and second cyber-caused blackouts did occur, not only was the damage far less than prophesized, but the operations also failed to convey much nuance. It is hard to know if they were messages, tests, failed attempts at more powerful attacks (especially in the case of 2016), or something else.

The blackouts did make one thing clear, however: relative to the cases that had come before, cyber operations were only getting more powerful and hackers were only getting more aggressive. The attackers in Ukraine may not have chosen to exercise their capabilities to the fullest, but their operations hinted that malicious code was growing ever more powerful. It could be employed to attack discrete targets—whether movie studios, banks, or nuclear facilities—and deployed to broad and destabilizing effect. On this point, still more was to come.

PART THREE

DESTABILIZATION

10

Election Interference

IT WAS THE EVE OF THE REPUBLICAN CONVENTION IN JUNE 1940. The party's members were in heated dispute over the potential nominees. Most seemed strongly to prefer isolationist candidates who wanted to keep the United States out of World War II, which was raging in Europe. Then, at a critical moment, the *New York Herald* reported surprising news: three-fifths of surveyed convention delegates backed extensive support to Great Britain in its uphill battle against the Nazis. The article cited a poll supposedly conducted by Market Analysts, Inc., an "independent research organization."

This organization, and its poll, never existed. British intelligence operatives had made it up and circulated it as part of their efforts to push the Republican Party toward choosing a pro-war candidate. The British fabrication efforts, lending weight to arguments made by Republicans aligned with British interests, helped catapult the candidate Wendell Willkie, previously a definite underdog, to the nomination. Willkie, a former Democrat, proved to be an enormous asset to Britain, acquiescing during the presidential campaign to Franklin Roosevelt's transfer of American destroyers to the Royal Navy. Maybe most importantly, he lost the November election, leaving Roosevelt and his strong support for Britain in charge.

The British election interference campaign did not stop there. British operatives and their American allies sustained the effort, focusing on top isolationist members of Congress. They falsely accused them of, among other things, taking money from and coordinating with Nazis and Nazi supporters. The operatives timed key revelations to come to light just weeks before the fall elections, forcing candidates not sufficiently supportive of the war onto the defensive. Each week, they reported back to London on how many stories they were able to plant in American papers, understanding fully that their remit was to spread "subversive propaganda." In the eyes of British spymasters, their efforts vastly increased the amount of support the United States was able and willing to provide to its European allies before Pearl Harbor.[1]

The British operation was not the world's first example of foreign election interference, and neither would it be the last. During the Cold War, the United States and Soviet Union interfered in a combined total of more than one hundred elections in other countries.[2] Autocrats all over the world have also long manipulated their own elections at home. Eventually, hackers would participate in election interference, too; it seems that in 2014, Russians wiped computers in Ukraine's election infrastructure days before the election and tried to disseminate false results on election night. Their fake results showed a pro-Russia candidate winning, and aligned with stories pushed through other Russian propaganda channels, though the Ukrainians were able to mitigate most of the harm and the pro-Russia candidate did not succeed.[3]

Even after eight decades, however, the British effort stands above all—and neatly foreshadows the Russian interference in the 2016 US election. Here was direct interference in United States presidential politics by a foreign actor, aided by the spread of false information, the manipulation of popular media, the clever timing of leaks and lies, and the creation of propaganda that aligned with preexisting narratives—with lingering uncertainty, even in retrospect, about the overall impact. The Russian hacking and leaking mission has justifiably become one of the most-discussed cyber operations of all time, but its British antecedent lends much-needed historical context. More than anything, the British effort serves as a reminder that the true importance of cyber operations comes not from their damage to machines, but from their destabilizing effects on humans and societies.

In 2016, the Kremlin's preferred messages cascaded throughout the electorate via traditional and social media. Russian operators played a part in boosting these messages, but unwitting citizens and reporters also spread them widely. What is too often characterized as a campaign of "fake news" was in fact a multipronged, ambitious, and aggressive effort to hack private information, put it to potent use, and drive wedges between key groups in American society. All told, the combination of cyber operations and influence campaigns interfered in a highly charged election and, in the opinion of more than a few experts, shaped the result.

For as much discussion as the 2016 operation has generated, it still deserves further attention, both to show how the Russians carried it out and to understand why it worked to the degree that it did. Like Stuxnet, this operation expanded the art of the possible for all to see. It provided an archetypal case of modern election interference, showing how propaganda and information operations can supercharge the long-established tradition of foreign meddling. The operation's narrative is too important to ignore, if not because of what it meant in 2016, then because of what it might herald for the future of democracy.

Democrats in the Crosshairs

For spy agencies, hacking the computers of electoral candidates is not particularly new. Chinese hackers reportedly penetrated both the Obama and McCain campaigns in 2008.[4] Mitt Romney's presidential campaign in 2012 perceived the threat of foreign hackers to be so severe that for key decisions, such as the vice-presidential selection, the team devised code names for potential selections and communicated using only computers disconnected from the internet.[5] Such precautions make sense, given the great international interest in American elections. Intelligence agencies all over the world want insight into what potential future American leaders and their advisors are thinking.

The US signals intelligence apparatus is likewise tasked with understanding who the future leaders of other countries might be and what they are likely to do while in office. Cyber operations help achieve this task. In the summer of 2012, for example, the NSA hacked the email accounts of Mexican candidate Enrique Peña Nieto and his close associates, gaining insight into the politics, policies, and inner circle of the future president.[6] Similarly, it seems that the NSA's surveillance of Angela Merkel began well before she became chancellor of Germany, when she occupied other government positions.[7]

It was not entirely unusual, then, when a group of Russian hackers penetrated the servers of the Democratic National Committee, or DNC, in 2015. The cybersecurity industry had tracked these hackers during their years-long espionage campaign against other United States targets. Most analysts believe they are tied to the Russian FSB, the successor to most elements of the famed KGB, likely working with another intelligence service, the SVR.[8] Once inside the DNC's network, the hackers made their first move: they deployed a stealthy persistence module on the target computers, indicating their intention to remain for the long haul.

The malicious code was hard to detect and provided a firm foothold in the DNC's networks. Elegant in its power and simplicity, the code enabled the FSB hackers to deploy additional malicious software, including modules for encrypted communications with command-and-control servers. They plugged directly into the mechanisms in the Windows operating system that system administrators use for managing large groups of computers, giving the hackers scalable control of the systems they compromised.

With that foundation in place, the hackers built toward further action, deploying password-stealing tools to swipe DNC employee credentials. Using these passwords to aid their lateral movement within the DNC network, they expanded their control to more computers and gained still greater access to the organization's internal documents. As they moved, the hackers took care to ensure operational security. For example, on each system they breached, they deployed an array of encryption tools to hide their actions from any investigators or network administrators. These signs of operational deftness and care indicate a group of experienced hackers.

But these precautionary steps did not entirely cloak the hackers from the US counterintelligence apparatus. At some point in 2015, the American government became aware of the intrusion at the DNC and alerted the committee's network administrators. In September 2015, an agent from the FBI called the main phone line at the DNC with the news. The person who answered transferred him to the IT help desk, where his call was eventually addressed.

Afterward, an internal DNC memo passed along the news: "The F.B.I. thinks the D.N.C. has at least one compromised computer on its network and the F.B.I. wanted to know if the D.N.C. is aware, and if so, what the D.N.C. is doing about it." The FBI agent had also specifically linked the intrusion to "the Dukes," a common name in the cybersecurity community for the well-known group of hackers. A quick internet search at that point would have turned up significant private-sector reporting that identified the group as Russian and likely from the FSB.

The DNC employee tasked with investigating did his best to understand what was happening within the penetrated network. Using the limited cybersecurity tools available to the committee, he found nothing. As a result, and in part due to the fact that the FBI agent had not provided proof of his identity, he did not return subsequent follow-up phone calls from the bureau. Despite the ongoing silence from the DNC, the FBI did not call any high-ranking officials there, nor did it show up in person to press the case at the offices, which were located just a mile away from the FBI field office. The bureau chose not to send follow-up emails, likely due to the strong possibility that the Russians were capable of accessing the DNC's mail servers. The investigation stalled. The hackers remained in place.

In November, the FBI called again. This time, agents issued a more strident warning. The infected computers at the DNC, the bureau told the committee, contained malicious code that was sending information back to hackers in Russia. Illicit communication of this sort is a telltale sign of an intrusion. Alarm bells should have sounded forcefully at both the FBI and the DNC, but still the response seemed sluggish at best. Over the ensuing months, representatives from the two institutions finally managed to meet in person. The DNC realized that the message from the FBI was not some kind of prank, and it could not be ignored any longer.

At long last, the committee understood that it was in the line of fire. What the Watergate burglars had tried to do to the DNC in 1972, Russian hackers were now doing at a much greater scale. Ironically, the file cabinet of interest to the Nixon-era burglars, still kept as a memento, was not far from one of the servers targeted by the hackers. With all of this finally made clear, the DNC began to try to fix things. By April 2016, it had made several upgrades to its lackluster cyber-security defenses. By then, however, it was much too late.[9]

A New Arrival

It was too late because another group of hackers had already arrived. Beginning at the end of March 2016, the GRU, the Russian military intelligence agency tied to the blackout operations in Ukraine, got in on the action. The NSA and broader cybersecurity community had watched these hackers for years, too.[10] The GRU's efforts were well organized, with clear division of labor. Some units focused on developing malicious code, while others focused on gaining access to targets. Still others focused on mining cryptocurrencies such as bitcoin, which the GRU used to pay for online hacking infrastructure that made operations harder to trace. Other units focused on public-facing efforts, which would soon be quite important.[11]

Whether the GRU knew of the other Russian intelligence activity against the DNC is uncertain.[12] The GRU began an operation against the Democratic Party, targeting the DNC, the Clinton campaign, and the Democratic Congressional Campaign Committee, or DCCC, which helps Democrats win elections to the House of Representatives. The hackers studied these organizations' technical configurations in an effort to better inform the operations to come.[13] They also began spear-phishing employees. But while other hackers, such as the North Koreans who targeted Sony, had focused on using socially engineered emails to deliver malicious code to their targets, the Russians used the emails to get key Democratic officials to surrender their passwords.

The GRU hooked their biggest fish early: Clinton campaign chairman John Podesta. Podesta had long been a leader in Democratic politics, serving as chief of staff to President Bill Clinton, founding a major DC think tank, and acting as senior counselor to President Obama. His legendary Rolodex, passion for policy, and senior status in the party made him invaluable to the Clinton campaign. Few names were bigger—and few people had more interesting email accounts. It was those emails that the GRU was after.

The spear-phishing email to Podesta seemed innocent enough. "Hi John," it said, "Someone just used your password to try to sign into your Google account. . . . Google stopped this sign-in attempt. You should change your password immediately." Podesta was suspicious, and forwarded the message to his information technology staff. Inexplicably, a campaign aide wrote back that the warning was genuine, and Podesta needed to change his password. Podesta then followed the fake warning's instructions and surrendered his password as part of the fake password-change process. This gave the Russian hackers access to a decade of his emails, numbering more than fifty thousand messages, which they copied to their own computers around March 21, 2016. The aide later blamed the misunderstanding on a typo. He said he meant to write that the warning Podesta received was *not* real, because he knew the campaign was being flooded with similar spear-phishing attempts. If it was a typo, it was a cata-strophic one.

Although Podesta was the Russians' most famous victim, he was far from the only one. On March 22, William Rinehart, a former DNC field director working on the Clinton campaign, opened an email similar to the one Podesta had received. It also claimed to have thwarted an intrusion, which it said had been attempted by someone in Ukraine. Rinehart was traveling and checking his email at 4:00 AM in Hawaii; he later told the *New York Times* he must have clicked the link in the message and given up his password while half-asleep.[14] In any case, the GRU was now armed with Rinehart's credentials, and began systematically vacuuming up his emails of interest, too.

The Russians had drawn up quite a target list. From early March to early April of 2016, the spear-phishing attempts persisted. In this period, GRU hackers targeted at least 109 members of Hillary Clinton's campaign staff, sending a total of 214 individualized spoofed emails. They attempted contact with her top policy advisor, Jake Sullivan, fourteen times, hoping to get access to any of his several email accounts. Twice, they sent messages to Hillary Clinton's personal email, which were ignored. Among her campaign staffers, however, thirty-six did click the malicious links, and a subset of those went on to give their credentials to the GRU.[15] The hacking attempts would continue all summer, with the Russians repeatedly trying their luck against new targets. Between the efforts specifically related to the upcoming election and spear-phishing for other purposes, the hackers sent nine thousand malicious links to more than four thousand accounts.[16]

Not all of their emails pretended to be from Google. Some impersonated Clinton campaign members. The Russians created an account with a name that was nearly identical to the email address of a Clinton staffer, and then used that to email more than thirty different campaign employees. Within the email was a link that purportedly directed users to a spreadsheet with information on Hillary Clinton's approval rating. When clicked, it brought the target to a website maintained by the GRU that presumably served up malicious code.[17]

On April 12, the GRU gained access to the DCCC network, using the spear-phished password of a DCCC employee. Once inside the network, they installed a piece of malicious code known as X-Agent on at least ten DCCC computers. Cybersecurity researchers had watched the GRU deploy, use, and refine X-Agent for years. It had served the Russians well in hundreds of operations, with some modules of the code dating back to 2004.[18]

X-Agent could perform many of the functions common to state-created malicious code. It permitted the GRU to gather documents, harvest passwords, and track individual targets as they went about their work. The hackers sent instructions to X-Agent to capture every keystroke typed by certain DCCC employees, take screenshots of important activities, and pilfer files from target computers so that the hackers could store them.[19]

Some employees at the DCCC also had access to the DNC network, as is fairly common in political circles where allied organizations share information and resources. The GRU hackers realized this and took advantage. On April 18, the GRU used X-Agent to gather the credentials of a DCCC employee who could also log in to the DNC network. Armed with this username and password, the GRU gained access to the national committee's network, which the FSB had already successfully hacked. Once there, the hackers installed more copies of X-Agent, and went on to infect at least thirty-three computers in the DNC network.[20] They then went to some effort to cover their tracks and confuse investigators, deleting logs and resetting timestamps on other files.[21] There is no doubt that the GRU, with its penetration of key Democratic officials, various committees, and the presidential campaign, achieved enormous access. In the world of cyber operations, that kind of access confers significant power.

Going Public

Once it had penetrated its targets, the GRU was ready to put its access to use. It already had numerous emails from Podesta and other Democratic staffers, but it wanted to mine the political organizations' files, too. Working within the DNC and DCCC networks, the GRU took thousands of screenshots and recorded large quantities of keystrokes. The GRU, studying the two committees from the inside, learned how they collaborated in boosting Democrats' chances in the coming elections. From their privileged perch, the hackers could view wide expanses of normally hidden information.

But, just as their information-gathering operation was hitting full stride, the hackers made a curious move: on April 12, they tried to register the web domain name electionleaks.com, paying $37 in cryptocurrency to a Romanian company to do so. But, having somehow botched the registration and lost the right to that domain, they came back a week later, on April 19, to register a second choice, DCLeaks.com.[22] DCLeaks remained dormant throughout April and May of 2016, but in hindsight, the registration was an early clue that the GRU had aims beyond simple espionage.

The second clue to the GRU's ambitions is that it sought certain kinds of information in the Democratic networks. The hackers weren't after the sort of intelligence gathered in traditional cyber espionage operations against candidates. They did not seem to care much about predicting how Hillary Clinton would act as president or understanding her policy priorities, perhaps because they already perceived her to be hostile toward Russia. Instead, the GRU's focus was on content that was politically explosive, even if it offered little forward-looking insight.

The GRU hackers sifted through the networks using search terms like "Hillary," "Trump," and "Cruz." They copied entire folders related to the Benghazi investigations, a politically hot topic that had little relevance to substantive foreign policy matters. They snapped up opposition research on Republican candidates and plans for field operations to increase Democratic turnout in the fall. The finances of the Democratic organizations also seemed particularly interesting to them.[23]

The documents of interest to the GRU hackers amounted to many gigabytes of information. Moving that much data out of the network at once might have attracted the attention of network defenders and revealed the GRU's illicit presence. To better hide their activities, the hackers used a technique called file compression to reduce the size of the documents they wanted to exfiltrate. They then deployed encryption to obscure the true contents of the files before copying them en masse off the Democratic organizations' networks and back to Russia.[24]

The GRU was also after the DNC's messages. In May, the hackers targeted the organization's email servers housing many thousands of employee messages. With their privileged access to DNC systems, the hackers were able to access many emails at once, without having to compromise the passwords of individual employees. They vacuumed up these messages, exfiltrated them via their command-and-control system, and stored them for later use.[25] They also found their way into the DNC's cloud-based systems, and copied information from them, as well.[26] The targeted organizations had been thoroughly compromised.

With so much information in hand, the GRU made its next move. In early June, its operatives put public content on DCLeaks.com for the first time. On the site, they disavowed any foreign connection, and instead claimed to be "American hacktivists who respect and appreciate freedom of speech, human rights and government of the people." Their sole aim, they said, in poor English, was "to find out and tell you the truth about US decision-making process as well as about the key elements of American political life."[27] This was the first platform the GRU would use to release its ill-gotten files, gathered from operations against Democratic organizations and other targets.

The individuals featured in the files published on DCLeaks were for the most part prominent Democrats, anti-Russian figures, or both. Early leaks on the site included files from George Soros's Open Society Foundations, emails from then-NATO Supreme Commander Philip Breedlove, and files about a general and a major who worked at United States Central Command. DCLeaks also hosted a small number of files about Bill and Hillary Clinton, as well as some on the Republican Party. At first, the site did not attract much attention.

In June of 2016, the Democratic Party took action. Working with CrowdStrike, a leading cybersecurity firm that had long battled Russian intelligence agencies, it tried to decontaminate the Democratic systems. The use of a firm like CrowdStrike was fairly typical, but the party also did something unusual: in a *Washington Post* story on June 14 and a CrowdStrike report on June 15, it announced that Russia had hacked the DNC. The party pointed the finger directly at Russian intelligence agencies, based on the strong technical evidence that was already available.[28]

From there, things escalated rapidly. On June 16, an anonymous party appeared online using the screen name of Guccifer 2.0—an apparent homage to an earlier Guccifer, who was a well-known Romanian hacker. This Guccifer declared, using profane language, that CrowdStrike got it wrong. He claimed he was Romanian, not Russian, and had worked alone to hack the DNC. To prove it, he released eleven files from inside the organization, which were quickly verified as authentic. He had many thousands more, he said, that he had already shared with WikiLeaks.

Right away, holes in this story began to appear. Cybersecurity researchers noticed that someone using Russian-language settings and the name Feliks Dzerzhinsky had edited some of the files posted by Guccifer; Dzerzhinsky was the founder of the Soviet secret police. With more investigation, a group of cybersecurity companies and researchers solidified the early leads. Among other things, they noted overlaps in the hacking infrastructure used to target the Democratic organizations and other operations attributed to Russia, including a notable one against the German Parliament.[29] As an amusing extra sign that something was amiss, when a journalist interviewing Guccifer online asked him to switch over to his native Romanian, it quickly became apparent that he did not speak the language.[30]

Enter WikiLeaks. Even prior to the Democrats' announcement and Guccifier's creation, the group's founder, Julian Assange, had sought to be relevant to the 2016 election. On June 12, he promised that WikiLeaks would release damaging Democratic emails. Why he said this remains a mystery, since the first known direct contact between the GRU and WikiLeaks occurred on June 14, though it is possible there had been a previous undetected transfer of information through intermediaries.[31]

The GRU and WikiLeaks continued to talk. On June 22, WikiLeaks messaged Guccifer, requesting access to any new material. WikiLeaks promised to distribute it with a higher profile and impact than Guccifer could. On July 6, the group reached out to Guccifer again, highlighting the upcoming Democratic convention and asking for any information related to the Clinton campaign. Time was of the essence, the message said, because the damaging material had to leak before Hillary Clinton could win over Bernie Sanders supporters in her run toward the general election.[32] On July 14, the GRU provided WikiLeaks with a large encrypted batch of hacked files in an email with the subject "big archive" and the message "a new attempt."[33]

After all the discussion, Assange delivered for the GRU. On July 22, just three days before the Democratic convention that would officially nominate Hillary Clinton, WikiLeaks posted the largest and most significant trove of DNC files. This batch included almost twenty thousand copies of emails stolen by the GRU hackers. The most damaging emails were the ones that showed some staffers at the DNC, which is not supposed to take sides in intraparty contests, clearly supporting Clinton and not Sanders in the presidential primaries. Two days after the publication of these messages, and one day before the convention was set to begin, DNC Chair Debbie Wasserman Schultz resigned.

The leaks continued all summer, as Hillary Clinton marched toward what many thought was her inevitable November victory. More than a dozen new troves of files from various Democratic entities appeared on online platforms. The leaked documents were authentic, though, in a few cases, the Russian hackers modified them before release to suit their own purposes. In one case, the hackers added "Confidential" to the cover of an opposition research report, presumably to make it more alluring to reporters.[34] They forged and modified

other documents to make it appear that shocking political dona-
tions had been made, one purporting to show a $150 million Bradley
Foundation gift to the Clinton campaign—which would have been
illegal—and another adding a line to a budget from the Open Society
Foundations that indicated funding of anti-regime activities in Russia.[35]

Three groups deserve particular attention for their responses to
the GRU operation during this period. The first is the group Donald
Trump had assembled to run his campaign, which some evidence
suggests was inclined to cheer on the Russian operation. Michael
Cohen, Trump's lawyer, later testified that he was in Trump's office
when Roger Stone, formerly in the campaign's employ, called to pass
along what he had just learned: that Assange was about to release a
"massive dump" of damaging emails from Clinton's campaign. In Cohen's words, "Mr. Trump responded by stating to the effect of
'wouldn't that be great.'"[36] It has been alleged that Stone contacted
WikiLeaks during the summer of 2016 at the Trump campaign's behest, and relayed whatever information he gained to the campaign.
He is apparently one of the "multiple links" between the Trump campaign and individuals tied to the Russian government that special
counsel Robert Mueller investigated, although the final report of
that investigation ultimately "did not find that the Trump campaign,
or anyone associated with it, conspired or coordinated with the Russian government" in its election interference.[37]

Mueller's report also indicates that, after the first set of email leaks,
a senior Trump campaign official "was directed" by an unspecified
individual "to contact Stone about any additional releases and what
other damaging information [WikiLeaks] had regarding the Clinton
Campaign." The government's indictment of Stone quotes specific
communications between him and WikiLeaks, sometimes directly
and sometimes through intermediaries, throughout the summer and

fall of 2016. Stone used the information he learned to give the campaign advance notice about the timing of future leaks.[38]

Candidate Trump did not keep his hopes for more leaks to himself. "Russia, if you're listening," he crowed at a July 27 press conference, "I hope you're able to find the thirty thousand emails that are missing," in obvious reference to the emails that had been selectively deleted from the unsecure private server Clinton used as secretary of state in President Obama's first term.[39] Within five hours, the Russians launched spear-phishing attempts at the Clintons' family office accounts for what appears to be the first time.[40]

The second notable group is other political campaigns. While most ignored the leaks, one actively reached out to the GRU for information they might be able to use. Aaron Nevins, a Republican consultant to Florida candidates, contacted Guccifer through Twitter, writing, "Feel free to send any Florida based information."[41] The Russians complied, sending over several gigabytes of voter turnout information and population modeling taken from the DCCC. These files provided insight into the committee's understanding of certain Florida congressional races and indicated where the party intended to focus its voter turnout efforts.

Nevins's efforts may have had impact. A campaign consultant for the Republican candidate in one local race said that the leaked data helped inform his vote-targeting strategy. After winning the race, however, the candidate himself denied that it had any influence. For Nevins, the choice to use leaked data for partisan purposes was easy. All was fair in a competitive campaign: "If your interests align," he said, "never shut any doors in politics."[42]

The third and most important group is the United States national security community. It was strangely silent. There was little public communication or apparent response during the summer of 2016.

Michael Daniel, who was at the time the White House cybersecurity coordinator, later said that the United States had been preparing response options during the late spring and early summer as the Russian activity became evident. These included some options to retaliate against the Russians and thereby reestablish deterrence, and others to interfere directly with the Russian operations.

Yet the leadership of the National Security Council decided instead to prioritize assistance to US election administrators as they worked to defend their infrastructure against Russian intrusions. The White House worried that if it confronted Russia too directly the situation might escalate into full-scale cyber conflict, including the potential manipulation of votes on Election Day. Unsure of its ability to send a signal of determination without risking escalation, the United States stood down.[43]

A series of August and September meetings between intelligence officials and congressional leaders attempted but failed to forge a bipartisan statement condemning the Russian hackers. This failure seems in large part to have been due to Senate Majority Leader Mitch McConnell's skepticism about the intelligence agencies' assessments of Russian state involvement.[44] The Obama administration chose to call out the activity on its own. In September 2016, President Obama told reporters that he warned Vladimir Putin at an international meeting to "cut it out, there were going to be serious consequences if he did not."[45] On October 7, the Department of Homeland Security and the Office of the Director of National Intelligence issued a statement blaming the Russians for the hacks and leaks.[46] The United States government seemed unable or unwilling to muster more opprobrium than that.

The statement barely registered in the media ecosystem given the frenetic pace of subsequent events. The *Washington Post* had unearthed a recording of Donald Trump making remarkably crude comments about assaulting women. "I don't even wait," he told the host of *Access Hollywood* as they were on their way to the studio for an interview. "And when you're a star, they let you do it. You can do anything. Grab them by the pussy. You can do anything." Damaging leaks of candidates' unguarded comments are a staple of politics—such as Mitt Romney's characterization of the 47 percent of Americans who pay no federal income tax as people who "are dependent upon government, who believe that they are victims, who believe the government has a responsibility to care for them," and Obama's 2008 observation of small-town Americans that "they get bitter, they cling to guns or religion or antipathy to people who aren't like them."[47] But Trump's words were exceptionally shocking. The bland government press release about Russia quickly faded from view.

One hour later, another breaking news story appeared, further burying the government's words and even distracting attention, to some extent, from Trump's seeming admission of sexual assault: WikiLeaks began publishing John Podesta's emails.[48] These emails included excerpts from Hillary Clinton's speeches to Wall Street banks, a subject of intense controversy during the Democratic presidential primary. As WikiLeaks parceled tens of thousands of his emails across the month of October, media coverage kept pace. No detail was too small, it seemed. Even Podesta's advice on how best to cook risotto garnered many media mentions, as if the country had no bigger things to worry about.[49] The *Access Hollywood* tape, and certainly the United States government's condemnation of the Russian activity, were yesterday's news.

It is hard to say whether WikiLeaks timed the Podesta leaks to bury the other stories that were less favorable to Trump. The available evidence suggests both that WikiLeaks had long planned for an

October operation independent of other events and that senior officials in the Trump campaign knew about it. In the days prior to the October 7 email dump, Trump's friend Stone told an unnamed senior Trump campaign official and other Trump supporters that WikiLeaks would imminently dump many more embarrassing files, and would commence with weekly releases. After the release of Podesta's emails, an unnamed associate of a high-ranking official in the Trump campaign texted Stone, "Well done."[50]

Amplification

By the tail end of the election cycle, the Russians' focus was less on hacking additional systems and more on propaganda and disinformation. Perhaps this shift in approach was a response to the warnings from President Obama, including a hotline message a week before the election.[51] More likely, however, it was the culmination of a multiyear effort to project and amplify divisive and pro-Trump messages inside the United States. This part of the Russian campaign both drew on and supported the hacking efforts. Thanks to the Mueller investigation and indictments, it is possible to reconstruct key pillars of the amplification activity in a way that goes beyond much of the contemporaneous news reporting and initial after-the-fact reconstructions.

It began in 2014, if not before. At the time, Russian operatives started studying how various groups in the United States used social media. They kept track of online group sizes, frequency of posts, and audience engagement, including comments and other responses. These operatives worked for a nebulous St. Petersburg-based organization known as the Internet Research Agency, the most well-known—but likely not the only—Russian group running disinformation campaigns in the United States.[52] Internet Research Agency employees made several trips to the United States in mid-2014 under false pretenses. As early as May 2014, they began discussing the 2016 presidential election as a target.[53]

In 2016, they posed as Americans and communicated with political activists and organizers in the United States to get a better sense of American politics. One of these communications resulted in a subsequent focus on states where Trump and Clinton were perceived to be in tightest competition—the "purple states," to use the phrase the Russians frequently repeated.[54] The Russian operatives next started to create hundreds of fake social media accounts. For each of these accounts, they crafted a persona, including time zone, interests, and political views. The goal was to amplify various radical groups and other opposition forces in the United States expressing dissatisfaction with the status quo.[55] Some of these accounts seemed to be primary vehicles for posting new content, whereas others only shared messages by reposting and linking.[56]

The Russians were careful to blend in as much as possible. Wary of operating from Russian IP addresses, they rented servers inside the United States and arranged relays so that their traffic appeared to originate on American soil. They also set up hundreds of disguised email accounts, all with United States-based providers, to hide their true identities.[57] Managers of the effort distributed additional cultural information, such as a list of US holidays, to operatives so that the posts they composed on a day-to-day basis could sound more like what an actual US citizen might write.[58]

They worked continuously to refine their operations, devising quantitative methods to provide feedback on how different operatives, posts, techniques, and accounts had performed. Managers discerned the patterns in the data and distilled lessons learned. For example, the Russians discovered the ratio of text, images, and video most common in posts that went viral.[59] It was the sort of message-testing that one would expect of a well-run marketing campaign—which, in effect, the Russian effort was.

Creating groups under false pretenses on Facebook was a natural next step. While pretending to be Americans, the Russian operatives set up and administered groups on a wide range of fraught political subjects, including border security, race, religion, and geographic identity. Noteworthy examples of their groups include "Secured Borders," "Blacktivist," "United Muslims of America," "Army of Jesus," and "Heart of Texas," among many others. By the time of the 2016 election, many of these groups had hundreds of thousands of members. Some of the members were Russian operatives with fake accounts, but many were Americans who did not know they had fallen for a foreign influence campaign.[60]

The purpose was clear. In 2016, managers gave the operatives who were managing the fake profiles and groups a clear directive: "use any opportunity to criticize Hillary and the rest (except Sanders and Trump—we support them)." When the Russian-administered groups on Facebook had an insufficient number of posts that condemned Clinton, managers criticized the operatives and demanded improvement, reminding them that such criticism was "imperative."[61]

There is no doubt that some of the Russian products found their way into the official communications of candidates' organizations. Trump campaign staffers and affiliates picked up and passed along certain anti-Clinton and pro-Trump messages created by the Russian operatives. Using their own accounts, these individuals reposted and retweeted the propaganda, extending its reach. The Russian operatives carefully studied the propagation of the material as it continued to grow in popularity.[62]

As the election approached, the Russians' political messages attempted to influence voters more pointedly. Some targeted minority groups known to lean Democratic and told them not to bother going to the polls. One post on the Russian-administered Instagram account called "Woke Blacks" declared, using a derogatory nickname for Hillary Clinton, that a "particular hype and hatred for Trump is misleading the people and forcing Blacks to vote Killary. We cannot resort to the lesser of two devils. Then we'd surely be better off without voting AT ALL."[63] Other messages posted in the Blacktivist Instagram group urged minorities to vote for Jill Stein, a third-party candidate who was deeply unlikely to win. "Trust me," one reassured them, "it's not a wasted vote."[64] All told, the Facebook campaign of inflammatory posts on Russian-controlled pages reached more than 126 million people.[65]

Fake news was part of the campaign, too. One retrospective analysis of Facebook sharing during the period before the election showed that the most popular fake news stories (from all sources, not limited to Russia) were more widely shared among users than the top news stories from legitimate outlets. Among the most popular fakes were stories attacking Clinton, accusing her of selling weapons to the Islamic State, of being legally disqualified from holding office, and of orchestrating the murder of an FBI agent. Another widely shared story claimed that Pope Francis had endorsed Donald Trump.[66] One study estimates that about 25 percent of Americans visited a website that published fake news in the month before the election, with conservatives much more likely to have done so.[67] A 2016 survey found that three-quarters of Americans who recalled seeing fake news headlines considered them to be at least somewhat accurate.[68]

In parallel with the Facebook operation, the Russians created thousands of fake accounts on Twitter. Here, too, they pretended to be American.[69] As the 2016 election approached, they amplified a series of hashtags designed to hurt Clinton, such as #Hillary4Prison, #MAGA, #TrumpTrain, #Trump2016, and #IWontProtectHillary.[70] They deployed some of the most popular of their accounts to claim that Clinton was orchestrating key voter-fraud efforts in competitive states such as North Carolina and Florida.[71]

Paid advertising complemented all these efforts. Beginning in 2015, the Russians began spending thousands of dollars each month on Facebook and Twitter. This use of foreign funds to influence an election is illegal under United States law, but Facebook and other companies did not properly verify the purchases and reveal the Russian activity.[72] In 2016, the Russians stole the identities of several United States citizens to prevent their illegal ad buys from being detected. With stolen social security numbers and other information, they could open accounts with financial providers and make purchases posing as Americans.[73]

From at least April 2016 through the election, Russian ads began appearing that advocated against Clinton and for Trump. Many evoked themes seen in other Russian messaging: accusing Clinton of supporting terrorism, of not deserving the votes of minorities, of wanting to ban guns, of corruption, of being hostile to Christianity, and much more. Others praised Trump as a leader capable of defeating terrorism, standing up for gun rights, and protecting the country. The Russians relied on Facebook's microtargeting algorithms to deliver most of these ads to specific groups interested in particular issues, just as a legitimate political campaign would. The Russians purchased at least 3,500 ads on Facebook.[74]

It is hard to know how much this advertising drove behavior, although Facebook's sales managers argued generally that paid ads and content on Facebook could swing elections. In a case study, the company highlighted the reelection campaign of Senator Patrick Toomey of Pennsylvania, who had spent big on Facebook in 2016 and squeaked out a narrow win. Facebook claimed based on its data analysis that Toomey's ad spending had made voters more likely to turn out and more likely to vote for him.[75] If Facebook is right that American ads on its platform influence voter behavior, it stands to reason that Russian ads probably did, as well.

A final part of the Russian campaign was designed to turn discord online into protests offline. Beginning in November 2015 with a "confederate rally," Russian operatives began organizing dozens of demonstrations throughout the United States, including in key states such as Florida and Pennsylvania. While some rallies were sparsely attended, others drew hundreds of Americans unaware of the rallies' provenance. Russian managers "closely monitored" how these gatherings went.[76]

They appeared to have had some success. At one event, ostensibly designed to show Clinton's support for Muslims, they convinced participants to hold signs falsely quoting Clinton saying she supported the imposition of Islamic law in the United States. They then used those images in other messages suggesting that Americans should not trust Clinton. At other rallies, under the banners "Down with Hillary" and "March for Trump," Russian operatives pretending to be Americans paid actual American citizens to perform political acts. One was paid to dress up as Clinton in a prison uniform and to ride in a cage that another person was paid to haul on his flatbed truck. In some cases, the Trump campaign promoted the rallies on the candidate's Facebook page.[77]

In still other cases, the Russians organized protests and counter-protests in the same place at the same time. They successfully brought American followers of competing Russian-administered groups face to face to scream at one another, even as the Russian organizers were nowhere in sight. In one case, a Russian-run Facebook group planned a rally called "Save Islamic Knowledge" in Houston while another Russian-run group organized the counterprotest: "Stop the Islamization of Texas."[78] Police had to be deployed to keep the groups from physically clashing.

It is likely that the Russians could not predict the relative success of these various efforts—divisive posts, fake news, paid ads, and political rallies—in reaching American voters, but they had the luxury of not having to choose among them. They could simply try a lot of different approaches to sowing division and aiding Sanders and Trump, and refine their efforts over time. Undoubtedly, as in commercial marketing, the different components reinforced one another, making it hard to disentangle the specific impacts of each part of the mix, but adding up to potent interference overall. The hacks and leaks helped advance an underlying theme of Clinton's corruption. As fake accounts pushed these ideas and also fostered groups under false pretenses, real Americans were drawn in, creating the potential for live events within the United States. Paid ads helped each part of the process, getting out the message in general but also boosting turnout for rallies. For the Russians, it was a virtuous cycle—for the United States, vicious subversion.

A Simple Machine

The Russian operation in 2016 was an attempt to shift the ground beneath the feet of American democracy. It was not an attempt to signal to policymakers, but rather to divide the public and swing an election, shaping the geopolitical environment in which Russia would operate. The assessment of the United States intelligence community and a series of Justice Department indictments was that the Russian effort had two overarching goals: to increase discord in the United States and, starting in early- to mid-2016, to help elect Donald Trump. On the first count, it seems clear that the operation was at least moderately successful. One large-scale study of social media activity showed that posts from Russian trolls caused observable increases in the polarization of the subsequent online conversation.[79]

The second point is more complex. Donald Trump won the election, prompting a contemporaneous text sent by an individual whose name is redacted to a top Russian official that said, "Putin has won."[80] This may be too self-congratulatory; history is filled with propagandists and intelligence officers dramatically overestimating the impact of their efforts. Yet, in a 2019 tweet, even President Trump seemed to acknowledge the role of Russian operatives in "helping me to get elected," though he emphasized that he "had nothing to do with" it and later walked back any claim of Russian influence.[81]

Nevertheless, uncertainty clouds analysis of the 2016 election.[82] Most likely, in an election that turned on a razor-thin difference— seventy-seven thousand votes spread across three states—altering any one of several components could have changed the outcome. Factors including the letters from FBI Director James Comey in October 2016, the Clinton campaign strategy, voter apathy, breathless media coverage of leaked emails, and many others all contributed to voters' decisions, and if any of them had played out differently, the final Electoral College tally might have gone the other way.[83]

It is more tractable to consider why the Russian shaping effort was able to work to the extent that it did. To focus only on the Russian activity is to ignore other dimensions of the problem. Any influence effort is like a type of simple machine: a wedge. It is most effective when it is driven into an already-existing crack, widening it inch by inch. The effectiveness of its application depends not just on the nature of the wedge and how forcefully it is applied, but also on the vulnerability of the target. Thus, perhaps more than in other kinds of cyber operations discussed in this book, the harm in a cyber influence effort depends on the victim.

Soviet propagandists learned this long ago.[84] They realized that the most effective influence operations use falsehoods that are not cut out of whole cloth, but built on preexisting notions. Fairly or not, Hillary Clinton had a reputation in some quarters of the American electorate as corrupt and selfish. The leaks of emails showing DNC senior staff discussing ways to undermine Sanders's primary challenge played into this preconception. The social media campaign and real-world rallies exacerbated it still further. More generally, the Russian wedge widened underlying divisions in the United States on hot-button issues. It did not have to create racial tensions and ideological differences; they were already there waiting to be exploited.

The media environment helped the operation succeed. GRU operatives communicated with reporters and gave them advance access to nonpublic documents they were about to make public through DCLeaks.[85] The journalists then wrote stories that publicized the leaks. Indeed, even though the files that WikiLeaks dripped out over the summer and fall of 2016 contained few major scandals, they attracted widespread media coverage.

Amy Chozick, a leading reporter for the *New York Times* covering the Clinton campaign, captured the prevailing journalistic wisdom well. She wrote that, at the time of the Podesta leaks, everyone in the newsroom "agreed that since the emails were already out there—and of importance to voters—it was *The Times's* job to 'confirm' and 'contextualize' them." It was only after the election that she realized the degree to which she and many others had served as "a de facto instrument of Russian intelligence."[86]

It was not just the media that drew more attention to the Russian leaks. Candidate Trump helped advance the Russian effort, too, with his public statements. In the final month of the campaign, as the Podesta leaks were underway, he explicitly drew attention to WikiLeaks at least 137 times in speeches and rallies. Three days after the Podesta emails first appeared, he exclaimed to a cheering crowd, "I love WikiLeaks!"[87] Yet, despite his earlier wish that the Russians deliver Clinton's missing emails, Trump disputed credible assessments of Russian involvement in the leaks that followed. In a presidential debate, he said that no one was capable of knowing who had carried out the operation, famously suggesting that a four-hundred-pound hacker might be responsible.[88]

The situation has not gotten much better since the frantic days of 2016. The United States could have treated the Russian operation as a harbinger of greater cyber destabilization to come. The two political parties could have come to agreement about the need for a united front against foreign interference. But the underlying divisions in the United States have only deepened. Perhaps worst of all, the differences seem to be not only of opinion or values, but of truth; Trump advisor Kellyanne Conway's famous line about "alternative facts" highlights this divide.[89] A democracy that cannot agree on fundamental realities—a foundation of truth that can prove impervious to foreign manipulation—is one that is highly susceptible to the shaping power of future wedges.

11

Exposure

ACCORDING TO LEGEND, Israel's famed intelligence service Mossad wished an old curse upon its adversaries: "May we read about you in the newspapers." For those working in the murk of intelligence and counterintelligence, one of the most dreaded outcomes is unexpected exposure to the light. Public scrutiny can spoil powerful capabilities, reveal covert operations, and impose damaging constraints on future action.

Though Mossad's pox of publicity long predated cyber operations, it resonates even more deeply in the digital domain. As Chapter 5's discussion of counterintelligence showed, when defenders understand the specifics of an adversary's network intrusion efforts, they can do more to thwart those operations. When an intelligence agency cannot keep the tools and methods of its cyber operations covert, its adversaries can undermine operational security or even deploy them for their own use.

Given this paramount importance of secrecy, the news stories that began appearing in the summer of 2016 caused panic in the United States government. In August, a *New York Times* headline asked:

"Was the NSA Hacked?" Another one at the *Washington Post* was declarative: "Powerful NSA Hacking Tools Have Been Revealed Online."[1] Each publication carried new details on classified American cyber capabilities and their use. Other outlets rapidly picked up the story. Cybersecurity experts followed with published analyses of tools and operations once thought secret and secure. As with the Snowden revelations, the NSA was back in the news, and not in a good way.

The bad press continued. Rumors swirled that senior military and intelligence officials recommended firing the head of the NSA, Michael Rogers, in part due to the breaches.[2] By May of 2017, it was clear that hackers from around the world were repurposing the NSA's tools for their own destructive use, bringing further embarrassment to the agency that lost control of them in the first place. The *Washington Post* published a deep dive on one powerful exploit under a long banner: "NSA Officials Worried About the Day Its Potent Hacking Tool Would Get Loose. Then It Did."[3] A few months after that, the *New York Times* followed with an investigation of its own, replete with quotes from influential former NSA employees, outlining the failures in operational security and the damage done. After the agency's brutal year, the *Times* headline captured the force of this new blow: "Security Breach and Spilled Secrets Have Shaken the NSA to Its Core."[4]

These leaks and headlines were part of a calculated campaign against US intelligence agencies. It was exposure deployed as a means of doing harm, a mix of counterintelligence and sabotage.

Exposure is powerful. The enigmatic group forcing American hacking tools into view degraded the United States' cyber capabilities. It damaged the reputation of the NSA with repeated broadsides of criticism and misinformation. The group's members seemed to operate unchecked and unseen, releasing classified code and associated documents at opportune moments. Eventually, these leaked tools helped enable two of the most devastating cyber attacks in history. All of this was made possible because the group had somehow, despite the extensive security precautions of the NSA, gotten their hands on a panoply of American secrets and decided to share them with the world. This is that story, one of the deepest mysteries in modern cyber operations.

The Shadow Brokers

As noted in the Introduction to this book, the Shadow Brokers began with a post online. On August 13, 2016, amidst the drama of the summer election campaign and the slowly unfolding Russian election interference operation, they announced that the NSA's tools were up for auction.

The Shadow Brokers went on to clarify that they were talking not just about the kind of malicious code samples that cybersecurity researchers sometimes share with one another. No, they had access to something much more valuable: the full tools themselves, which they had obtained, they boasted, by watching the NSA's hacking operations and by hacking the agency. Now they were going to sell the best of those tools to the highest bidder. These tools, they presciently suggested, were so powerful that they could spread quickly to computers all over the world, granting enormous power to any hacker who wielded them.

This had some precedent, if only in fiction. In the videogame series *Mass Effect*, a character called the Shadow Broker leads an organization that deals in intelligence. Its motto is "I know your every secret, while you fumble in the dark." By continually accessing and selling information across a range of customers, the Shadow Broker maximizes its own profits. It does so while protecting itself, always working through disguises or agents. Even the subordinates in its own organization do not know its identity. More importantly, it structures its transactions such that no one customer can ever learn enough to gain a decisive advantage on the others. They all must keep coming back to buy more insight. The Shadow Broker, with access to such a wide range of secrets, can always stay one step ahead.[5]

The real-life Shadow Brokers offered proof of their bona fides. They posted links to NSA hacking tools and screenshots of folders laden with NSA code names. The tools included powerful exploits against firewalls, which security researchers and journalists quickly realized came from the American hacking arsenal.[6] News raced through the cybersecurity community: as outlandish as their claims seemed, the Shadow Brokers were for real.

The Shadow Brokers anticipated the NSA's interest. Calling the NSA by the name Equation Group, a label the Russian cybersecurity company Kaspersky had coined, the Shadow Brokers taunted the agency directly. In answer to their own mocking question about which stolen files might be available for auction, the Shadow Brokers wrote, "Equation Group not know what lost. We want Equation Group to bid so we keep [what we've taken] secret."[7] If the NSA wanted to find out which files had been compromised, the Shadow Brokers were saying—in an echo of *Mass Effect*—that it would just have to pay more than anyone else.

The intrigue tempted journalists. From the very beginning, the Shadow Brokers desired wide attention, though they did not always receive as much as they wanted. In their first tweets, they tagged the Twitter accounts of major media organizations, such as the *New York Times*, the BBC, CNN, the *Wall Street Journal*, *Time*, and many others—including, perhaps most interestingly, the Russian news service RT, WikiLeaks, and the conspiracy site *InfoWars*. They also sought particular attention in the cybersecurity community, tagging technology publications like *Wired* and *Vice,* as well as companies such as Kaspersky and Symantec.[8] And in a lengthier message, the Shadow Brokers made it clear what they expected the press and cybersecurity companies to do now that the files had been posted online: "You write many words."[9]

The Shadow Brokers also knew, however, that others would do more than write about the hack. The publication of the NSA's tools would help other hackers all over the world penetrate computer systems. Even just with the first set of exploits they released for free, the Shadow Brokers said, "You break many things." The winner of the auction could go much further, using the tools on offer to "hack networks as like equation group." What once only the NSA could do, now ordinary hackers would be able to do. The Shadow Brokers revealed at least the partial erosion of the Nobody But Us principle.[10]

Just thirty minutes before the Shadow Brokers' first appearance, a Twitter user with the name HAL999999999 sent two researchers at Kaspersky odd messages. In one, he seemed to suggest that he needed to speak with Eugene Kaspersky, the company's enigmatic founder. In another, he suggested the time-sensitive nature of the need, warning "shelf life, three weeks." The Kaspersky researchers did not see any of these communications until after the Shadow Brokers released their tweet. When the Kaspersky team did read the messages, however, they guessed that the mysterious requests might be related to the Shadow Brokers' offer. Based on the Twitter username, which appeared on other web sites, the researchers traced the messages back to Hal Martin, an employee with the NSA contractor firm Booz Allen Hamilton. Kaspersky tipped off the NSA.[11]

Two weeks later, on August 27, almost two dozen FBI agents and SWAT team members raided Martin's house and arrested him. Quickly, it became clear to the government that Martin had been hoarding terabytes of classified NSA files at his home, including what media reports would later estimate as three-quarters of the agency's hacking tools.[12] Martin had even taken home classified documents just three days before the Shadow Brokers' first post. In the aftermath of the Snowden leaks, any investigator applying Occam's Razor at the moment of the arrest would have come to an obvious conclusion: Martin was the Shadow Brokers.

Occam's Razor would have been wrong. While Martin was in custody, the Shadow Brokers released their second message in September. Written in a mock Kim Jong-un voice, using a stereotypical Asian accent, the message contained no new NSA files. Instead, the Shadow Brokers just ranted that there were not enough bidders on the auction and claimed that their aim was to make money. The message closed with an ominous warning of what would happen if bidding did not pick up: "we assume no one interested and we start serring on the underground. Rots of transparency and discrosure there." The Shadow Brokers were threatening to sell the tools not to a single buyer like the NSA but to all comers in the darkness of the hacking world, enabling more criminals to employ what were once the Five Eyes' powerful and secret offensive capabilities.[13]

The Shadow Brokers' third missive dropped the Kim Jong-un character but kept the rage. It excoriated the media for not giving the group enough exposure, especially given the magnitude of the exploits in the files. The auction, this post insisted, "is sounding crazy but is being real." Again, the Shadow Brokers emphasized that they did not want fame but were out to make money. They also touted the value of what they were in a position to sell. While the free sample distributed during the summer included firewall exploits, the full batch would include the NSA's hacking tools for use against "Windows, Unix / Linux, Routers, Databases, Mobile, Telecom"—in other words, basically everything.[14]

October 2016 was a fateful month. As outlined in Chapter 10, the *Washington Post* reported on Donald Trump's lewd comments caught on tape before his *Access Hollywood* appearance, and the leaks of Democratic files accelerated. The US government also called out the Russian government for meddling in American elections. President Obama again warned the Kremlin to halt its aggressive activities, and a leak to *NBC News,* reinforced by Vice President Joe Biden's comments in an interview, indicated the United States was preparing its own cyber strike against Russia to unleash at a time of its choosing.[15] Adding to the commotion, on October 5, the arrest of Hal Martin became public, sparking another round of worry about the NSA's inability to keep secrets and renewed speculation about just who the Shadow Brokers might be.[16]

The Shadow Brokers continued to add fuel to the fire. On October 15, they announced the end of the hacking tools auction without the sale of the tools and posted a fake transcript of a conversation between Loretta Lynch and Bill Clinton featuring crude sexual discussion.[17] Two weeks later, they reappeared with continued political commentary. They condemned corruption in America, highlighted the large number of Americans who do not vote, and suggested that hacking or otherwise disrupting the upcoming presidential election would be a good thing. They pointed out that the United States had itself interfered in elections overseas and was hardly blameless. They also suggested that the 2016 election interference was retaliation from Iran for American cyber attacks against its nuclear program.

Along with their outraged polemic, the Shadow Brokers included more information on NSA activities, which they called, a day before Halloween, their "trick or treat." They posted a list of NSA targets from all around the world, especially in China, and advised those who had been breached on what they could do to preserve evidence so that network defenders could spot the NSA. They waved off Biden's threats of cyber attacks as ravings of a "DirtyGrandpa." Instead, the Shadow Brokers asked a question that seemed to imply they were still in control: "How bad do you want it to get? When you are ready to make the bleeding stop, pay us, so we can move onto the next game."[18]

As with their earlier messages, the Shadow Brokers retained their focus on American media. They complained that they were not receiving enough attention for their activities and speculated that adjusting their style might help: "TheShadowBrokers is making special effort not to using foul language, bigotry, or making any funny. Be seeing if NBC, ABC, CBS, FOX is making stories about now?"[19] Nonetheless, in the week before the election and even in its aftermath, coverage of election interference far surpassed reporting on the Shadow Brokers' activities in the mainstream press. The comparative silence was not because journalists chose to ignore the Shadow Brokers out of patriotism, but rather because too much else was going on. If Shadow Brokers wanted attention, they would have to do more.

The Escalation of Exposure

As 2016 turned to 2017, the United States entered a period of tumult. The Obama administration gave way to the Trump team. Newspapers outdid each other with juicy leaks about Russian election interference, the presidential transition, and other forms of political intrigue. "Fake news" and "post-truth" became household terms; the latter was *Oxford English Dictionary*'s 2016 word of the year.[20] The Shadow Brokers tried to make themselves heard, especially to their target audience at the NSA, over the din.

On December 14, 2016, a user with the pseudonym Boceffus Cleetus posted on Twitter and Medium. His brief message was laced with American pop culture references and written in a cartoonish cowboy voice. Boceffus pointed to a new site utilizing ZeroNet, a peer-to-peer web-hosting technology that is hard to take offline and popular with cryptocurrency devotees, where the Shadow Brokers had very recently posted a list of NSA tools for sale. Boceffus said he was just a "ZeroNet enthusiast" who had "found" the Shadow Brokers' site—but his portrayal of himself as unassociated with the group strains credulity.[21]

Whether he was a sock puppet account or not, Boceffus was right: the Shadow Brokers had begun selling more NSA exploits on a ZeroNet site. The group had evidently abandoned the auction model from the previous August. Instead, they would offer an à la carte menu of hacking tools, with prices listed for each. To verify the sale was real and prove that they were the same Shadow Brokers, they posted some new screenshots of NSA capabilities and signed their message with a cryptographic key to which only they had access. To gain more attention, the Shadow Brokers sent out a flurry of tweets and gave a brief interview to the technology publication *Motherboard*.[22]

The collection of exploits on offer was vast. Confirming some claims the Shadow Brokers had made in August, this latest trove proved they had access to much more than the firewall-hacking code they had released at first. It indicated that they had obtained a wide range of NSA tools capable of breaching many different kinds of tar-

gets, and that hundreds of cyber capabilities were compiled and prepared for use. Supplementing the tools themselves were NSA user
guides to stealthy cyber operations. Classified code names laced the
uploaded files. Though the tools and manuals were often a few years
old, they provided substantial insight into how the NSA went about
its business of global espionage.

A well-established security analyst known only as thegrugq
summed up the situation as "definitely a gut punch" for the NSA,
one that exposed "a lot of operational detail and lessons" even if the
tools were slightly out of date.[23] The Shadow Brokers, for their
part, once again indicated that they knew the harm they were
doing and could stop it—for the right price. "TheShadowBrokers is
not being irresponsible criminals," the group said in their *Motherboard* interview. "TheShadowBrokers is opportunists. TheShadowBrokers is giving 'responsible parties' opportunity to making
things right."[24]

Evidently the responsible parties did not step up, at least not to
the Shadow Brokers' satisfaction. The group began the new year
with a series of tweets mocking those who thought Russians interfered in the 2016 American election.[25] On January 7, they posted
another message announcing they would now also sell NSA tools
for hacking Windows.[26] Only a few days later, the Shadow Brokers
issued what they called a "farewell" post, claiming that since not
enough people were paying them, they were going to shut down
rather than bear the risk of continued operations. "Despite theories, it always being about bitcoins for TheShadowBrokers," they
wrote. "Free dumps and bullshit political talk was being for marketing attention."[27] To back this up, they posted their bitcoin address one more time, suggesting that the NSA's tools would still be
for sale if the right buyer came along.

Two links at the bottom of the farewell message were small but packed a mighty punch. These links enabled anyone to download sixty-one different NSA hacking tools, including some that could bypass the leading antivirus software without detection. With these powerful signals intelligence wares abruptly dumped online, cybersecurity companies reacted to the threats to their users, and rushed to bring out security updates. Maybe worse for the NSA, skilled cybersecurity professionals all over the world gained the ability to look through their logs of network activity and, using the leaks as a guide, detect any NSA operations and American hacking techniques hidden in them.

Even if the dump of exploits did not create the national media splash the Shadow Brokers had long sought, it attracted enormous attention in the technology press. Former NSA hacker Jake Williams called it a "burn-it-to-the-ground moment," remarking on how the Shadow Brokers had chosen such a bold move for the closing days of the Obama administration.[28] The group had fired a potent parting shot and, with the advent of the Trump presidency, seemed prepared to fade from view.

Indeed, the Shadow Brokers stayed silent in the ensuing months. They did not reappear until April 2017, after President Trump ordered an airstrike on Syrian air bases in retaliation for the Syrian use of chemical weapons. This time, they addressed their message directly to the new commander in chief: "Respectfully, what the fuck are you doing? TheShadowBrokers voted for you. TheShadowBrokers supports you. TheShadowBrokers is losing faith in you. Mr. Trump helping theshadowbrokers, helping you. Is appearing you are abandoning 'your base,' 'the movement,' and the peoples who getting you elected."

What followed was a screed entitled "Don't Forget Your Base," stretching to more than fifteen hundred words. Reflecting an apparent knowledge of political cleavages in the United States, the Shadow Brokers' text touched on a wide range of American policies and issues, from Russia relations to white privilege. It criticized the Trump administration for kowtowing to "globalists" and suggested that Trump focus only on what his die-hard supporters wanted. Among other suggestions, the Shadow Brokers advised that Trump should "double-down" on his relationship with Putin, should support nationalist and isolationist policies, and should ignore any probes into whether the 2016 election was hacked or rigged.

Yet the most significant aspect of the Shadow Brokers' post was not its political advice or its half-baked policy ideas. It was the indecipherable part of the message, near the very end: CrDj"(;Va.* NdlnzB9M?@K2)#>deB7mN.[29] This was the long-hidden decryption password to the file the Shadow Brokers had first posted in their auction the previous August. The password enabled anyone to access the package of tools that supposedly could have fetched the group millions of dollars. Now, the once-prized hacking toolkit was freely available for everyone else to use for their own purposes and largely worthless for the NSA.

The next day, the Shadow Brokers posted another lengthy message, touching on Edward Snowden, the Supreme Court, and much more. Reversing their "always being about bitcoin" claim, they now outlined a different reason for the persistent revelation of NSA capabilities: "No more classifying bullshit. No more black budgets and black ops."[30] In other words, by exposing the agency's capabilities and by subjecting it to public scrutiny again and again, they hoped to degrade and limit what the NSA could do. For all the Shadow

Brokers' criticism of US foreign policy, they left no doubt that it was the country's signals intelligence capability that was most in their sights.

And the drumbeat continued. Next, the Shadow Brokers escalated still further by calling out Jake Williams, the cybersecurity analyst who had analyzed their activities, as a former member of an elite NSA hacking unit. This move came just a few weeks after the US Department of Justice indicted two Russian intelligence officers and two Russian criminal hackers for their breach of Yahoo. It also came amid concerns expressed by former NSA employees that foreign governments could identify and prosecute them in retaliation.[31]

The Shadow Brokers seemed to play on these fears. They said that, while they did not plan to make a "habit" of identifying those who had worked in secret roles for the NSA, they would make "exception for big mouth."[32] The threat was clear: not only could they leak the NSA's tools, but they could identify its people; not only could they damage the larger organization, but they could expose the usually out-of-view individuals who helped make it tick.

Throughout the spring of 2017, the flow of information was largely in one direction. The Shadow Brokers continued to expose NSA capabilities and shape the public narrative. They seemed to be playing a two-level game, communicating with the media and the public on one hand and with the NSA on the other. Parts of their missives seemed tailored to one group or the other. In their next post, the Shadow Brokers seemed both to acknowledge the multiple purposes behind their messages and to toy once more with the NSA. They left no doubt that they were in control: "TheShadowBrokers showing you cards theshadowbrokers wanting you to be seeing. Sometime peoples not being target audience."[33] They released this warning just before Easter, on Good Friday.

The Good Friday post was more than words. It was a body blow. The Shadow Brokers released twenty-three more NSA hacking tools, including some with immense power. One of these, DOUBLE-PULSAR, was malicious code capable of hiding itself deep within a computer's operating system and allowing a hacker to issue a wide range of commands to the machine while avoiding detection. Security analysts who reverse-engineered DOUBLEPULSAR noted the sophistication and power of its technique, calling it one of the most potent pieces of malicious code released in the previous decade.[34]

Hackers all over the world quickly put DOUBLEPULSAR to use. In just the two weeks after the Shadow Brokers' release of the code, other hackers collectively used it to infect almost half a million computers, the vast majority of them in the United States.[35] The NSA had once used DOUBLEPULSAR to great effect in its mission to spy silently on targets all over the world. By exposing the capability, the Shadow Brokers had turned the agency's tool back on the United States. The chaos from DOUBLEPULSAR diminished internet security and disproportionately hurt Americans.

The Shadow Brokers also released ETERNALBLUE, another key Five Eyes exploit. It targeted Windows computers and did so with great effectiveness. The NSA and its partners had deployed the tool for more than five years as a key part of their arsenal. ETERNAL-BLUE was so powerful, a former agency employee told the *Washington Post,* "it was like fishing with dynamite." Another former agency employee described the intelligence haul gained from deploying the tool as "unreal."[36] Once again, the Shadow Brokers had removed powerful arrows from the NSA's quiver and distributed them around the world for anyone to use. The leak of ETERNAL-BLUE helped enable two massive cyber attacks, as Chapters 12 and

13 will discuss, as well as operations by financially motivated cyber criminals.[37]

For good measure, the Shadow Brokers also revealed still more about NSA operations and targets. They released tools the agency's hackers had used to gather information from worldwide financial networks, and files revealing that the NSA had hacked key banks in Qatar, the United Arab Emirates, Palestine, Kuwait, and Yemen. One of these files showed the list of network administrator accounts at various overseas financial institutions compromised by the NSA, which journalists quickly confirmed as belonging to real employees.[38]

In May, the Shadow Brokers continued to taunt the NSA. At the same time, they offered more justifications for their behavior, claiming to be responsible entrepreneurs and nothing more. More significantly, they announced yet another change in their approach to making money: they would move to a subscription service. Their new business model, as they put it, was "being like wine of month club. Each month peoples can be paying membership fee, then getting members only data dump each month." Instead of wine, the members of this proposed club would receive newer and more powerful NSA exploits, as well as information about the NSA's hacking operations against banking systems and against the nuclear programs of Russia, China, Iran, and North Korea.

Once again, however, the Shadow Brokers offered an alternative, undoubtedly with the NSA in mind. Practically yelling, they wrote, "OR IF RESPONSIBLE PARTY IS BUYING ALL LOST DATA BEFORE IT IS BEING SOLD TO THEPEOPLES THEN THESHADOWBROKERS WILL HAVE NO MORE FINANCIAL INCENTIVES TO BE TAKING CONTINUED RISKS OF OPERATIONS AND WILL GO DARK PERMANENTLY."[39] Of course, whether anyone could trust the Shadow Brokers to hold up their end of a deal was, at best, an open question. But it was a moot point. The NSA, at least in public, kept its silence.

Who, What, and How?

With the advent of their private monthly subscription service, the Shadow Brokers faded from public view. They released no new hacking tools to the wider internet in the summer of 2017, though they claimed to have continually provided copies of the NSA's exploits to their subscribers—a claim for which there is no evidence. Perhaps most significantly, they threatened to identify another former NSA hacker and link him to a specific operation in China, prompting further concern that the Shadow Brokers had penetrated the agency so deeply that they could determine which employees had carried out which operations. But, despite the threat, the group did not seem to follow through.[40] All in all, the saga of the Shadow Brokers seems to have ended with a whimper rather than a bang.

It continues, however, to be a tremendous mystery. Tracking all the moving pieces, it can be easy to lose focus on critical questions: Who are the Shadow Brokers? What did they pilfer from the NSA? How did they manage to do it? The answers are still unknown, but some informed speculation can lay out plausible theories.

The *who* question attracted the most interest from the start. Immediately after the Shadow Brokers' first appearance in August 2016, analysts offered two theories. Some thought it likely that the Shadow Brokers were a cover for a disgruntled NSA employee or contractor.[41] This person might have been looking to profit off their access to some of the agency's important capabilities. The Shadow Brokers' apparent access to a wide array of tools and documents lent support to this theory. In 2019, someone with an anonymous Twitter account, who seemed to have intimate knowledge of NSA lingo, claimed that a group of former government insiders was responsible for the Shadow Brokers, but offered no evidence.[42] If that tweet was accurate, there was no foreign hand behind the operation.

Other well-known cybersecurity analysts suspected that an adversarial foreign government orchestrated the Shadow Brokers' campaign. Given the Kremlin's penchant for hacking and leaking operations and the Shadow Brokers' elevated risk tolerance, Bruce Schneier and Matt Tait both theorized that the Shadow Brokers might be a direct Russian government operation.[43] To these and other analysts, the group's increasingly political statements in the fall of 2016 and into 2017 indicate something beyond just a disgruntled employee.

Even if a Russian intelligence agency was not directly controlling the account, leaks from the United States' investigation suggest some Russian government involvement.[44] What form this took is unclear. Russian intelligence agencies may have run the operation themselves, just as they operated the Guccifer 2.0 persona in 2016. Or the agencies may have provided some pilfered NSA files to a profit-seeking intermediary who conducted the Shadow Brokers operation; there is ample evidence generally that Russian government cyber operations mix freely with the world of organized crime.[45]

The "what" mattered, too. Even if the United States government had, according to news reports, at least a provisional sense of who was responsible for orchestrating the leaks, it apparently still had questions about what exactly the perpetrators had taken. It was a matter of great importance to determine just what was in that stolen cache and what was not. The Shadow Brokers' haul, from exploits to manuals to operational notes, had already proved itself to be stunning, but the possibility lingered that even more had been taken than had thus far been released.

All of this leads to the obvious question: how did the Shadow Brokers get their hands on this top-secret data? One guess that gained wide circulation for much of the summer and fall of 2016 was known as the staging server theory. This assumed that the Shadow Brokers were unlikely to have penetrated the classified networks of the NSA. Instead, the theory suggested, when the NSA's own hackers moved tools, during some routine operational preparation, from its most protected classified systems onto the staging servers from which they would launch operations against targets, a foreign intelligence agency observing NSA efforts might have detected the activity and seen its chance to gain access to NSA tools. As Chapter 5 described, the NSA has targeted Chinese hop points in a similar way.

But the staging server theory had big flaws. First, it was and is standard practice at the NSA to rename hacking tools before using them in operations, in part to obfuscate their underlying code names. Second, the NSA—like all intelligence agencies with good operational security—did not stage large amounts of material outside of classified networks, and certainly would not have done that on just one server. Third, it was unlikely that NSA hackers would make so many operational mistakes that a foreign intelligence agency, even one as advanced as Russia's, could access so many of their tools.

The staging server theory looked less and less plausible as the releases continued. With the December file dump, it lost even more credibility. The collection of pilfered files at that point was so broad and included tools that targeted such a wide range of systems that it was very improbable they had come from just one staging server.[46] In the spring of 2017, when the NSA's operational notes and plans began appearing in the Shadow Brokers' releases, the staging server theory seemed entirely debunked; there would have been no operational value in placing those kinds of files, which were not hacking tools, on a server outside the classified NSA network.

The August 2016 arrest of Hal Martin provided another, more plausible theory: even if he himself were not the entirety of the Shadow Brokers—and he couldn't be, since the messages and releases continued during his imprisonment—perhaps the Shadow Brokers had obtained the information from him, with or without his knowledge. Over a twenty-year career, including stints as a contractor supporting the NSA's Tailored Access Operations intrusion team, Martin certainly had had extensive access. Indeed, prosecutors alleged that he had brought home "many thousands of pages" of classified material as well as terabytes of sensitive digital data.[47] But while investigators concluded that Martin had taken copies of large numbers of the agency's hacking tools, they could find no evidence that he had sold or distributed them.

In 2017, another theory gained more credence: that a different NSA employee, Nghia Hoang Pho, had also taken home troves of files starting sometime in 2014 or 2015, using removable media such as USB drives. Pho eventually pled guilty to unauthorized removal of classified information, telling the judge that he had worked from home to improve his job performance. There is no evidence that Pho was motivated by malice, or that he knowingly shared the files with a foreign government.

Still, on the home computer on which Pho stored the files, he also ran a copy of antivirus software made by none other than Kaspersky, the Russian firm that had tipped off the NSA to Hal Martin in the first place.[48] As a popular antivirus company, Kaspersky has wide access to the files of clients all over the world. The company was investigating a large set of NSA hacking operations at the time Pho loaded the files to his computer.[49] As a result, the Kaspersky software on Pho's computer identified the NSA files as worthy of further study and sent copies of them back to Kaspersky's headquarters, though it is not clear if these are the files that the Shadow Brokers ultimately leaked. From there, an Israeli counterintelligence operation that had hacked Kaspersky reportedly discovered the files on the company's servers, raising alarm bells among Western intelligence agencies.[50]

What happened after the files made their way to Kaspersky is not clear. Court documents suggest that Pho's files plausibly ended up in the hands of a potential adversary, presumably Russia, though they do not specify how. Admiral Mike Rogers, NSA director at the time, cast the harm of the exposure in stark terms. He said that Pho took and compromised "some of NSA's most sophisticated, hard-to-achieve, and important techniques of collecting [signals intelligence] from sophisticated targets of the NSA, including collection that is crucial to decision makers when answering some of the Nation's highest-priority questions." Rogers added an ominous warning: "Compromise of one technique can place many opportunities for intelligence collection and national security insight at risk."[51] After Pho received a sentence of sixty-six months in prison, the Department of Justice noted that Pho "forced NSA to abandon important initiatives to protect itself and its operational capabilities, at great economic and operational cost."[52]

Kaspersky disputes, however, that it was the mechanism through which the files made their way to Russia or any other potential adversary. Once the matter became public, the firm claimed that, at the direction of CEO Eugene Kaspersky, it had destroyed its copies of the files after realizing that they were classified NSA documents. Yet the company would not confirm when that destruction took place.

Kaspersky also suggested that the data logs from its product on Pho's computer indicate that he disabled the company's antivirus at some point in order to load pirated versions of Microsoft Office, which came with malicious code from unknown hackers. Kaspersky indicated that hackers breached Pho's computer on several occasions after that. The firm implied that any of those hackers could have either been responsible for the Shadow Brokers' releases or given the pilfered files to someone who was.[53]

There are reasons to doubt Kaspersky's theory of the case, however. Skeptics have long suspected Kaspersky of having ties to the Russian government, though direct public evidence of a link was scant before the Shadow Brokers saga, and though the firm's supporters point to its having helped the United States by turning in Martin. For years, Eugene Kaspersky has vehemently denied helping any government with cyber espionage efforts, but those protestations may be untrue. Alternatively, other Kaspersky employees might have, without their boss's knowledge, provided information to Russian intelligence services, perhaps including files taken from Pho's computer. Finally, Kaspersky itself could well be a target of surveillance; the company's telecommunications infrastructure was in Russia at the time and was likely subject to Russian passive collection.[54] The truth could even be a combination of some of the above.

The question of how the Shadow Brokers obtained their illicitly gained wares may not have just one answer. The Shadow Brokers might have drawn on years of counterintelligence activities, especially if they were a front for the Russian intelligence community or some criminal group with an arm's-length relationship with the Kremlin. Just as the NSA has long studied and tracked other states' hackers, the Russians have long observed American hackers in action. The source for the Shadow Brokers might not have been one breach, one compromised staging server, or one employee with the wrong antivirus software. It might have been a dedicated adversary conducting counterintelligence operations for years and meeting with at least some success. It should always be kept in mind how tireless and aggressive the NSA's counterparts are. But there remained one big question.

Why?

Whether the Shadow Brokers sourced the NSA's secrets from one breach or several, whether the operation was orchestrated directly by the Kremlin or through some proxy, why did they reveal the stolen secrets? Doing so meant passing up serious opportunities. Armed with tools like ETERNALBLUE and intelligence pilfered from the NSA's networks, whoever was behind the Shadow Brokers could have hacked an enormous number of targets all over the world. They could have run sophisticated counterintelligence operations against the NSA, watching the agency when it thought it was operating unobserved. As well as foreclosing these possibilities, going public also meant that the backlash from exposure would inevitably force the NSA to investigate, possibly leading to the discovery and remediation of some of the agency's security vulnerabilities. The exposure of capabilities might also have prompted some major retaliation by the NSA, or by other levers of American power, although that does not appear to have happened.

One possibility—aligned with the theory that the Shadow Brokers was a Russian government effort—is that the operation intended to send a signal. As the NSA and other American intelligence agencies tracked Russian hacking activity in the summer of 2016, the posting of NSA files may have been a warning to back down; if so, the massive releases were quite aggressive signals.[55] During the run-up to the election and then the transition to the Trump administration, the Shadow Brokers' increasingly political posts may have attempted to deter American retaliation, with the lingering threat of further exposure as punishment. Yet there is not nearly enough public evidence to support this view over other possibilities. If it was a signal, the case provides very little clarity on what specifically the signal was, much less whether the United States government received it as intended.

Alternatively, money may have been the motivation. The Shadow Brokers' multiple reminders that, for the right price, they would hand over what they had taken do not particularly fit with the theory that the Shadow Brokers saga was purely an operation controlled by the Russian government, which likely did not need the cash. It more readily suggests that behind the Shadow Brokers' operation was a profit-seeking intermediary partially tied to the government, or a criminal group that was entirely separate, or a disaffected insider. Any of these possibilities would also be more consistent with the Shadow Brokers' constant complaints about a lack of media attention and too few auction bidders.

One final theory seems to be the simplest and likeliest: this was sabotage in the form of exposure—and sabotage is a classic form of shaping. By dragging the NSA's capabilities into the light of day, the Shadow Brokers eroded the agency's capacity to use its powerful hacking tools. In the words of Leon Panetta, a former head of the CIA and former Secretary of Defense, "these leaks have been incredibly damaging to our intelligence and cyber capabilities." The operational effect of a leak is devastating, he said. "Every time it happens, you essentially have to start over."[56] It would certainly make sense for a hostile foreign intelligence agency to want to inflict this kind of setback on the United States, and perhaps it would make sense for a traitorous insider to feel similarly.

The timing of the Shadow Brokers' releases was devastating, too. As the group methodically burned NSA capabilities, the United States was trying both to resist aggressive Russian influence operations and to deploy cyber capabilities alongside its military operations against the Islamic State. In the end, the cyber operation against the Islamic State fell far short of expectations, according to an after-action review by Secretary of Defense Ash Carter.[57] This failure was probably for reasons unrelated to the Shadow Brokers, but it is certain that the exposure of American cyber capabilities did not help.

Maybe even worse, by emphasizing how the NSA had lost its secrets, the Shadow Brokers subjected the agency to withering criticism. Privacy advocates had long railed against the agency's practices, but now leading technology companies also voiced their concerns. Referring to ETERNALBLUE and its role in enabling another massive cyber attack, discussed in Chapter 12, Microsoft president Brad Smith said, "this vulnerability stolen from the NSA has affected customers around the world. Repeatedly, exploits in the hands of governments have leaked into the public domain and caused widespread damage. An equivalent scenario with conventional weapons would be the US military having some of its Tomahawk missiles stolen." Smith believed the NSA's aggressiveness in exploiting computers and the agency's inability to secure its systems had led to increased cybersecurity risks for users everywhere.[58]

The Shadow Brokers almost certainly did more harm to United States security and intelligence collection capabilities than Snowden did. Snowden took his documents to journalists and let them determine what was in the public interest to publish. While the NSA strenuously disagreed with many of those journalists' decisions, the

United States government was at least often consulted and alerted prior to publication. It could make the case for why some documents should be partially or entirely redacted.[59] Indeed, as a result of these redactions, the published Snowden documents are comparatively silent on some notable categories of operations, especially the NSA's active hacking efforts against non-democracies.

The Shadow Brokers, by contrast, took their pilfered haul directly to the internet. Despite their protests to the contrary, they seemed to revel in releasing NSA tools that would have explosive secondary effects, such as ETERNALBLUE and DOUBLEPULSAR.[60] They also revealed operations against specific systems and organizations, such as those in the Middle East, which appeared to be clearly legitimate intelligence targets by any standard. Even worse, they threatened to reveal operations against still more sensitive targets, such as the Chinese and Russian nuclear and ballistic missile programs, a threat they do not seem to have carried out.[61]

The Shadow Brokers' exposures fit into an intriguing and alarming pattern. During the years of Snowden revelations, some published documents that were widely assumed to have come from his trove in fact did not. This set of leaks from someone other than Snowden included some of the more operationally useful files, such as the Advanced Network Technologies directory of NSA tools that the German magazine *Der Spiegel* published in December 2013.[62] The exposure of this catalog likely forced the agency to reconfigure its operational practices. Other articles accused the NSA of spying on German Chancellor Angela Merkel and on internet users using privacy-protecting software. These stories appear to contain material from the Snowden trove but also from other unknown sources.[63]

One provocative possibility is therefore that the Shadow Brokers saga is the latest and most significant iteration of a damaging trend of exposure orchestrated by the same foreign actor. The evidence to support this is thin but intriguing. Combine this possibility with others—that the Russian government had a hand in the Shadow Brokers operation and that the source was ongoing counterintelligence operations rather than a single breach—and the pieces seem to fit together in a theory that makes sense. If true, it would provide a long-sought explanation for the non-Snowden leaks. An emboldened Russia, especially after their successes in the 2016 election interference, might have decided to escalate a leaking campaign to sabotage everything it could.

Whatever the source and the primary motivation, exposure does damage. Most significantly, as Panetta noted, the NSA must rebuild a great deal of its tooling and operational procedures in the aftermath of any serious breach. It must notify vendors of the pilfered hacking tools so that they can issue security updates to protect American computers. But if the NSA is unable to determine just what the intruders took, then it might overcompensate for the breach. Out of an abundance of caution, the NSA might surrender information to vendors on exploits the Shadow Brokers did not in fact obtain, stripping itself of capabilities that otherwise would be useful.[64] The uncertainty the Shadow Brokers created, coupled with the NSA's responsibility for public security, could lead the agency into harming itself.

Of course, it is impossible to know based on public information whether the US government has better answers to these who, what, how, or why questions. Leaks to reporters from the investigation suggest that intelligence agencies see the hand of the Russian government, at least in some form, behind the Shadow Brokers. Leaks suggest, as well, that the presence of Kaspersky on Pho's computer also provided a source of classified information to the Russians, but it was possibly not the only one. The confidence of these internal assessments is also not known, and the US government may still have deep unanswered questions.

Some of those questions relate to what the Shadow Brokers took and perhaps why they released what they did. It seems that, at least into 2018, the United States was still trying to get answers. According to multiple media reports, the CIA spent months running a European operation aimed at discovering what was in the Shadow Brokers' haul. The effort began in 2017, just as the Shadow Brokers' releases intensified. The CIA met with a Russian intermediary who appeared to be well-connected within the Russian intelligence community and who offered to sell the agency copies of the files the US intelligence community had lost.

The deal meandered through twists and turns. The Americans struggled to determine if the intermediary had access to all that he claimed. They grew alarmed when he kept offering to share information on Donald Trump's ties to Russia—a politically fraught topic, given the Trump White House's already poor and suspicious relationship with its own intelligence community. The CIA made clear that such information was "unsolicited," but still feared that the intermediary was part of a Russian influence operation to drive a wedge between different parts of the US government. The agency worried that, if the operation leaked, Trump would see it as an attempt to undermine him. As it turns out, the CIA was right to fret, since the operation did come out and Trump made just that accusation.

The Russian intermediary wanted reassurance that the US intelligence community was behind the effort, not rogue operators. To reassure him, the Americans gave him advance notice of a series of tweets the NSA would post to its Twitter account. This foreknowledge of social media posts established their bona fides, convincing the intermediary that the operation had official approval.

Ultimately, it appears the intermediary did not deliver. After receiving a first payment from the Americans, he provided files that were genuinely from the Shadow Brokers' trove—but that had already been released. Even after a reported additional payment of $100,000, routed through an indirect channel, the intermediary could provide information only on what he said were Trump's ties to Russia. He offered little insight on matters related to the pilfered files. When pressed, he told the Americans that his instructions from Russian intelligence officials were to hold back any information about the Shadow Brokers.

The American operatives reportedly confronted the intermediary and gave him a choice: change sides and provide information on his contacts in Russian intelligence, or leave Europe and return to Russia for good. Without hesitation, the man chose the latter option.[65] As he walked out the door, the damage of exposure was clear: some of the NSA's deepest secrets were plastered all over the internet, but the Shadow Brokers' own workings remained as mysterious as ever. They had reshaped the game.

12

Theft, Ransom, and Manipulation

THE BILLS ARE CALLED SUPERNOTES. Their composition is three-quarters cotton and one-quarter linen paper, a challenging combination to produce. Tucked within each note are the requisite red and blue security fibers. The security stripe is exactly where it should be and, upon close inspection, so is the watermark. Ben Franklin's apprehensive look is perfect, and betrays no indication that the currency, supposedly worth one hundred dollars, is fake.

Most systems designed to catch forgeries fail to detect the supernotes. The massive counterfeiting effort that produced these bills appears to have lasted decades. Many observers tie the fake bills to North Korea, and some even hold former leader Kim Jong-Il personally responsible, citing a supposed order he gave in the 1970s, early in his rise to power.[1] Fake hundreds, he reasoned, would simultaneously give the regime much-needed hard currency and undermine the integrity of the US economy. The self-serving fraud was also an attempt at destabilization.

At its peak, the counterfeiting effort apparently yielded between $15 million and $25 million per year for the North Korean government.[2] The bills ended up all over the world, allegedly distributed by an aging Irish man and laundered through a small bank in Macau. The North Koreans supplemented the forging program with other illicit efforts. These ranged from trafficking opiates and methamphetamines, to selling knockoff Viagra, to smuggling parts of endangered animals in secure diplomatic pouches.[3] All told, United States government experts suggest that the regime at one point netted more than half a billion dollars per year from its criminal activities.[4]

During the first decade of the 2000s, the United States made great progress in thwarting North Korea's illicit behavior, especially its counterfeiting operation. A law enforcement campaign stretching to 130 countries infiltrated the secret trafficking circles and turned up millions of dollars in bogus bills. In one dramatic scene, authorities staged a wedding off the coast of Atlantic City, New Jersey, to lure suspects and arrest them when they showed up. The US Treasury Department also deployed its expanded Patriot Act powers, levying financial sanctions on the suspect bank in Macau and freezing $25 million in assets.

The wide-reaching American operation seemed to work. By 2008, the prevalence of supernotes had declined dramatically. One FBI agent involved in the United States effort offered an explanation: "If the supernotes have stopped showing up, I'd venture to say that North Korea quit counterfeiting them. Perhaps they've found something else that's easier to counterfeit after they lost the distribution network for the supernote."[5] Under pressure from American investigators, and challenged by a 2013 redesign of the $100 bill, the North Koreans moved on to newer tricks for illicitly filling their coffers.

It should be no surprise that hacking would be one of these. North Korean leadership has taken care to identify promising young people and get them computer science training in China or even—undercover as diplomats to the United Nations—in the United States. Once trained, the North Koreans often live abroad, frequently in China, as they carry out their cyber operations. This gives them better internet connectivity and more plausible deniability of North Korean government ties, while still keeping them out of the reach of United States law enforcement.[6]

These North Korean hackers have carried out a systematic effort to target financial institutions all over the world. Their methods are bold, though not always successful. In their most profitable operations, they have manipulated how major financial institutions connect to the international banking system. By duping components of this system into thinking their hackers are legitimate users, they have enabled the transfer of tens of millions of dollars into accounts they control. They have tampered with log files and bank transaction records, prompting a flurry of security alerts and upgrades in international financial institutions. Most publicly, and perhaps by accident, the hackers have disrupted hundreds of thousands of computers around the world in a ham-fisted effort to hold valuable data for ransom. Through their successes and failures, they learned to modify and combine their tricks, evolving their operations to be more effective.

Even with a mixed track record, these attempts at manipulating the global financial system have literally paid off. The bounties from North Korean hacking campaigns are huge; the United Nations estimated the total haul at $2 billion, a large sum for a country with a gross domestic product of only about $28 billion.[7] As North Korea continues to develop nuclear weapons and intercontinental ballistic missiles, cyber operations help fund the regime. The scale of these operations is tremendous, at least relative to their past illicit efforts. Hackers now turn a far larger profit than the supernotes ever could.

But, as with the supernotes, the potential value of financial manipulation for North Korea goes at least somewhat beyond profit-seeking. It is also an attempt to undermine the integrity of worldwide markets by deleting transaction records and distorting financial truth. Such tactics are tempting for government agencies but carry enormous risk. In the run-up to the Iraq War, the United States considered draining Saddam Hussein's bank accounts, but decided against it, fearful of crossing a Rubicon of state-sponsored cyber fraud that would harm the American economy and global stability.[8] In 2014, President Obama's NSA review commission argued that the United States should pledge never to hack and manipulate financial records. To do so, it said, would have a tremendously negative impact on trust in the global economic system.[9] This was not a risk the North Koreans feared.

Billion-Dollar Fraud

Bank robbery is a terrible idea. Not only is it illegal, but it also yields an awful return on investment. In the United States, the average bank robbery nets around $4,000 in cash, and the average bank robber pulls off only three heists before getting caught.[10] Prospects are a little better overseas, but not much. Strikingly bold capers, like the 2005 theft at Banco Central in Brazil that required months of secretive tunnel-digging, can fetch tens of millions of dollars, but the vast majority of significant attempts end in catastrophic failure.[11]

North Korean operatives found a better way to rob banks. They did not have to break through reinforced concrete or tunnel under vaults to get at the money, and they had no need to use force or threats. Instead, they simply duped the bank's computers into giving it away. To do this, they set their sights on a core system in international business called the Society for Worldwide Interbank Financial Telecommunication, or SWIFT. The SWIFT system has been around since the 1970s. Its eleven thousand financial institutions in more than two hundred countries process tens of millions of transactions per day. The daily transfers total trillions of dollars, more than the annual gross domestic product of most countries. Many financial institutions in the SWIFT system have special user accounts for custom SWIFT software to communicate their business to other banks all over the world.

The Central Bank of Bangladesh stores some of its money in the Federal Reserve Bank of New York, which the Central Bank uses for settling international transactions. On February 4, 2016, the Bangladeshi bank initiated more than three dozen payments. Per the transfer requests sent over the SWIFT system, the bank wanted some of its New York money, totaling almost a billion dollars, moved to a series of other accounts in Sri Lanka, the Philippines, and elsewhere in Asia.

Around the same time and halfway across the world, a printer inside the Central Bank of Bangladesh stopped working. The printer was an ordinary HP LaserJet 400, located in a windowless, twelve-by eight-foot room. The device had one very important job: day and night, it automatically printed physical records of the bank's SWIFT transactions. When employees arrived on the morning of February 5, they found nothing in the printer's output tray. They tried to print manually, but found they could not; the computer terminal connected to the SWIFT network generated an error message saying it was missing a file. The employees were now blind to transactions taking place at their own bank. The silent printer was the dog that did not bark: a sign that something was deeply wrong, but not immediately recognized as such.

This was not an ordinary machine failure. Instead, it was the culmination of shrewd North Korean preparation and aggressiveness. The hackers' clever move was to target not the SWIFT system itself, but a system connected to it. The special accounts used by the Central Bank of Bangladesh to interact with the system had enormous power, including the capacity to create, approve, and submit new transactions. By focusing their espionage on the bank's network and users, the hackers were eventually able to gain access to these accounts.

The reconnaissance required to figure out how the SWIFT system worked and to gather the necessary credentials for authentication was time-consuming. Yet even as the hackers were moving through the bank's network and preparing their operation—a process that took months—the Central Bank of Bangladesh failed to detect them. In part, this was because the bank was not looking very hard. After the hack, a police investigation identified several shoddy security practices, including cheap equipment and a lack of security software, which made it easier for hackers to reach sensitive computers.[12]

Once the hackers gained access to the bank's SWIFT accounts, they could initiate transactions just like any authorized user. To further avoid detection, they wrote special malicious code to bypass the internal antifraud checks in SWIFT software. Worse still, they manipulated transaction logs, making it harder to figure out where the bank's money was going and casting doubt on the veracity of the logs upon which this, and every, high-volume financial institution depends. The North Korean strike against these logs was a dagger to the heart of the system. They sidelined the printer with additional malicious code, buying themselves time while the system processed their illicit transfer requests.

The hackers thus sent their payment requests to New York unbeknownst to anyone in Bangladesh. But employees at the New York Fed realized something was amiss. When they noticed the sudden batch of Bangladeshi transactions, they thought it was unusual that many of the receiving accounts were private entities, not other banks. They questioned dozens of the transfers and sent requests for clarification back. But the Bangladeshi bankers, distracted and apparently still trying to recover from the hack, did not respond.

It was not until the Bangladeshis managed to get their computer systems working again that they realized the severity of the situation. The newly repaired printer spit out the backlog of transaction records, including many that immediately looked suspicious. By the time the central bankers urgently reached out to their counterparts in New York, it was too late. The weekend had come, and the American workers had gone home; the North Korean hackers had either gotten very lucky with the timing of their operation or had planned it remarkably well. The Bangladeshi bankers had to sweat out the days until the Fed staff came back to work.

Monday brought mixed news. On the positive side was that vigilant New York Fed analysts had stopped most of the transactions, totaling more than $850 million. This included one $20 million transfer request with an especially odd intended recipient: the "Shalika Fandation" in Sri Lanka. It appears the hackers intended to write "Shalika Foundation," though no nonprofit by that name, even properly spelled, seems to exist. To the extent that this typo helped alert analysts to the fraud, it must count as one of the most expensive in history, at least for the hackers.

The bad news was that four transactions had gone through, worth a total of $101 million. Three payments sent $81 million to accounts at Rizal Bank in the Philippines, and one payment sent $20 million to Pan Asia Bank in Sri Lanka. The Central Bank employees in Bangladesh, working quickly, convinced Pan Asia Bank to stop the transaction and send the money back. They were less fortunate with Rizal Bank, which had already placed the money in several accounts tied to casinos. Someone, acting as a so-called money mule, had made withdrawals from these accounts on February 5 and February 9—the latter even after the Bangladeshis had warned Rizal Bank of the fraud. Of the $81 million sent to the Rizal accounts, only $68,000 remained. The rest was gone.

Investigators from the British firm BAE Systems began tracking the bank hackers and uncovered several important clues that identified the North Koreans as perpetrators. They linked some of the code used in the Bangladesh intrusion to earlier North Korean hacks, most notably the 2014 operation against Sony. Even some of the typos in the code exactly matched typos in the code that damaged the movie studio, suggesting that the same perpetrators were reusing the tools.[13] The investigation reached a clear verdict: from a world away, and from the comfort of their homes and offices, North Korea's hackers had manipulated transaction records, exploited the system of interbank trust, and pulled off one of the biggest bank heists in history.[14]

A Campaign Emerges

As remarkable as the Bangladesh operation was, it was just one part of what was eventually recognized as a worldwide campaign. A parallel target of that campaign was a Southeast Asian bank that has not been named in public.[15] In this second operation, the hackers followed a series of fairly well-orchestrated steps. They appear to have initially compromised their target via the server that hosted the bank's public-facing website.

In December 2015, they expanded their malicious presence from that server to a different server within the bank. This one ran the powerful SWIFT software that connected the bank to the global financial system. The next month, the hackers deployed additional tools to begin moving within the target network and positioning malicious code to interact with the SWIFT system. On January 29, 2016, the hackers tested some of these tools. They did so almost precisely at the same time that they performed similar activity in their Bangladesh operation.

On February 4, just as the hackers began initiating payment requests in Bangladesh, they also manipulated the Southeast Asian bank's SWIFT software. However, unlike in the parallel Bangladesh campaign, they did not yet initiate any fraudulent transactions. Slightly more than three weeks after that, the hackers caused a halt in operations at the second bank. Little is known about the circumstances surrounding this disruption.

Even after they took the money from the Central Bank of Bangladesh, the hackers kept up their focus on their second target. In April, they deployed keylogging software to the bank's SWIFT server, presumably to gain additional credentials to the most powerful user accounts. These credentials, the keys to the bank's SWIFT kingdom, would be essential to stealing money.

But by now the world of international banking sensed danger, in part aided by BAE's investigation. SWIFT released new security updates in May in response to the alarm surrounding the Bangladesh incident and worries about the integrity of the financial system. The hackers would have to circumvent these updates to carry out their mission. By July, they began testing new malicious code for that purpose. In August, they once again began deploying code against the bank's SWIFT server, presumably with the goal of soon transferring funds.

It was here that, despite all their careful testing and deployment of malicious code, the North Koreans hit a fatal snag: the Southeast Asian bank was better prepared and better defended than the Bangladeshi one had been. In August 2016, more than seven months after the hackers had made their initial entry, the bank found the breach. They hired Kaspersky, the high-profile Russian cybersecurity company, to investigate. The hackers, realizing that investigators were in hot pursuit and acting quickly to shut down the operation against the bank, deleted a large number of files to cover their tracks, but missed some. This mistake allowed Kaspersky to discover that much of the malicious code overlapped with that used in the bank hacking incident in Bangladesh.

BAE Systems' and Kaspersky's investigations brought the contours of North Korea's campaign into view. It had ambitions much larger than just the two banks. Notably, in January 2017, the North Koreans compromised a Polish financial regulator's systems and caused it to serve malicious code to any visitors to its websites, many of which were financial institutions. The North Koreans preconfigured that malicious code to act against more than a hundred institutions from all over the world, primarily banks and telecommunications companies. The list of targets included the World Bank, central banks from countries such as Brazil, Chile, and Mexico, and many other prominent financial firms.[16]

Nor did the North Koreans limit themselves to seeking out traditional currencies. Their campaign included a series of efforts to steal increasingly valuable cryptocurrencies like Bitcoin from unsuspecting users all over the world. They also targeted a significant number of Bitcoin exchanges, including a major one in South Korea known as YouBit. In that case, the exchange lost 17 percent of its financial assets to North Korean hackers, though it refused to specify how much that amounted to in absolute terms.[17] One estimate from Group-IB, a cybersecurity company, pegged North Korea's profit from some of their little-noticed operations against cryptocurrency exchanges at more than $500 million.[18] While it is impossible to confirm this estimate or the details of the hacks on cryptocurrency exchanges, the size of the reported loss emphasizes the degree to which the North Koreans have plundered smaller and more private financial institutions, almost entirely out of view.

The cybersecurity companies reached a consensus: the North Koreans had clearly reoriented some of their hacking tools and infrastructure from destructive capabilities to financially lucrative and destabilizing ones. The same country that had launched denial-of-service attacks against the United States in 2009, wiped computers across major South Korean firms in 2013, and hit Sony in 2014 was now in the business of hacking financial institutions.[19] The most isolated and sanctioned regime on the planet, as it continued to pour money into acquiring illicit nuclear weapons, was funding itself in part through hacking. It was yet another way in which statecraft and cyber operations had intersected. Far more was to come.

Ransomware and Beyond

In 2016 and 2017, the ambitions and capabilities of the North Korean hackers were apparent. The technical reports from BAE Systems and Kaspersky had revealed them. But, even as the threat became a major subject of conversation in circles of international finance, it was not clear what anyone could do about it. Beyond upgrades in cybersecurity defenses, there were few good options. North Korea was already an international pariah due to its pursuit of nuclear weapons. Additional sanctions, such as those levied by the Obama administration after the Sony hack, seemed to do little to slow its hacking campaigns.[20]

The North Koreans then raised the stakes. For their next trick, they took another old-fashioned crime online: taking hostages for ransom. The hostages were not people, though, but pieces of data. While traditionally spies would have sought to copy the data stored within big organizations, like many modern profit-motivated criminals, the North Koreans were not after secrets. They instead deployed a technique known as ransomware, in which hackers encrypt the hard drive of their target computer and delete any backups. The decryption key remains unknown to the target. If the target does not have a surviving backup of the data, the only way to recover the information is to pay the hackers a ransom in return for the decryption key. Given the value of the data, institutions are often willing to do this.

In February of 2017, North Korean hackers started testing the early stages of their new ransomware. They infected a single organization, still unknown, in which the code spread quickly to around a hundred computers. In the scheme of global cybersecurity, this was an imperceptible rounding error, and scarcely anyone noticed. In March and April, the hackers deployed new code and infected an additional five organizations, seemingly chosen at random. Once again, the operation was too small to attract much attention.[21]

Then, in May of 2017, North Korean hackers decided to deploy yet another version of the code. This one had an innovative twist: rather than rely on socially engineered emails or other manual methods of spreading from computer to computer, this ransomware would propagate itself automatically. Each computer the code infected would go on to infect more, which would go on to infect still more. Exponential growth would mean many more victims and thus many more ransoms. Similar to Stuxnet, this self-propagating code was a worm. Like the supernotes and the manipulation of financial transaction records, the North Korean worm would be a profitable attack that also had the benefit of destabilization: organizations all over the world would worry about connecting to the internet or engaging with one another, fearful of how a rapidly spreading threat might metastasize through a channel they thought was safe.

Though the concept and power of worms had been known for some time, good ones are hard to write.[22] North Korean hackers realized that they could take a shortcut. They found the propagation technique embedded in one of the NSA's powerful exploits, ETERNALBLUE, which the Shadow Brokers had leaked just a few months before. While some network administrators had patched their systems to defend against the exploit, surely many had not. By targeting the same vulnerability that the NSA had long exploited, the North Koreans could build a worm of their own. They deployed this new version of their ransomware on May 12, 2017, with the new propagation code tucked inside.[23]

Immediately, the entire cybersecurity world knew about it. Supercharged by the power of the NSA's exploit, the North Korean worm spread rapidly around the globe, aided by the large number of unpatched systems. Cybersecurity researchers carefully studied the code. Due to the worm's devastating effects and artifacts in the code that referred to software known as WanaCryptor, they named the operation WannaCry. Additional forensic examination found strong similarities to earlier North Korean operations. Researchers concluded that WannaCry was a state-sponsored attack of unprecedented proportions.

Before long, the worm had infected hundreds of thousands of computers in more than 150 countries, encrypting their files and locking out their users. One of the organizations most severely disrupted was Britain's National Health Service, which delayed some medical operations and diverted patients from emergency rooms as it scrambled to respond.[24] Some hacking victims quickly paid the ransom.[25]

But word soon got out: don't pay. Those who paid did not get their files back. The ransomware code contained no mechanism to determine who had coughed up the cryptocurrency demanded by the hackers. This omission was either a sign of remarkably amateurish engineering, or, more likely, an indication that the malicious code was still under development and was not supposed to spread as widely as it did. The hackers might have been unaware of how powerful the NSA's exploit was or how quickly it would spread the worm once they included it in the code. In any case, the power of exponential growth in infections took over like a runaway train headed downhill. The worm became harder and harder to stop, even for those nominally in control.[26]

The Five Eyes did not mean for ETERNALBLUE's power to be used in this way. They intended for it to be a valuable tool for carefully and quietly spreading malicious code within target networks, not running amok on the internet. The WannaCry outbreak was thus one of the most publicly devastating consequences of the Shadow Brokers' actions. If it had not been for the mysterious group's penetration of the agency and its aggressive decision to dump American hacking tools for anyone to study and use, the seemingly unstoppable cascade of infections would not have happened.

Suddenly, however, the onslaught of new infections did stop, or at least dramatically slowed. A British security researcher, Marcus Hutchins, noticed a web address buried in the malicious code: iuqe rfsodp9ifjaposdfjhgosurijfaewrwergwea.com.[27] Given its incomprehensibility, this was clearly not a website meant for humans to visit. In fact, Hutchins noticed, it was not even a website at all. No one owned the domain name. He paid around $10 to register it himself. He then went back to work analyzing the malicious code.

Four hours later, a friend also working on the problem pointed out to him that the infections had stopped. In fact, so long as the malicious code could connect to Hutchins's newly registered domain, it no longer executed its malicious attack. But if the WannaCry code could not connect to the domain, the attack would execute. In effect, by registering the domain name, Hutchins had activated a secret and likely unintentional kill switch that stopped the worm's spread.[28] As a result, the North Koreans' first major ransomware experiment—from premature spread to ignominious end—inflicted at least $4 billion in damages but ultimately brought in only a pittance for the regime.[29]

This initial failure did not keep the North Koreans down for long or deter them from using ransomware in the future. By October 2017, they were ready to try again. This time, their plan was different: they would deploy ransomware not to get money directly, but instead as cover for an operation like the one they performed in Bangladesh. By causing a lot of disruption with digital hostage-taking, they could proceed, right under the noses of distracted bankers, to execute illicit transactions and take money from well-stocked accounts.

Their new target, located in Taiwan, was the Far Eastern International Bank. North Korean hackers spent time doing detailed reconnaissance of the bank's network, just as they had against their other victims. They gathered usernames and passwords and, on October 1, 2017, readied their malicious code for the operation. It had several interlocking components.

The malicious code would first make itself hard to remove, burrowing into an operating system and establishing a way to persist there. Another component would spread through the bank's network, using information likely gained from earlier reconnaissance efforts to establish a presence in important areas. A third component systematically enumerated the user's files and encrypted them before displaying a message demanding a ransom. Other components established command-and-control mechanisms with the North Korean hackers, permitting them to dictate the malicious code's activities from afar.

While the bank was, at least in theory, distracted by the apparent ransomware attack, the North Korean hackers initiated a series of financial transactions. Their commands to the SWIFT system authorized transfers to Cambodia, the United States, and Sri Lanka. Early indications were that the hackers had tried to steal $60 million.[30] But the hackers put incorrect values in some of the message fields, causing those transfers to fail. Some other transfers did go through, however, totaling more than $14 million. This included transfers to the Bank of Ceylon in Sri Lanka on October 3, as well as transfers to banks in Cambodia and the United States.

The next day, a money mule arrived in Sri Lanka and withdrew several hundred thousand dollars without incident. But two days after that, when he returned for more cash, Sri Lankan police were ready for him. They arrested the mule and eventually an accomplice, as well.[31] The Far Eastern International Bank was reportedly able to recover most of the stolen money.[32] Nonetheless, the hackers themselves remained free, out of the reach of international law enforcement and ready to strike again.

Worldwide Withdrawals

The North Korean hackers had clearly mastered several key hacking tasks that once would have been far beyond them. They could get deep access to banks' computer networks in countries all over the world by deploying malicious code, conducting extensive reconnaissance, and remaining largely undetected. They had also developed an exceptional understanding of the SWIFT system and how banks connected to it, updating their tactics and tools to keep pace with the urgent security upgrades SWIFT and financial institutions kept rolling out.

But they had a problem: in too many cases, they issued a fraudulent transaction without being able to actually get the pilfered funds. With the notable exception of operations against cryptocurrency exchanges, banks had thwarted the theft operations in their final withdrawal stages time and time again. The North Koreans needed a better way to cash out.

In the summer of 2018, the hackers tried a new tactic. The operation began with the compromise of Cosmos Cooperative Bank in India sometime around June. Once inside Cosmos, they developed a thorough understanding of how the bank functioned and gained secret access to significant parts of its computing infrastructure. Throughout the summer of 2018, they seemed to be preparing for a new kind of operation. This time, they would use ATM cards as well as electronic funds transfers to get the money out.

The premise of an ATM cash-out is quite straightforward and predates the North Koreans' operations: hackers gain access to the credentials of a bank's customer, and then a money mule shows up to an ATM and withdraws money from that account. With no bank teller to talk to or physical branch to enter, the chance of arrest is substantially lower. Previous ATM cash-outs by different criminal hackers had worked at a small scale, including against the National Bank of Blacksburg in Virginia.[33] The challenge was getting the target's card and PIN to dupe the ATM into disbursing the money.

But before the North Koreans could act, United States intelligence agencies caught a whiff that something was amiss. While it seems the United States government did not know specifically which financial institution the North Koreans had compromised, the FBI issued a private message to banks on August 10. In it, the Bureau warned of an imminent ATM cash-out scheme due to a breach at a regional bank. The breach fit into a pattern of what investigators often called "unlimited operations" because of the potential for many withdrawals.[34] The FBI urged banks to be vigilant and to upgrade their security practices.

It did not matter. On August 11, the North Koreans made their move. In a window that lasted only a little over two hours, money mules in twenty-eight countries sprang into action. Operating with cloned ATM cards that worked just like real ones, they withdrew money from machines all over the world in amounts ranging from $100 to $2,500. Whereas previous North Korean attempts had failed because large bank transfers were hard to miss and easy to reverse, this effort was designed to be broad, flexible, and fast. The total take was around $11 million.

One question immediately surfaced: how did the North Koreans manage this? For each withdrawal, they would have had to trick Cosmos Bank's authentication system into permitting the disbursal of money at the ATM. Even if they had some information for each customer's account, it is exceptionally unlikely that they had managed to get the PINs of so many individuals. Without those numbers, every attempt at authenticating the withdrawal requests should have failed.

BAE Systems' researchers offered a theory that fits available evidence quite well. They surmised that the North Korean compromise of the Cosmos computer infrastructure might have been so thorough that the hackers were able to manipulate the fraudulent authentication requests themselves. As a result, when each withdrawal request made its way through the international banking system to Cosmos Bank, it was likely misdirected to a separate authentication system set up by the hackers.[35] This system would approve the request and bypass any fraud-detection mechanisms Cosmos had in place. A senior police official in India later confirmed this supposition.[36]

Once the cash-out was successful, the hackers also went back to Plan A: two days later, they initiated three more transfers using the SWIFT system from Cosmos Bank to an obscure company in Hong Kong, netting around another two million dollars. The firm, ALM Trading Limited, had been created and registered with the government just a few months before. Its nondescript name and apparent lack of web presence makes it exceptionally difficult to learn more about it or about the fate of the money transferred to it, though it seems likely that the North Koreans collected the cash.[37]

The Cosmos operation shows how the North Koreans' tactics of theft, ransom, and financial-record manipulation can have impacts that go beyond just the acquisition of funds for the regime. Cosmos

Bank took major online systems offline for almost nine days in response to the attack—an eternity in the banking world.[38] Future operations may try to exploit this potential for destabilization more directly, perhaps by flooding the SWIFT system with fraudulent transactions to cause still-greater doubts about its integrity.

There is no reason to think that the North Korean financial campaign will stop. For years, its operational hallmark has been code that continually evolves and improves. What the North Koreans lack in skill, at least when compared to their counterparts at the NSA, they partially make up for in aggressiveness and ambition. They seem mostly uninhibited by worries of blowback and appear to welcome the consequences of disrupting thousands of computers or modifying vitally important financial records. In gaining much-needed cash, they slowly reshape and advance their position geopolitically. They incur setbacks, to be sure, but over time their hackers have garnered vast sums for the regime while threatening the perceived integrity of global financial systems. The days of supernotes are gone, but North Korea has brought together fraud and destabilization once again.

13

Widespread Disruption

EVERY JUNE 28, Ukraine celebrates Constitution Day. As the name suggests, the public holiday marks the Parliament's 1996 approval of the country's constitution, which solidified Ukraine as an independent post-Soviet state. The commemoration resonates most strongly in the western regions of the country, where citizens tend to favor greater alignment with Western Europe and the United States. In these regions, the population's suspicion of Russian influence is comparatively strong.

In 2017, Constitution Day was different. While for Ukrainians it was an opportunity to celebrate, for Russia it was an opportunity to flex its muscle. At a time when Russian and Ukrainian forces were years into their simmering territorial conflict in eastern Ukraine, Constitution Day offered a symbolic occasion for a broader and bolder move: disruption and destabilization on an international scale.

Indeed, the Russians did not really aim their disruption operation, which quickly acquired the name NotPetya, at any one specific target. In contrast to previous cyber attacks that targeted one facility, one company, or even the power grid for one city, this one was indiscriminate and widespread. The Russian hackers endowed the attack code with the capacity to copy and spread itself. In this sense, it was like Stuxnet, but unlike Stuxnet, it contained no target verification mechanisms to limit its force; pervasive damage was the goal. Unlike WannaCry, which might have spread by accident, NotPetya was undoubtedly intentional. The attack was a broadside that damaged everyone doing business in Ukraine and everyone paying taxes to the Ukrainian government. Launched on the eve of the Constitution Day holiday, it was unlike any cyber attack seen before.

The indiscriminate nature of the assault meant that it did not stop at the Ukrainian borders, but spread all over the world. As a result, it thrust itself into Western consciousness in a way that so many other parts of the conflict in Ukraine did not. Multinational brand-name corporations like Maersk, FedEx, and Merck suffered huge losses.

Beyond the corporate losses, NotPetya was significant for a number of reasons. It served as a reminder of the potency of Russian government hackers and the aggressiveness of the Russian state. It was yet another illustration of how ordinary businesses and individuals can find themselves on the front lines of geopolitically motivated cyber operations. And it foreshadowed what might come next: increasingly powerful and autonomous cyber attacks, in which hackers load digital equivalents of unguided rockets, aim in a general direction, light the fuses, and watch to see what unpredictable but serious damage results. For those who want to disrupt global order and do not care about proportionality or targeting, this kind of attack fits the bill.

NotPetya ranks as the costliest and possibly the most important cyber attack in history. It caused more than $10 billion in clearly quantifiable damage and sent companies all over the world scrambling to strengthen their cybersecurity practices.[1] It built on the Shadow Brokers' efforts and embarrassed the NSA once more, turning the agency's leaked tools against American and allied computers. It prompted condemnation from major governments, as policymakers worried that it might herald an age of increasingly devastating and haphazard attacks. The conclusion seems inescapable: because of cyber operations' possibility for automation and rapid propagation, disruption can scale.

A Wolf in Weasel's Clothing in Sheep's Clothing

The message is familiar: apply software updates. Sometimes the appeal comes from a security professional, someone who knows security patches are essential to defending against hackers' new tricks. Often it comes in the form of an annoying dialog box, too often minimized again and again, indicating that some new version of Microsoft Office, Windows, or some other software is ready to install. Sometimes, code patches itself in the background without bothering the user. Whatever the mechanism, updating software makes sense, as it usually does improve security.[2]

Hackers working for the GRU, Russia's military intelligence agency, turned that notion on its head in 2017. These hackers seem to have been part of the same group that caused the blackouts in Ukraine in 2015 and 2016.[3] Now, they had a new kind of attack in mind. To begin, they identified a piece of software, known as MeDoc, that enjoyed significant market share in Ukraine. MeDoc was essential for paying taxes and so, according to one estimate, more than 80 percent of the domestic corporations in Ukraine used it.[4] These were the firms the hackers wanted in their crosshairs. It was the soft-

ware's reach, rather than its function, that made MeDoc an ideal vehicle for their attack.

Next, the hackers compromised Linkos Group, the company
behind the software. The GRU gained access to critical systems and
stole administrator passwords, then moved on to their more powerful
trick: source code manipulation. Just as hackers had manipulated
Juniper's code to insert backdoors in 2012 and 2014, Russian hackers
manipulated the code that made up MeDoc. To do so was an impressive feat, since the code was substantial, about one and a half gigabytes in size; if the code were made up entirely of text, it would run
to some quarter of a million pages long. Amidst this digital expanse,
the hackers cleverly made their malicious modifications without
detection.

As a result, some of the software updates the company pushed out
in April, May, and June 2017 actually made its software less secure.
Users who thought they were downloading a new and improved iteration got a version of MeDoc that included the GRU's latent malicious code. But while the Juniper hackers had only changed some
encryption and inserted a backdoor, the Russian hackers went further. The poisoned versions of MeDoc enabled the hackers to perform remote reconnaissance on everyone who downloaded them.
More worryingly, the Russian additions permitted the hackers to
deploy additional malicious code and run it on many thousands of
computers spread across Ukraine and the world.

The GRU hackers were deliberate and savvy. They spent the spring
of 2017 subtly refining their illicitly placed code. Rather than set up
a separate mechanism for sending and receiving messages to the
hacked computers, they subverted the channel the MeDoc software
used to communicate with the company's servers, blending in and

avoiding detection. By the end of June, after one final tune-up to the malicious code—which MeDoc's update mechanisms dutifully, though unwittingly, delivered on June 22—they were ready to act.

On the morning of June 27, the hackers launched the attack. First, they put their stolen administrative passwords to work, logging into one of the company's vital servers and gaining full access. Next, they deployed a new server configuration they had prepared in advance. This new configuration redirected all the data and web traffic intended for the legitimate MeDoc update servers to another server controlled by the hackers. As usual, the users of MeDoc had no idea that anything nefarious was happening.

This other server was apparently based in Latvia. Little is known about it. A company that specialized in renting server space and reselling it to others operated the server, yet the machine seemed to serve no websites. Its registration information lists a name that does not appear elsewhere on the internet and a phone number that is similarly inconclusive. Investigators eventually determined that the server was wiped clean on the evening of June 27, obscuring the investigative trail.

In the short time that the server was online, though, it packed quite a punch. As computers running MeDoc all over the world connected to the hacker-controlled machine, the Russian code within MeDoc suddenly became important. The hackers used a preconfigured set of commands to distribute still more malicious code and launch their attack. For three hours, until the hackers reverted the MeDoc systems back to their original configuration, they sent this payload through the trusted MeDoc update channel to computers all over the world. Those computers and their users did not realize that, instead of downloading a legitimate security patch, they had just been drawn into a rapidly unfolding cyber attack.

The payload was itself a powerful piece of code, which soon acquired the name NotPetya. The Russian hackers had fashioned it as a variant of an already known piece of ransomware for criminal use known as Petya.[5] Once the malicious server loaded NotPetya onto a corporate computer that ran MeDoc and downloaded the poisoned update, the code began a series of damaging and destructive tasks. For the most part, it completed these tasks on its own, showing a significant degree of preplanned automation.

First, it searched each computer for administrator passwords, which operating systems store in memory, using a combination of tricks that hackers have long deployed. These passwords are the lifeblood of any computer network. They are a natural target for hackers because they enable further operations. The fact that just a few administrative passwords can grant control to a company's domain of computers is an opportunity that is usually too irresistible to pass up. By acquiring these passwords early in the attack, the NotPetya code could do more damage later.

Next, the NotPetya code attempted to access and exploit other computers connected to the one it had just infected. Like Stuxnet and WannaCry before it, NotPetya was a worm, spreading on its own throughout networks all over the world. The machines affected by the MeDoc backdoor were merely patient zeroes setting off a much larger and growing infection. To achieve this lateral movement and thus exponential growth in infections, the NotPetya code deployed several clever tricks. For one, the code tried to deploy the administrator passwords it had just stolen, since some of these could work on other machines, as well. Once the NotPetya code was on its next machine, it would make copies of that system's passwords and spread itself again. Each infection begat many more infections.

The Russian hackers also had a second propagation technique. They repurposed ETERNALBLUE, the powerful NSA exploit leaked by the Shadow Brokers and used by the North Koreans in WannaCry a little more than a month before. Even though many companies had applied patches and fixed the software weaknesses ETERNALBLUE exploited, others remained vulnerable. Against these unpatched computers and networks, NotPetya's code sometimes used the pilfered NSA tool to spread itself still further. It was yet another devastating public consequence of the Shadow Brokers' penetration of the agency and exposure of American secrets.

Coupling ETERNALBLUE with potent password-stealing techniques proved to be quite a powerful combination. NotPetya moved quickly. Once it spread to a new target network, it moved throughout that network sometimes in a matter of not minutes but seconds.[6] One leading cybersecurity firm, Cisco Talos, concluded that it was the fastest-spreading malicious code it had ever seen. "By the second you saw it, your data center was already gone," Cisco analyst Craig Williams said.[7]

NotPetya also took care to hide itself from computer defenses. It checked to see if antivirus software was running on the system. If it found antivirus software from a few major companies, most notably Norton or Symantec, the code would do its best to cover its tracks, including by loading itself into more transient memory and deleting its presence from the hard drive. NotPetya would also delete key activity log files from the system, making it as hard as possible to reconstruct what had happened.

All these infections, which numbered in the hundreds of thousands, would have been bad enough if NotPetya were simply an espionage tool. The code would have enabled the hackers to collect an enormous amount of information about parties doing business in

Ukraine and to steal a significant number of corporate secrets. The powerful distribution channel of the MeDoc update mechanism paired with the hackers' lateral movement capabilities would have enabled tremendous reach across the globe. The special code designed to evade antivirus systems would have helped reduce the risk of detection and aided the surreptitious collection of information.[8]

The GRU hackers, however, did not want to spy. They wanted to disrupt and destroy. They decided to expose the valuable MeDoc update channel and all the possible access it entailed, making it public as they launched a devastating cyber attack. The decision to give up such enormous opportunity for future espionage in favor of launching a near-term attack is not an unprecedented one, and it provides insights into the hackers' mindset. Either they had so many penetrations of Ukrainian systems and software that powerful espionage channels like MeDoc were not special to them, or they so prioritized sabotage over spying that it was worth sacrificing the backdoor access they enjoyed.

NotPetya, once it had obtained passwords and done its best to spread itself to other computers, often started attacking the host computer.[9] Like the Petya ransomware from which it drew inspiration, NotPetya displayed a screen to the user saying that a necessary hard drive repair was underway. This was nonsense. Instead of repairing the hard drive, NotPetya was in the process of decapitating it, overwriting the critical master boot record, just as the Iranians and North Koreans had done in their attacks, and encrypting the user's data to render it inaccessible. Eventually, after this was done, NotPetya would inform the user that a ransom had to be paid for the files to be restored.

Unfortunately for the users, as with WannaCry, there was no decryption key—although, this time, that decision seemed to be intentional. For NotPetya victims, paying the ransom accomplished nothing. Even if the hackers wanted to decrypt files for a victim, they could not do so. It quickly became clear that, though the hackers disguised NotPetya as money-making ransomware, it was really a disruption operation, designed to erase vital files from a gigantic range of targets in a way that all could see.

The Damage Is Done

The global shipping business is like a giant game of *Tetris*. The flow of goods never ends. From shippers to ports to boats to trucks to customers, all the pieces have to fit together. Small problems left unaddressed can quickly compound.

Maersk is the world's largest shipper, with about 15 percent of the global market. The company employs thousands of logistics and finance experts, making sure its massive container ships get their cargoes where they need to go on time. One of these employees had installed MeDoc on a computer in Odessa, a Black Sea port city on the coast of Ukraine. When one of the compromised updates of MeDoc in 2017 landed on this computer, it became a beachhead for NotPetya. From there, NotPetya expanded throughout Maersk's worldwide network. Soon after the attack started on June 27, the firm's employees realized that something had gone very wrong. Before long, they were running down hallways and jumping over locked key card gates trying to disconnect as many computers as they could before the code dealt its blow. Within two hours, the entirety of Maersk's global network was either destroyed or disconnected.[10]

Everything ground to a halt. Shipping gates closed at seventeen of the company's seventy-six ports, from North America to Europe to Asia and beyond. Hundreds of eighteen-wheel tractor-trailers, many filled with perishable goods, lined up for miles outside these ports. Employees accustomed to tapping into a powerful corporate network that spanned the globe found themselves using WhatsApp on personal cell phones to communicate. Workers rushed into electronics stores to buy whatever new computers they had available.[11] A company used to sending a ship bearing twenty thousand containers into some port around the world every fifteen minutes was now facing a logistical nightmare—one that was, in the words of its chairman, "impossible to imagine."[12]

Recovery was hard and slow. The interconnectedness of Maersk's networks had enabled NotPetya to spread quickly. The attack had wiped out many key backups, especially of the critical domain controllers the company needed to function; the 150 controllers that managed the worldwide network continually synced with one another, and thus all had gone down together. Maersk employees called office after office, looking for intact copies of the controllers' proper configuration. Again and again, the answer was negative. It was only when the employees called the office in Ghana that they discovered a lucky break: a power outage had taken a single controller offline before the attack, disconnecting it from the company's network and sparing it from NotPetya's blow. The vital data had survived.

Because it would take days to upload the lone backup through Ghana's low-bandwidth connections, Maersk employees had to come up with a different plan. Their office workers in Ghana did not have visas to visit the United Kingdom, the headquarters of the recovery effort. Instead, an employee from Ghana took a hard drive with the backup to Nigeria, where another employee picked it up. That employee then flew from Nigeria to London. It was a twenty-first century echo of the famous 1925 sled dog expedition to deliver anti-diphtheria serum to Nome, Alaska.

Maersk estimated the direct cost to the company at between $250 million and $300 million in just one fiscal quarter, though some media reports suggested that these were low-balled numbers. The company had to reinstall or replace its entire computing infrastructure: four thousand servers, forty-five thousand computers, and twenty-five hundred applications. In some cases, it took three months to disentangle the logistical mess and find containers.[13] Customers took their business elsewhere. Maersk paid millions of dollars to other shippers who moved critical goods for the company during the attack. Afterwards, Maersk spent millions more on improved cybersecurity. As a result of these expenses and losses, the firm reduced its profit forecasts for 2017 and cited NotPetya as one of the reasons its stock price fell.[14]

Maersk was not the only shipping company in the line of fire. FedEx, one of the world's major package delivery companies, also took heavy losses. In 2016, the company had finalized its acquisition of TNT Express. At the time, TNT was an independent shipping company with a strong presence in European markets. The firm employed more than eighty thousand people who collectively handled more than a million deliveries per day.[15] The deal seemed like a boon for FedEx, especially since FedEx's main rival, UPS, had tried and failed to acquire TNT just four years before. No doubt, the promise of greater interconnection across a global logistics operation was alluring.

Unfortunately, one of the downsides of ever-tighter integration is the greater accumulation and expansion of risks. In such a united system, what once might have been a local issue confined to a small network can instead snowball into something more fearsome, crippling a global corporation. Corporate consolidation can also create unforeseen dangers, in which new subsidiaries specifically pose surprising problems. Indeed, FedEx had unwittingly assumed quite a significant cybersecurity risk by integrating TNT into its main technology functions in June 2017, one year after the acquisition.

TNT did business in Ukraine and thus used the MeDoc software the Russian hackers compromised. When the NotPetya code burned through TNT's network, it encrypted the firm's files, locking the data up without a key. TNT's incident responders raced to react. They activated contingency plans of all sorts to limit the damage. With computers not functioning, the company resorted to manually sorting packages.[16] FedEx estimated that the costs of recovery in just the six months following the attack amounted to $400 million. Although growth in other parts of the business softened the blow somewhat, this was a direct and substantial hit to the firm's bottom line.[17]

Maersk and FedEx were the two most visible victims, but far from the only ones. Merck, a major pharmaceutical company valued at more than $200 billion, lost fifteen thousand computers in the first ninety seconds after it was infected.[18] The company had to temporarily shut down its production of the Gardasil 9 vaccine, which is essential for guarding against the sexually transmitted disease HPV. The attack hit at a bad time, as demand for the Gardasil 9 vaccine turned out to be higher than previously forecast. As a result, Merck found itself borrowing reserve doses from the United States' stockpile at the Centers for Disease Control. Unable to replenish the government reserves quickly, it struggled with a shortfall into 2018. That a cyber attack could do such damage to pharmaceutical production was unprecedented. The company later estimated the total damage at more than $670 million.[19]

NotPetya's attack code slithered into hundreds of thousands of computers in corporate networks all over the world. The erratic way in which the code spread itself intersected with the wide variety of corporate network configurations. The unfolding damage was not only extensive but unpredictable; one only had to be doing business in Ukraine and to be in the wrong place at the wrong time. A wide variety of other global firms experienced losses of hundreds of millions of dollars, with some losing all their Windows computers and having to start from scratch. The attack directly interfered with their businesses, from construction to healthcare to manufacturing and beyond.[20]

Despite NotPetya's global consequences, Ukraine was clearly the central target. MeDoc had approximately four hundred thousand customers in the country, including the vast majority of domestic businesses. More than one million Ukrainian computers ran its software. With the compromise of the MeDoc update channel, each machine permitted a modern-day Trojan horse onto its hard drive. Every new infection was both a victim of attack and a vector for further propagation of the NotPetya code throughout its network and beyond.

The damage cascaded across Ukrainian society. One estimate indicated that NotPetya struck more than three hundred major organizations in the country, affecting 10 percent of Ukraine's computers. The National Bank of Ukraine reported that it was having difficulty with customer service and banking operations. The second largest-bank, Oschadbank, lost about 90 percent of its computers to the attack. At least twenty other banks were affected, too. In one city after the next, ATMs displayed NotPetya's fake ransomware messages. Four hospitals in Kiev found themselves in the digital line of fire. Other medical clinics shut down or chose to turn off their computers, forcing some doctors back to paper-and-pen recordkeeping.

The attack affected nearly every federal government agency in Ukraine. Many ministries, including critical ones responsible for healthcare, disconnected themselves from the internet and from society in a desperate attempt to avoid the digital blast. Other offices weren't so lucky; the post office, which in Ukraine also handles pension payments and financial transfers, tried to disconnect itself but lost 70 percent of its computers before it could act. Airport information boards ceased functioning and, on the metro in Kiev, customers found themselves unable to pay. Just under sixty miles away, at the site of the 1986 Chernobyl nuclear meltdown, workers switched to manual radiation-monitoring systems as loudspeakers urgently instructed employees to disconnect and turn off their computers. The Ukrainian minister of infrastructure later summed it up bluntly: "The government was dead."[21]

For American policymakers, however, the most significant harm might not have been damage to computer systems. The use of the NSA's leaked tools forced the agency back into uncomfortable public scrutiny. It reignited many of the concerns about operational security raised by the Shadow Brokers and increased calls for additional restraints on the NSA's activities. Even agency allies recognized the risk that attacks like NotPetya posed and the role that leaked tools played in enabling it. Michael Hayden, a former director of the NSA, said this of his own former charges: "If they cannot protect the tools, I just can't mount the argument to defend that they should have them. This is the one that, unless resolved, I think actually could constitute a legitimate argument to do less."[22]

An Unanswered Blow

NotPetya was the most destructive cyber attack in history. The fact that NotPetya's damage was so far-reaching highlights a reality that seems only to grow: ordinary people and businesses cannot escape geopolitically motivated cyber operations. With worms, it is easy to extend attacks and hard to contain them, and countries like Russia do not bother trying to limit the damage. The distinction between targets and collateral damage fades away when everyone is seen as an acceptable victim. Even if the damage is unpredictable and erratic, the mission's objective is still achieved. The GRU did not need to know its targets in advance to have success, at least as the agency defined it.[23]

Of all the cyber attacks to date, NotPetya seemed most poised to burst out of the gray zone between peace and war in which so many cyber operations reside, and spark some kind of escalation. But it did not. Ukraine, used to suffering Russian aggression, took the attack in stride as best it could. Its government pinned the blame on the Kremlin, then set about working to remediate the damage and bring services back online. NATO announced it was sending additional aid to Ukraine, but otherwise did little to deter or punish Russia. For all of 2017, the United States and other major states aired little evidence publicly about the source of the attack, and made no indication that they planned to respond. The Russian government, as always, disclaimed any role in the operation, though few believed its thin denials.

Against this backdrop of comparative silence, it was not even clear how to interpret NotPetya's widespread disruption. Some cybersecurity experts suggested it was a cleanup effort designed to wipe away evidence of other Russian cyber operations. Perhaps it had gotten out of control. Others thought it was a warning. "Anyone who thinks this was accidental is engaged in wishful thinking," said Cisco's Craig Williams, the researcher who had studied the code in depth. "This was a piece of malware designed to send a political message: If you do business in Ukraine, bad things are going to happen to you."[24]

If NotPetya was a warning, it is worth parsing exactly what kind of warning it was. It was not so much a signal to the Ukrainian government or the United States government, but rather a message to business leaders all over the world. In this sense, it was an attempt to shape the economic environment, making Ukraine less palatable as a place for foreign investment. The attack likely did not reveal anything new to Ukrainian policymakers, who were quite familiar with Russia's animosity, and indeed were engaged in a bloody war.

Crucially, NotPetya lacked the kind of calibration that good international signals require. Had certain unanticipated factors been different, the damage could have been so much greater; for example, had Maersk's office in Ghana not had its power outage, the damage borne by the firm likely would have been much higher. On the other hand, the damage could also have been so much less. For example, if Maersk's global domain controllers did not sync with one another in a way that let NotPetya wreak global havoc on the firm's networks, the company would have suffered only a glancing blow. The hackers likely did not know how Maersk had configured its system—it seems they did not spend much time doing reconnaissance on it—so these outcomes may have resulted in large part from luck.

For as overtly destructive as it was, NotPetya also lacked clarity. An after-action investigation revealed that, in some target networks, the hackers had placed a peculiar file on up to 10 percent of the computers. This file served as a vaccine of sorts, instructing the NotPetya attack code not to target those particular machines. The motivation behind this vaccine is deeply ambiguous. It may have been meant to soften the blow and implicitly serve as a threat that the attackers could return. More likely, in the eyes of technical investigators, the spared computers served as a way for the hackers to maintain access to the target networks, ensuring that they would not have to hack their way in again later.[25]

Fundamentally, the haphazard and volatile nature of an operation like NotPetya reduces its value in calibrated signaling. With the unpredictability of signals like this, it is hard to know in advance what the effects will be and thus what message will be sent. History offers a striking parallel: inaccuracy in early aerial bombing campaigns during World War II often caused unwanted escalation since the raids could not be targeted well and caused variable and unpredictable amounts of damage.[26] Like these early air raids, indiscriminate disruption operations are powerful but blunt instruments.

It was not until February 2018, more than seven months after the attack, that the Trump administration finally came up with a response. In a display of press releases coordinated with allies like Great Britain, the White House confirmed what the intelligence community had long known: Russia was responsible for the operation. The Trump administration promised that the Russian attack, which it called "reckless and indiscriminate," would "be met with international consequences."[27] One month later, the administration announced new sanctions on Russia, though most of those seemed to have little to do with NotPetya.[28]

As a result, the most significant American retaliation for NotPetya was exposure, calling out the Russians for what they did. For some actors, this kind of exposure is indeed a serious cost. The NSA and its partners have for decades taken great pains to elude detection and establish plausible deniability. This desire to stay hidden was, in part, what made the Shadow Brokers' leaks so damaging. Some actors, once caught, have quickly destroyed their own infrastructure, erasing whatever tracks they could and giving up the operation rather than risking further scrutiny.[29] In general, hackers from democratic governments seem to fear exposure the most.

To other hackers, exposure means much less. Especially for those oriented toward flash-fried attacks rather than slow-cooking espionage, the threat of public revelation is not much of a concern. Russia in particular seems to be content with its own implausible deniability, and other authoritarian hackers appear not to feel any bite from public exposure and international condemnation. In addition to Russian hackers, the United States has indicted Chinese, Iranian, and North Korean hackers on various occasions since 2014 and levied sanctions at other times. These indictments offered significant evidence that the foreign governments had authorized or carried out a wide range of activities, from economic espionage to probing American critical infrastructure to launching major cyber attacks.[30] Yet none of those states appear to have much diminished their overall cyber operations in response. If anything, they seem to be doing more, not less.[31]

The Trump administration may have thought that, in condemning NotPetya, it was reasserting a boundary of acceptable cyber operations. It may have thought that coordinating the press releases with other allies created more international pressure on the Kremlin. Yet, absent any real force, the words and limited sanctions seem misguided and empty. No other consequences have materialized. The world's most destructive cyber attack has gone largely unanswered.

Conclusion

THREE REPEATEDLY OBSERVED CHARACTERISTICS of hacking animate this book: its versatility as a tool of geopolitical shaping, its weakness as a means of geopolitical signaling, and its ambition, which has become increasingly aggressive as modern cyber operations grow in capability.

The cases in this book demonstrate the flexibility of hacking. Some of these, like Stuxnet and the 2016 election interference, are high-profile and have attracted enormous attention. Others, such as those oriented toward passive collection and counterintelligence, have not. Taken together, the multiplicity of operational objectives illustrates the range of what hackers can do. The chapters have shown how states have relied on cyber operations time after time to gain advantages over other states by spying, attacking, and destabilizing. Hacking has earned its place in the playbook of statecraft.

There is potential for cyber operations to expand still further as tools of shaping. Most provocatively, hacking may be of direct use in joint operations with conventional military capabilities. Though this possibility has long been discussed, there is not nearly enough evidence on which to evaluate it. As mentioned, cyber attacks against Georgia in 2008 appear to have worked alongside traditional Russian military operations, but it is hard to know their effects.[1] With much of the work of United States Cyber Command and military units like Joint Special Operations Command's "Task Force Orange" mostly out of view, it remains difficult to judge the degree to which states have successfully integrated hacking into their traditional military campaigns.[2]

For as much as these chapters highlight what is different between cases, they also underscore their common elements. In important respects, much of the process of hacking is conceptually similar from operation to operation: performing reconnaissance on a target, developing malicious code to exploit a vulnerability, making entry to the target network, establishing command and control, moving laterally within the target network, deploying additional tools, and monitoring effects. By tracing these operational similarities through various incident narratives and geopolitical contexts, this book aims to make them more recognizable and more widely understood.[3]

Signaling and Shaping Revisited

But, as this book has shown, the cyber operations that achieve such a broad range of objectives often fail at one important task: signaling. Cyber capabilities are ill-suited for communicating with other states to encourage or discourage future behavior. In this way, they depart from their predecessors, like conventional military arms and nuclear weapons. States sometimes try to signal with cyber operations, but usually fail. The rhetoric around topics like cyber deterrence can sometimes outrun the reality, which is that cyber capabilities rarely offer clear, credible, or calibrated means of signaling and coercion. There are four reasons for this.

First, visibility enhances signaling, but cyber capabilities often benefit from or require secrecy. For decades, canonical international relations scholarship and policymaking has focused on those activities that all can see. Presidential summits and international diplomacy are fixtures in the minds of scholars and the public. Widely examined cases such as the Cuban Missile Crisis center on the capacity of leaders to walk up to—and then back from—the geopolitical brink in a way that shows resolve, benefits their own interests, and ultimately averts a war. For decades, this has been the art of modern statecraft.

Conventional military activities are often far more oriented toward visible signaling than toward direct combat. There is a repertoire of American military action that is effective because it is visible but does not directly harm an adversary. This includes activities like force mobilizations, joint exercises with regional allies, freedom of navigation patrols, and overt weapons development. When United States policymakers want to signal commitment to their near-peer counterparts in China and Russia, these are most often the approaches on which they rely. They are also the subjects that receive a great deal of scholarly attention.

Crucially, when these conventional military signals are sent, the underlying capabilities become more useful, not less. Joint exercises enhance operational abilities. Mobilizing forces places them in a better position to attack. Building more and better weapons increases a state's overall power projection capability. Preparing credible threats makes it easier to deliver on them when required. Signaling thus makes the use of force more credible.

By contrast, many cyber operations can't meet their goals—such as passive collection, surreptitious decryption, source code manipulation, and counterintelligence—if the operations come into view. Even in some acts of sabotage, such as Stuxnet and Wiper, perpetrators have tried to remain invisible as long as possible to increase operational effectiveness. "If you know much about it, [cyber is] very easy to defend against," explained Michael Daniel, cybersecurity coordinator during the Obama administration, adding, "that's why we keep a lot of those capabilities very closely guarded."[4] As seen throughout this book, exposing particular hacking capabilities tends to render those capabilities much less useful, especially against well-secured targets. Shrouding cyber capabilities in secrecy is such a crucial principle that it underpinned the "Nobody But Us" philosophy of the NSA, whose edge partially eroded after the revelations of some collection efforts. Because revealing one's own hacking efforts to send a signal generally makes those tools less effective, savvy actors are unlikely to do it frequently.

In this respect, cyber operations are more akin to some less widely studied parts of the traditional military playbook: special operations and other forms of covert action. These efforts, which are often visible to the adversary, are effective because of their force, targeting, and timing. They have strategic effects, cumulatively and sometimes individually. The thousands of special operations raids that the United States conducted in Iraq, Afghanistan, Pakistan, and beyond show the power of direct shaping in the right circumstances; most obviously, they kill people who aim to harm the United States and they gather intelligence on terrorist cells. Yet these missions, carried out by separate elite units, are not seen as part of mainline military activity, receive less scholarly attention, and sometimes have less oversight by Congress and other public bodies. They are relegated to the sidelines of statecraft as it is studied and commonly understood. So, too, are cyber operations.

The second reason cyber operations are poor for signaling is that they do not lend themselves to predictable and easily calibrated force. Conventional tools of statecraft are much better at inflicting carefully chosen amounts of harm. In his classic work on coercion, Thomas Schelling explained that the most effective way to compel a change in an adversary's behavior is to use a visible form of harm that can be carefully increased. For example, when the Truman administration needed allied France to withdraw from territory taken in the waning days of World War II, the United States forced France's hand by cutting off supplies, knowing how the cost to France of operating without support would steadily increase. Before long, the French backed down. This was masterful signaling, averting a crisis and a disastrous fight between allies.[5]

Contrast this with cyber operations, which, even as they become more public and powerful, are poorly suited for communicating well-defined "latent violence," or the possibility of more harm to come. For example, many cyber attacks lack control over how much damage they do. The attacks on Sands Casino and Operation Ababil likely did less damage than the hackers anticipated, as did perhaps CRASH-OVERRIDE. WannaCry probably did more than anticipated.

NotPetya was completely unpredictable. It was a poorly targeted attack lobbed in the general direction of an adversary, designed to inflict damage on whoever happened to be in the wrong digital place at the wrong time, with uncertain consequences. Had major companies set up their information technology differently, the cost of Not-Petya might have been an order of magnitude less; had some companies been less lucky, things could have turned out much worse. While many cyber operations are more precise, in general it is hard to signal when the operational effects cannot be anticipated and ratcheted up over time.

In addition, defenders can interfere with the hackers' ability to escalate, which also reduces capacity to threaten latent harm. Usually, as seen in several cases discussed in this book, defenders can take targeted systems offline once they realize an attack is underway or imminent, though not all systems can be quickly disconnected or disabled. Notably, this does not apply to any operation that inflicts harm by leaking already-acquired documents.

Third, even visible and controllable cyber operations are much harder to interpret than conventional tools of statecraft. Robert Jervis argued that, even with conventional weapons, it is always easier to send signals than it is to interpret them, since policymakers assume that the nuances in their signals will be apparent to their counterparts.[6] That said, some signals are more interpretable than others. It is readily apparent what message the United States sends when it mobilizes an aircraft carrier battle group; decision-makers on the receiving end of the signal understand and fear the displayed readiness to attack. The deployment of thousands of American soldiers to the European continent during the Cold War is similarly obvious in meaning. As noted in the Introduction, these troops might not be capable of repelling a Soviet invasion, but they could die trying. Every Soviet leader knew that the death of thousands of Americans would precipitate war. There was little ambiguity.

Most cyber operations, however, are on the other end of the spectrum of interpretability. At least based on public information, there is still debate about whether the blackouts in Ukraine were a test or a demonstration or something else. No clear evidence provides an answer to why those attackers did not do as much damage as they could, or if they tried to do more and failed. Likewise, the case of the Shadow Brokers remains a mystery on many levels, starting with the identity of its perpetrators. The saga is rife with nuance and complexity, so much so that it is hard to unpack the underlying meaning.

Even in less complex cases, the fact that most policymakers and scholars do not understand the basics of how cyber operations work makes this task of interpretation much more difficult. For example, the more automated nature of the 2016 blackout in Ukraine might be plausibly seen as a threat to the United States, which uses similar systems in its electrical grid, but the manually orchestrated 2015 blackout cannot be seen as a threat in the same way. The attacks had similar effects but interpreting them correctly requires an understanding that most policymakers and scholars do not have of malicious code.

The fourth point is related: effective signaling requires not just communication but also credible commitment; to have meaning, a threat cannot be perceived as hollow. Conventional tools of statecraft show commitment easily, and have for millennia. The Greek soldier and historian Xenophon argued that deliberately boxing one's own army in a corner increased its chances of victory, in part because it signaled to the enemy that, with no retreat possible, the army would keep fighting, no matter how sustained the assault. "We may bless the ground that teaches us that except in victory we have no deliverance," he wrote.[7] This kind of demonstrated commitment is hard to muster in cyber operations that risk no lives, have unclear paths of escalation, frequently offer no clear last chance to avert conflict, and often become less effective when their preparations are made public.

The Expanding Art of the Possible

In lieu of much effective signaling, states have found it better to use their cyber capabilities to grapple with one another for advantage.

This book's narrative spans several decades of cyber operations. This history demonstrates an important pattern: the harm that hackers can do is expanding faster than the deterrence or defenses against them. For years, increasingly aggressive activities have in many cases gone unblocked and unmet by meaningful retaliation.

Intelligence agencies pioneered cyber espionage operations many years ago. They poked around adversaries' and even allies' computer networks in secret and tapped in as data transited fiber-optic cables. These agencies, and their military partners, eventually added a parallel track of targeted attack, using the same illicit access to foreign networks to destroy and manipulate information, not just gather intelligence. Eventually, this also expanded, adding a category of operations, including widespread disruptions like NotPetya, meant to destabilize broad swaths of a targeted society. At each turn, despite protestations and a few attempts to impose consequences, the scope of cyber operations grew mostly unchecked.

Within each of these three categories—espionage, attack, and destabilization—operations continue to become more powerful and more scalable. For espionage purposes, the Chinese have hacked military targets, valuable but obscure offices in the United States, key parts of the computing supply chain, major cloud service providers with gigantic amounts of data, and many other targets.[8] The success of companies like Huawei in manufacturing, building, and repairing undersea cables and new 5G telecommunications infrastructure raises fears that the Chinese government may try to match the advantages in passive collection that the Five Eyes enjoy, according to statements of former government officials and leaked documents.[9]

Russian agencies have likewise continued to expand their cyber espionage repertoire. They have penetrated American critical infrastructure companies, government agencies, and political institutions like the Democratic National Committee.[10] In 2019, Russian cryptographers submitted a proposed international encryption standard that contained flaws. Although they said the flaws were inadvertent, many other cryptographers doubt this claim, ever mindful of the Dual_EC backdoor that showed up in Juniper and RSA's products.[11]

Cyber attacks continue to grow in prominence, too. The United States announced with great fanfare in 2016 that it was launching a cyber campaign against the Islamic State. Senior defense officials, inclined to talk about cyber capabilities using comfortable analogies, bragged about dropping "cyberbombs" on jihadist targets.[12] The mixed results of the effort did nothing to abate the interest of major states in developing and deploying offensive hacking tools.[13] Iran has continued to launch cyber attacks against regional adversaries. China turned its Great Firewall into a tool of attack to take down an American website posting censored content.[14]

For its part, Russia has continued to be aggressive in its attacks, as well, apparently undertaking a major cyber operation against the 2018 Winter Olympics in South Korea that was mostly thwarted by strong cyber defenses.[15] More alarmingly, it appears that hackers from a Russian chemical lab were involved in a very sophisticated effort to disable safety mechanisms at a petrochemical plant in Saudi Arabia, which could have caused a massive explosion. Cybersecurity defenses prevented the attack, but analysts discovered that the malicious code's capabilities exceeded previous operations. Recalling Stuxnet and the 2016 blackout in Ukraine, the Department of Homeland Security warned that it "surpass[ed] both forerunners with the ability to directly interact with, remotely control, and compromise a safety system—a nearly unprecedented feat."[16]

Destabilization missions also continue to expand. Social media companies struggle to combat the threat to their platforms; in just one quarter of 2019, Facebook removed more than two billion fake accounts. But many more remain online despite the company's efforts. Overall, the percentage of accounts on the platform that are fake has increased, not decreased, reaching a high in 2019 of 5 percent, according to the company's own estimates. A series of news reports and academic studies showed that fake Facebook accounts were directly engaged in political operations in elections all over the world, such as advocating for the Russian-supported far-right party in Germany.[17] Russian operatives continue trying to buy ads on the platform, including to interfere in American elections, while Chinese operatives attempt to manipulate the political process in Hong Kong.[18]

Hack-and-leak operations are alive and well, too. In 2017 and 2018, Russian operatives conducted a series of influence campaigns, with mixed effectiveness, aimed at organizations they considered harmful to Russian interests. Their targets included the World Anti-Doping Agency, which had revealed Russian cheating in the Olympics; the Organization for the Prohibition of Chemical Weapons, which had examined Russia's poisoning of a former spy; and the investigation into Malaysia Airlines Flight 17, which Russian forces had shot down in Ukraine.[19] A network of outlets, including social media accounts and state propaganda platforms such as Sputnik, stand ready to push the Russian message.[20]

Iran and its supporters have used disinformation for their own purposes, too. Researchers found sprawling campaigns that relied on hundreds of fake accounts on Facebook and Twitter. These campaigns aimed to mislead individuals all over the world. One effort aimed to sow division in the United States, Saudi Arabia, and Israel. It included well-constructed fake news articles that revealed a sophisticated understanding of online media and politics in the targeted countries. Perhaps most impressively, the Iranian operators watched carefully for signs that online commenters had discovered that a given article was fake; if this happened, they deleted that content and replaced it with a legitimate news article, sowing confusion among readers and making it harder for investigators to follow their tracks.[21]

Iran also seems to be the victim of an exposure campaign. In 2019, an unknown perpetrator revealed secret information about Iranian hacking operations. The group posted Iranian hacking tools, in much the same way that the Shadow Brokers revealed American cyber capabilities. Furthermore, it revealed evidence of Iran's penetration of dozens of organizations all over the world, showed the digital infrastructure from which the Iranian intelligence agencies carried out their operations, and exposed identities and photographs of the Iranian hackers.[22] More overtly, United States Cyber Command also began sharing intelligence on Iranian capabilities.[23] This multifaceted exposure no doubt harmed Iran's operational capability.

A group called Intrusion Truth has similarly exposed Chinese hackers. The group's members remain anonymous, but in a series of reports beginning in 2017, they revealed a great deal about the organization, capability, and identity of Chinese hackers. In so doing, they disclosed more information than even private-sector cybersecurity analysts had access to. A statement issued by the group makes clear that the motivation for this exposure is to interfere with Chinese cyber espionage operations: "We are directly challenging this illegal and unfair activity by exposing those responsible, naming the hackers themselves and identifying the agencies that hide behind them."[24] The case shows the continued expansion of cyber operations and the continued overlap with information operations.

More generally, cyber capabilities have also expanded from great powers to smaller states. The United Arab Emirates and Qatar seem to have engaged in tit-for-tat hack-and-leak operations for several years, part of an increasing trend of leaked and forged documents globally.[25] Various authoritarian regimes have woken up to how cyber operations can suppress dissent at home and abroad, and generally serve as tools of repression. Saudi Arabia has hacked critics of the kingdom around the world, including the journalist Jamal Khashoggi, who was later brutally murdered by agents of the Saudi Arabian government.[26] Western and Israeli firms, many staffed by former government hackers, sell tools and services to these countries with abandon, rapidly increasing the number of states with mid-tier but effective cyber capabilities at their disposal.[27] Sometimes these tools leave the realm of national security in service of other missions; in 2017, cybersecurity researchers showed that hackers had carried out a campaign against supporters of an initiative to tax soft drinks in Mexico.[28]

These are operations that have only recently come to light, and their full stories cannot yet be told. No doubt, journalists and analysts (and perhaps other hackers) will find and reveal more information about them as time goes on. It is certain that there are even more operations happening now that no one has yet uncovered in public. The expansion of cyber operations shows no sign of stopping.

This expansion continues largely unchecked because states define the contours of acceptability. They decide what is a cause for conflict and escalation and what, like NotPetya, merits sternly worded statements months later. Thus far, most states seem to be content to hack each other in their endless struggle for advantage. The United States, perhaps in response to the growing ferocity of modern cyber operations and the continued erosion of Nobody But Us capabilities, has begun to express a more forceful stance. In 2018,

Cyber Command announced a shift to a more aggressive approach and received new authorities to more routinely conduct clandestine military cyber operations.[29]

The new strategy seeks what the Command calls "persistent engagement," as part of a daily "agreed competition" with other states.[30] The director of the NSA and commander of Cyber Command, Paul Nakasone, notes that adversaries act similarly below the threshold of war, "gaining strategic advantage through competition without triggering armed conflict."[31] Other American officials, including former White House officials, likewise hint at the possibility of American attacks on adversaries' critical infrastructure, saying, "we don't want to take any options for ourselves off the table."[32]

The strategy of persistent engagement and the normalization of powerful cyber attacks offer notable contrast to the era when policymakers and pundits feared catastrophic cyber war and treated every incident with alarm. For instance, in one of the earliest examples of public state-sponsored espionage—an effort called Moonlight Maze—Russian hackers penetrated a range of unclassified American networks and stole gigabytes of information. In 1999, in a secret session in the midst of the operation, Deputy Secretary of Defense John Hamre put it bluntly to Congress: "We're in the middle of a cyber war."[33] In hindsight, Moonlight Maze pales in comparison to every case discussed in this book.

The scale of operations today is orders of magnitude greater than what occurred just two decades ago. Former NSA Deputy Director Chris Inglis has alleged that the Russians control two hundred thousand pieces of malicious code in American critical infrastructure, and the United States no doubt has its own surreptitious presence in adversary networks all over the world, too. Yet, as in every other case in this book, policymakers on all sides have chosen to regard these operations not as acts of war or even public crises, but rather as parts of the everyday digital melee.[34]

In this sense, the current framework of persistent engagement might be misunderstood as under-hyping cyber operations; if something is daily, it is by definition not exceptional. But to dismiss cyber operations as less important because they occur every day and do not cross the threshold of war is to miss the point. This book shows how, again and again, hacking makes a difference in geopolitics. The crescendo of cases illustrates how hackers achieve missions that are ever more varied, and develop capabilities that are ever more powerful— motivated by the prospect of geopolitical advantage for their states and largely uninhibited by norms, treaties, or fear of retaliation.

One thing is certain: in states' conflict of interests, wills, and worldviews, they will continue to hack one another. They will build and deploy computer code that spies, attacks, and destabilizes. This is one key part of what Kennan's "perpetual rhythm of struggle" looks like in the digital age. All major powers seem unwilling or unable to stop it. To the contrary, they embrace it. Unfettered and undeterred, their hackers reshape the world.

Notes

INTRODUCTION

1. The tweets and original message have since been deleted but can be accessed via internet archives; this is true for many of the internet postings cited in this Introduction and in Chapter 11. "The Shadow Brokers Twitter History," https://swithak.github.io/SH20TAATSB18 /Archive/Tweets/TSB/TSBTwitterHistory/; theshadowbrokers, "Equation Group Cyber Weapons Auction—Invitation," *Pastebin*, August 13, 2016, archived at https://swithak.github.io /SH20TAATSB18/Archive/Pastebin/JBcipKBL/.

2. Ellen Nakashima and Craig Timberg, "NSA Officials Worried about the Day Its Potent Hacking Tool Would Get Loose. Then It Did," *Washington Post*, May 16, 2017.

3. Shane Harris, Gordon Lubold, and Paul Sonne, "How Kaspersky's Software Fell Under Suspicion of Spying on America," *Wall Street Journal*, January 5, 2018.

4. Fred Kaplan, *Dark Territory: The Secret History of Cyber War* (New York: Simon and Schuster, 2016), 2.

5. The limited scholarship that exists on the potential to signal with covert operations suggests that such signaling is much more complex and requires confidence that the signals will be interpreted as intended—a confidence that, as this book will show, is more misplaced in cyber

operations than in some other covert activities, such as secret foreign aid. Austin Carson and Keren Yarhi-Milo, "Covert Communication: The Intelligibility and Credibility of Signaling in Secret," *Security Studies* 26, no. 1 (2017): 124–156.

6. For examples of this vast signaling-centric literature, see James D. Fearon, "Signaling Foreign Policy Interests: Tying Hands versus Sinking Costs," *Journal of Conflict Resolution* 41, no. 1 (1997): 68–90; Andrew Kydd, "Trust, Reassurance, and Cooperation," *International Organization* 54, no. 2 (2000): 325–357; Scott D. Sagan and Jeremi Suri, "The Madman Nuclear Alert: Secrecy, Signaling, and Safety in October 1969," *International Security* 27, no. 4 (2003): 150–183.

7. Thomas Schelling, *Arms and Influence* (New Haven: Yale University Press, 1966), 47.

8. For example, see John Lewis Gaddis, *Strategies of Containment: A Critical Appraisal of American National Security Policy during the Cold War* (Oxford: Oxford University Press, 2005); Margaret MacMillan, *Paris 1919: Six Months That Changed the World* (New York: Random House, 2007); Michael J. Hogan, *The Marshall Plan: America, Britain and the Reconstruction of Western Europe, 1947–1952* (Cambridge: Cambridge University Press, 1987). For discussion of the "nuclear revolution" leading to a focus on signaling-heavy scholarship, see Robert Jervis, *The Meaning of the Nuclear Revolution* (Ithaca, NY: Cornell University Press, 1989).

9. George Kennan, "The Inauguration of Organized Political Warfare [redacted version]" April 30, 1948, Wilson Center Digital Archive, https://digitalarchive.wilsoncenter.org/document/114320.

10. For one study of this strategy, funded by the US Department of Defense, see Roger Beaumont, "Maskirovka: Soviet Camouflage, Concealment and Deception," Stratech Study Series No. SS82-1, Center for Strategic Technology, Texas A&M University, College Station, TX, November 1982.

11. For an excellent summary of this deception operation, see James H. Hansen, "Soviet Deception in the Cuban Missile Crisis," *CIA: Studies in Intelligence* 46, no. 1 (2002): 49–58. For more on how news of the missiles' presence was dismissed by agency senior leaders, see Sean D. Naylor, "Operation Cobra: The Untold Story of How a CIA Officer

Trained a Network of Agents Who Found the Soviet Missiles in Cuba," *Yahoo News*, January 23, 2019.

12. Gus W. Weiss, "The Farewell Dossier: Duping the Soviets," *CIA: Studies in Intelligence* 39, no. 5 (1996). Deception certainly cut the other way, too. It was not until after the Cold War ended that the United States realized that two members of its intelligence community, Robert Hanssen and Aldrich Ames, had independently sold reams of classified information to the Soviets, including information on which Soviet officers were American spies.

13. One person who did get this distinction right early on is Thomas Rid. His seminal book focuses on how cyber capabilities are an extension of spying, sabotage, and subversion. Thomas Rid, *Cyber War Will Not Take Place* (Oxford: Oxford University Press, 2013). Another scholar who identified key facets of the cyber domain early was Richard Harknett. See Richard J. Harknett and James A. Stever, "The New Policy World of Cybersecurity," *Public Administration Review* 71, no. 3 (2011): 455–460; Richard J. Harknett, John P. Callaghan, and Rudi Kauffman, "Leaving Deterrence Behind: War-Fighting and National Cybersecurity," *Journal of Homeland Security and Emergency Management* 7, no. 1 (2010); Richard J. Harknett and James A. Stever, "The Cybersecurity Triad: Government, Private Sector Partners, and the Engaged Cybersecurity Citizen," *Journal of Homeland Security and Emergency Management* 6, no. 1 (2009); Richard J. Harknett, "The Risks of a Networked Military," *Orbis* 44, no. 1 (2000): 127–143; Richard J. Harknett, "Information Warfare and Deterrence," *Parameters* 26, no. 3 (1996): 93–107.

14. Former NSA and CIA Director Michael Hayden wrote, "[T]hese weapons are not well understood by the kind of people who get to sit in on meetings in the West Wing . . . . I recall one cyber op, while I was in government, that went awry . . . . In the after-action review it was clear that no two seniors at the final approval session had left the Situation Room thinking they had approved the same operation." Michael Hayden, *Playing to the Edge: American Intelligence in the Age of Terror* (New York: Penguin, 2017), 147.

15. For some notable acknowledgment of related points, see Michael P. Fischerkeller and Richard J. Harknett, "Persistent Engagement and

Tacit Bargaining: A Path toward Constructing Norms in Cyberspace," *Lawfare* blog, November 9, 2018.

16. Many of these sources are imperfect. Despite generally being very informative, some of the slides leaked by NSA contractor Edward Snowden lack context and do not present an entirely accurate picture of what the agency does. Other files may be out of date in the fast-moving environment of cyber operations.

1. EXPLOITING HOME-FIELD ADVANTAGE

1. Neil MacFarquhar, "U.N. Approves New Sanctions to Deter Iran," *New York Times*, June 9, 2010.

2. The leaked slides referenced here redact the mention of China and Russia. There is no doubt, however, that the United States conducts espionage operations against those countries. Glenn Greenwald / MacMillan, "Documents from *No Place to Hide*," [Snowden NSA archive], May 14, 2014, PDF pages 56–57.

3. MacFarquhar, "U.N. Approves New Sanctions to Deter Iran."

4. Greenwald / MacMillan, "Documents from *No Place to Hide*," 56–57.

5. Glenn Greenwald and Ewen MacAskill, "NSA Prism Program Taps in to User Data of Apple, Google, and Others," *Guardian*, June 6, 2013.

6. Peter Koop, "What Is Known about NSA's PRISM Program," *Electrospaces* blog, April 23, 2014.

7. To disguise their cable-tapping operation even from the Americans, the British obtained another copy of the telegram from a Mexican source. For a good discussion of the case and its implications, see Christopher Andrew, *For the President's Eyes Only: Secret Intelligence and the American Presidency from Washington to Bush* (New York: Harper Perennial, 1996), ch. 2.

8. "Access: The Vision," Government Communications Headquarters, July 2010, posted by *The Intercept*, September 25, 2015, https:// theintercept.com/document/2015/09/25/access-vision-2013/.

9. Adam Satariano, "How the Internet Travels across Oceans," *New York Times*, March 10, 2019.

10. Jordan Holland, Jared Smith, and Max Schuchard, "Measuring Irregular Geographic Exposure on the Internet," Cornell University arXiv digital archive, arXiv:1904.09375v2 [cs.NI] rev. May 31, 2019.

11. Ryan Gallagher and Henrik Moltke, "TITANPOINTE: The NSA's Spy Hub in New York, Hidden in Plain Sight," *The Intercept*, November 16, 2016.

12. Gallagher and Moltke, "TITANPOINTE"; Sam Roberts, "The Secret behind a Mysterious Traffic Code? It's Made Up," *New York Times* City Room blog, July 15, 2013.

13. Gallagher and Moltke, "TITANPOINTE."

14. For more on Special Source Operations, see "SSO Corporate Portfolio Overview," National Security Agency presentation deck, n.d., published alongside Charles Savage, "Newly Disclosed N.S.A. Files Detail Partnerships with AT&T and Verizon," *New York Times*, August 15, 2015. Also see "Special Source Operations," National Security Agency, *Washington Post*, 2013, https://snowdenarchive.cjfe.org/greenstone /collect/snowden1/index/assoc/HASH5098.dir/doc.pdf.

15. Among other sources discussed below, see "SKIDROWE: Low Speed DNI Processing Solution Replacing WEALTHYCLUSTER2," National Security Agency, n.d. This presentation deck can be viewed via "SKID-ROWE Program," *The Intercept*, November 16, 2016, https:// theintercept.com/document/2016/11/16/skidrowe-program/. The UK's Government Communications Headquarters (GCHQ) also collects data from telecommunications sites in its territory. For reporting on this (albeit reporting that does not give as detailed discussion as it should of technical limitations on collection), see Ewen MacAskill, Julian Borger, Nick Hopkins, Nick Davies, and James Ball, "GCHQ Taps Fibre-Optic Cables for Secret Access to World's Communications," *Guardian*, June 21, 2013; and James Ball, "Leaked Memos Reveal GCHQ Efforts to Keep Mass Surveillance Secret," *Guardian*, October 25, 2013. For a partial listing of the cables to which GCHQ has access, see "Cables: Where We Are," UK Government Communications Headquarters, ca. 2012. This document was shared publicly in Frederick Obermaier, Henrik Moltke, Laura Poitras, and Jan Strozyk, "Snowden-Leaks: How Vodafone-Subsidiary Cable & Wireless Aided GCHQ's Spying Efforts," *Süddeutsche Zeitung International*, November 25, 2014.

16. Julia Angwin, Jeff Larson, Charlie Savage, James Risen, Henrik Moltke, and Laura Poitras, "NSA Spying Relies on AT&T's 'Extreme Willing-ness to Help,'" *ProPublica*, August 15, 2015.

17. Michelle Nichols, "United Nations Says It Will Contact United States over Spying Report," Reuters, August 26, 2013.

18. "2011 Acquisition Plan—Communications," United Nations Procurement Division, 2011, https://web.archive.org/web/20120108022955 /http:/www.un.org/depts/ptd/2011plan_coms.htm.

19. Greenwald / MacMillan, "Documents from *No Place to Hide*," 55.

20. "United Nations DNI Collection Enabled," National Security Agency, *ProPublica*, 2015, https://www.documentcloud.org/documents /2274328-sso-news-united-nations-dni-collection-enabled.html.

21. The NSA conducts surveillance on the internet backbone under at least three authorities: the Foreign Intelligence Surveillance Act, the FISA Amendments Act of 2008, and transit authority. Other documents on different parts of the collection program also refer to Executive Order 12333 as an authority, likely involving operations outside of the United States. "Report on the President's Surveillance Program," Interagency Offices of Inspector General, *New York Times*, 2015, https://assets .documentcloud.org/documents/2427921/savage-nyt-foia-stellarwind-ig-report.pdf. For an NSA classification guide on a related program, see "Classification Guide for WHIPGENIE," National Security Agency, *The Intercept*, 2014, https://snowdenarchive.cjfe.org/greenstone/collect /snowden1/index/assoc/HASHb285.dir/doc.pdf.

22. For general insight on an NSA tool to prioritize the collection of useful information, aptly named SCISSORS, see "SSO Collection Optimization," National Security Agency, *Washington Post*, 2013, https://snowdenarchive.cjfe.org/greenstone/collect/snowden1/index /assoc/HASHb720.dir/doc.pdf.

23. For more discussion of transit authority, see Peter Koop, "FAIRVIEW: Collecting Foreign Intelligence inside the US," *Electrospaces*, August 31, 2015; Peter Koop, "NSA's Legal Authorities," *Electrospaces*, September 30, 2015; "SSO Corporate Portfolio Overview," National Security Agency, 2015, https://snowdenarchive.cjfe.org/greenstone/collect /snowden1/index/assoc/HASH01a5/f29cea54.dir/doc.pdf.

24. "Special Source Operations Corporate Partner Access," National Security Agency, *ProPublica*, 2015, 21, https://www.documentcloud .org/documents/2275165-tssinfcorporateoverview.html.

25. This is sometimes also called network shaping. For more on the concept and a detailed example of how network shaping can be achieved

overseas, see "Network Shaping 101," National Security Agency, *The Intercept*, 2016, https://www.documentcloud.org/documents/2919677 -Network-Shaping-101.html.

26. Angwin et al., "NSA Spying Relies on AT&T's 'Extreme Willingness to Help.'" For an analysis of traffic shaping, see Sharon Goldberg, "Surveillance without Borders: The 'Traffic Shaping' Loophole and Why It Matters," Century Foundation, June 22, 2017.

27. "BRECKENRIDGE for STORMBREW Collection," *SSO Weekly* [internal National Security Agency newsletter], October 28, 2009. This document was posted by *ProPublica* in 2015 and can be viewed at https://www.documentcloud.org/documents/2274323-sso-news -breckenridge-for-stormbrew-collection.html. Also see the presentation deck "Cyber Threats and Special Source Operations," National Security Agency, March 22, 2013, accessible at https://www .documentcloud.org/documents/2274329-tssinfssooverviewforntoc25 march2013.html.

28. AT&T received twice as much money as Verizon, a sign of the tight ties between the company and the intelligence community. Craig Timberg and Barton Gellman, "NSA Paying U.S. Companies for Access to Communications Networks," *Washington Post*, August 29, 2013. Also see the NSA's own "Project Description" of the Special Source Operations Project at https://archive.org/details/pdfy-QKaJJLNUMq _dLGGE/page/n5. For context, see Barton Gellman and Ashkan Soltani, "NSA Surveillance Program Reaches 'Into the Past' to Retrieve, Replay Phone Calls," *Washington Post*, March 18, 2014.

29. Gallagher and Moltke, "TITANPOINTE."

30. James Ball, Luke Harding, and Juliette Garside, "BT and Vodafone among Telecoms Companies Passing Details to GCHQ," *Guardian*, August 2, 2013. Ryan Gallagher, "Vodafone-Linked Company Aided British Mass Surveillance," *The Intercept*, November 20, 2014.

31. For an early view on this discussion, see Jack Goldsmith and Tim Wu, *Who Controls the Internet? Illusions of a Borderless World* (New York: Oxford University Press, 2006).

32. After Snowden's revelations, the NSA said the threshold was not 51 percent, but offered no further information. "NSA's Implementation of Foreign Intelligence Surveillance Act Section 702," Office of Civil Liberties and Privacy, National Security Agency, April 16, 2014, 4;

Rachel Martin, "Ex-NSA Head Hayden: Surveillance Balances Security, Privacy," *NPR*, June 9, 2013.

33. The code-name has likely changed since it became public, but there is little doubt that the collection from internet companies continues.

34. The specific statistic and the reference to Indian targets comes from Shobhan Saxena, "NSA Targets Indian Politics, Space & N-Programmes," *The Hindu*, September 24, 2013. See the next note for more on these statistics generally and their analysis.

35. Most of the publicly-known information about PRISM comes from one leaked presentation deck. Various news providers published excerpts, but none published it in its entirety. The best assembly and analysis of the deck comes from Koop, "What Is Known about NSA's PRISM Program." Among the reported stories making the deck public, see Greenwald and MacAskill, "NSA Prism Program Taps in to User Data"; Barton Gellman and Laura Poitras, "U.S., British Intelligence Mining Data from Nine U.S. Internet Companies in Broad Secret Program," *Washington Post*, June 7, 2013; Jacques Follorou and Glenn Greenwald, "France in the NSA's Crosshair: Wanadoo and Alcatel Targeted," *Le Monde*, October 21, 2013.

36. James Bamford, "A Death in Athens," *The Intercept*, September 29, 2015; Vassilis Prevelakis and Diomidis Spinellis, "The Athens Affair," *IEEE Spectrum*, June 29, 2007.

37. Bamford, "A Death in Athens."

38. Quoted in Bamford, "A Death in Athens."

39. "FY 2013 Congressional Budget Justification: Vol. I: National Intelligence Program Summary: Special Source Access: Foreign Partner Access: Project Description," National Security Agency, February 2012. The document is available online via Anton Geist, Sebastian Gjerding, Henrik Moltke, and Laura Poitras, "NSA 'Third Party' Partners Tap the Internet Backbone in Global Surveillance Program," *Dagbladet Information*, June 19, 2014.

40. "DIR Opening Remarks Guidance for DP1," National Security Agency: Information, 2014. For further analysis of why Denmark is a likely participant, see Geist et al., "NSA 'Third Party' Partners Tap the Internet Backbone"; Greenwald / MacMillan, "Documents from *No Place to Hide*," 37–38.

41. "Visit Précis: Hr. Dietmar B——, Director SIGINT Analysis and Production," National Security Agency, April 30, 2013. This briefing on

the visit to the NSA of a high-ranking BND official was published online
by *Der Spiegel* in the context of its reporting. Spiegel Staff, "New NSA
Revelations: Inside Snowden's Germany File," *Der Spiegel,* June 18, 2014.

42. *Special Source Operations Weekly* [NSA internal newsletter], March 14,
2013, National Security Agency. This document was published online
by *Der Spiegel*, with Spiegel Staff, "Spying Together: Germany's Deep
Cooperation with the NSA," June 18, 2014.

43. [author name redacted], "Third Party Nations: Partners and Targets,"
Cryptologic Quarterly 7, no. 4 (1989): 15–22; "RAMPART-A Project
Overview," National Security Agency presentation deck from Oc-
tober 1, 2010, published online with Ryan Gallagher, "How Secret
Partners Expand NSA's Surveillance Dragnet," *The Intercept*, June 18,
2014, 3.

44. "RAMPART-A Project Overview," 12.

45. In a comment about specific agency operations, Edward Snowden said:
"An EU member state like Denmark may give the NSA access to a
tapping center on the (unenforceable) condition that NSA doesn't
search it for Danes, and Germany may give the NSA access to another
on the condition that it doesn't search for Germans. Yet the two tapping
sites may be two points on the same cable, so the NSA simply captures
the communications of the German citizens as they transit Denmark,
and the Danish citizens as they transit Germany, all the while considering it entirely in accordance with their agreements." Gallagher, "How
Secret Partners Expand NSA's Surveillance Dragnet."

46. "RAMPART-A Project Overview," 23; Gallagher, "How Secret Partners
Expand NSA's Surveillance Dragnet."

47. "Special Source Access: Foreign Partner Access: Project Description," 1.

48. Ryan Devereaux, Glenn Greenwald, and Laura Poitras, "Data Pirates of
the Caribbean: The NSA Is Recording Every Cell Phone Call in the
Bahamas," *The Intercept*, May 19, 2014.

49. Devereaux et al., "Data Pirates of the Caribbean"; "DEA-The 'Other'
Warfighter," National Security Agency, April 20, 2004, published online
as "SIDToday: DEA—The 'Other' Warfighter," *The Intercept*, May 19,
2014.

50. The NSA refers to this as "full content."

51. Devereaux et al., "Data Pirates of the Caribbean"; "MYSTIC: General
Information," National Security Agency, 2009, published online as

"MYSTIC," *The Intercept*, May 19, 2014; "SOMALGET," National Security Agency, May 2012. The latter, a memo written by an official in the NSA's International Crime and Narcotics division, was published online as "SOMALGET," *The Intercept*, May 19, 2014.

52. "COMSAT Background," Government Communications Headquarters, July 2, 2010, published online with Duncan Campbell, "My Life Unmasking British Eavesdroppers," *The Intercept*, August 3, 2015; "COMSAT Cyprus Technical Capability," Government Communications Headquarters, published online with Duncan Campbell, "My Life Unmasking British Eavesdroppers," *The Intercept*, August 3, 2015; Duncan Campbell, "GCHQ and Me," *The Intercept*, August 3, 2015; SIGINT Communications, "The State of Covert Collection: An Interview with SCS Leaders (Part 1)," *SIDToday,* National Security Agency, November 15, 2006, published online by *The Intercept*, May 29, 2019.

53. Unlike stories sourced from leaked documents, this one seems to have less public supporting evidence, hence the use of "apparently" in the text. The United States did not deny spying on Merkel, and it is likely that the activity occurred, though the claim of embassy-based espionage is not confirmed beyond this article. Jacob Appelbaum, Nikolaus Blome, Hubert Gude, Ralf Neukirch, Rene Pfister, Laura Poitras, and Marcel Rosenbach, "The NSA's Secret Spy Hub in Berlin," *Der Spiegel*, October 27, 2013.

54. For one example of an early station, see "Blast from the Past: YRS in the Beginning," *The Northwest Passage* [Yakima Research Station (YRS) newsletter] 2, no. 1 (2011); and "YRS Gears Up to Celebrate 40 Years," *The Northwest Passage* 3, no. 7 (2012). Both published online with Duncan Campbell, "My Life Unmasking British Eavesdroppers," *The Intercept*, August 3, 2015.

55. "Subject: NSA Intelligence Relationship with Saudi Arabia," National Security Agency information paper, April 8, 2013, published online with Glenn Greenwald and Murtaza Hussain, "The NSA's New Partner in Spying: Saudi Arabia's Brutal State Police," *The Intercept*, July 25, 2014.

56. Laura Poitras, Marcel Rosenbach, Fidelius Schmid, Holger Stark, and Johnathan Stock, "How the NSA Targets Germany and Europe," *Der*

Spiegel, July 1, 2013; Matthew M. Aid, "The CIA's New Black Bag Is Digital," *Foreign Policy*, July 17, 2013; Ewen MacAskill, Julian Borger, Nick Hopkins, Nick Davies, and James Ball, "Mastering the Internet: How GCHQ Set Out to Spy on the World Wide Web," *Guardian*, June 21, 2013.

57. Jacob Appelbaum, Laura Poitras, Marcel Rosenbach, Christian Stöcker, Jörg Schindler, and Holger Stark, "Inside TAO: Documents Reveal Top NSA Hacking Unit," *Der Spiegel*, December 20, 2013; "New Nuclear Sub Is Said to Have Special Eavesdropping Ability," Associated Press, February 20, 2005.

58. The program may be related to the UK's Government Communications Headquarters' efforts to tap cables in a similar area using sites on the coast of Oman. Duncan Campbell, "Revealed: GCHQ's Beyond Top Secret Middle Eastern Internet Spy Base," *The Register*, June 3, 2014.

59. Formally, the NSA refers to DANCINGOASIS as SIGAD US-3171, and the program appears on a chart showing overall collection outcomes. Glenn Greenwald made the chart public when he published *No Place to Hide: Edward Snowden, the NSA, and the US Surveillance State* (New York: Metropolitan Books, 2014), but the program is not discussed in the book, perhaps due to his agreement with Edward Snowden not to discuss programs related to military activities. Greenwald / MacMillan, "Documents from *No Place to Hide*," 79. For analysis, see Peter Koop, "NSA's Largest Cable Tapping Program: DANCINGOASIS," *Electrospaces*, June 7, 2015.

60. [Author redacted], "Utility of 'Security Conferences,'" posting on internal NSA discussion board, published as "I Hunt Sys Admins," alongside Ryan Gallagher and Peter Maass, "Inside the NSA's Secret Efforts to Hunt and Hack System Administrators," *The Intercept*, March 20, 2014, 2.

61. Ashkan Soltani, Andrea Peterson, and Barton Gellman, "NSA Uses Google Cookies to Pinpoint Targets for Hacking," *Washington Post*, December 10, 2013; "NSA Signal Surveillance Success Stories," *Washington Post*, December 10, 2013. The latter presents an excerpt from an April 2013 National Security Agency internal presentation.

62. "Tor Stinks," National Security Agency, internal presentation deck, June 2012, published as "'Tor Stinks' Presentation—Read the Full Document," *Guardian*, October 4, 2013.

63. "Mobile Apps Doubleheader: BADASS Angry Birds," Government Communications Headquarters internal presentation deck, n.d., published online alongside Jacob Appelbaum, Aaron Gibson, Claudio Guarnieri, Andy Müller-Maguhn, Laura Poitras, Marcel Rosenbach, Leif Ryge, Hilmar Schmundt, and Michael Sontheimer, "The Digital Arms Race: NSA Preps America for Future Battle," *Der Spiegel*, January 17, 2015.

64. "ICTR Cloud Efforts," Government Communications Headquarters presentation, July 2011, published online alongside Ryan Gallagher, "Profiled: From Radio to Porn, British Spies Track Web Users' Online Identities," *The Intercept*, September 25, 2015; "Pull-Through Steering Group Meeting #16," Government Communications Headquarters internal memorandum, February 29, 2008, published online alongside Ryan Gallagher, "Profiled." For other relevant tools, see the same article's links to "BLAZING SADDLES," "ICTR Cloud Efforts," "GCHQ Analytic Cloud Challenges," "SOCIAL ANTHROPOID," and "Demystifying NGE ROCK RIDGE."

65. For detailed analysis of the XKEYSCORE system in addition to the documents cited below, see Morgan Marquis-Boire, Glenn Greenwald, and Micah Lee, "XKEYSCORE," *The Intercept*, July 1, 2015; Micah Lee, Glenn Greenwald, and Morgan Marquis-Boire, "Behind the Curtain," *The Intercept*, July 2, 2015.

66. Each use of the internet (known as a web session) captured in XKEY-SCORE gets assigned exactly one AppID. On the other hand, each session can have many fingerprints, which are related to the content rather than the type of the message. "XKEYSCORE," National Security Agency internal presentation deck, December 2012, published online alongside Glenn Greenwald, "XKeyscore: NSA Tool Collects 'Nearly Everything a User Does on the Internet,'" *Guardian*, July 31, 2013. See presentation pages 11–13. "Introduction to XKS Application IDs and Fingerprints," National Security Agency internal presentation, August 27, 2009, published online alongside Morgan Marquis-Boire, Glenn Greenwald, and Micah Lee, "XKEYSCORE: NSA's Google for the World's Private Communications," *The Intercept*, July 1, 2015.

67. At the NSA, analysts are instructed not to run queries that would reveal information about persons in the Five Eyes.

68. XKEYSCORE can help with target discovery, too. Say the agency has intercepted an extremely sensitive document from a foreign intelligence target: it might want to identify everyone online who has downloaded that document to determine who might be involved in the hostile operation. XKEYSCORE can search the NSA's collections to help answer this question, potentially identifying new foreign targets worthy of more intrusive surveillance. "XKEYSCORE," presentation pages 19–21. Also linked to Marquis-Boire et al., "XKEYSCORE," find "Using XKS to Find and Search for Logos Embedded in Documents," memorandum prepared by Booz Allen Hamilton, n.d., labeled as "XKS Logos Embedded in Docs"; and "Free File Uploaders," National Security Agency internal presentation deck, August 13, 2009. For Canadian analysis in this area, see "LEVITATION and the FFU Hypothesis," Communications Security Establishment Canada presentation deck, published online alongside Amber Hildebrandt, Michael Pereira, and Dave Seglins, "CSE Tracks Millions of Downloads Daily: Snowden Documents," *CBC*, January 27, 2015.

69. "TRAFFICTHIEF Configuration Read Me," National Security Agency, published online alongside Marquis-Boire et al., "XKEYSCORE."

70. "Contact Mapping: Tip-Off to Diplomatic Travel Plans," Government Communications Headquarters internal presentation, January 2010, published online alongside Laura Poitras, Marcel Rosenbach, and Holger Stark, "'Royal Concierge': GCHQ Monitors Diplomats' Hotel Bookings," *Der Spiegel*, November 17, 2013.

71. Spiegel Staff, "Quantum Spying: GCHQ Used Fake LinkedIn Pages to Target Engineers," *Der Spiegel*, November 11, 2013; Appelbaum et al., "Inside TAO: Documents Reveal Top NSA Hacking Unit"; "Quantum Insert Diagrams," National Security Agency internal presentation deck, published online by *The Intercept*, March 12, 2014; "Tailored Access Operations," National Security Agency internal presentation deck, n.d., described in Spiegel Staff, "Inside TAO: Documents Reveal Top NSA Hacking Unit," *Der Spiegel*, December 29, 2013; "Foxacid," National Security Agency internal presentation, January 8, 2007, published online alongside Sam Biddle, "The NSA Leak Is Real, Snowden Documents Confirm," *The Intercept*, August 19, 2016; Ryan Gallagher

and Glenn Greenwald, "How the NSA Plans to Infect 'Millions' of Computers with Malware," *The Intercept*, March 12, 2014; linked to the same article find "There Is More Than One Way to QUANTUM," National Security Agency internal presentation deck, ca. 2010. Also see "NSA Quantum Tasking Techniques for the R&T Analyst," Booz Allen Hamilton presentation to National Security Agency, published online alongside Spiegel Staff, "Inside TAO"; and Nicholas Weaver, "A Close Look at the NSA's Most Powerful Internet Attack Tool," *Wired*, March 13, 2014.

72. Even if no credentials can be found, passive collection can still gather information about hackable computers all over the world. Training materials show how XKEYSCORE can generate lists of all the browser types and users that visit terrorist forums or Iranian government sites, and pass that information to hackers at the NSA, and how XKEY-SCORE can reveal the configuration of routers the NSA might want to hack, in essence providing a target list for the agency's digital intruders. "Using XKEYSCORE to Enable TAO," National Security Agency internal presentation, July 16, 2009, published online alongside Marquis-Boire et al., "XKEYSCORE"; "What Is HACIENDA?" Government Communications Headquarters internal presentation, published online alongside Jacob Appelbaum, Monika Ermert, Julian Kirsch, Henrik Moltke, Laura Poitras, and Christian Grothoff, "The HACIENDA Program for Internet Colonization," *Heise / c't Magazin*, August 15, 2014; "Pull-Through Steering Group Meeting #16," 2.

73. Marquis-Boire et al., "XKEYSCORE," 28.

74. David Cole, "'We Kill People Based on Metadata,'" *New York Review of Books*, May 10, 2014.

75. For the fruits of one of these reports, which drew on a variety of signals intelligence sources, see "MAKERSMARK (Russian CNE)," Communications Security Establishment Canada internal presentation, 2011, published online alongside Sam Biddle, "White House Says Russia's Hackers Are Too Good to Be Caught but NSA Partner Called Them 'Morons,'" *The Intercept*, August 2, 2017.

76. Jason Seher, "Former NSA Chief Compares Snowden to Terrorists," *CNN*, December 1, 2013.

2. DEFEATING ENCRYPTION

1. Contemporaneous news coverage was extensive. See, for example, Adam Nagourney, Ian Lovett, and Richard Perez-Pena, "San Bernardino Shooting Kills at Least 14; Two Suspects Are Dead," *New York Times*, December 2, 2015.

2. Cecilia Kang and Eric Lichtblau, "F.B.I. Error Locked San Bernardino Attacker's iPhone," *New York Times*, March 1, 2016.

3. US Department of Justice Office of the Inspector General, "A Special Inquiry Regarding the Accuracy of FBI Statements Concerning Its Capabilities to Exploit an iPhone Seized during the San Bernardino Terror Attack Investigation," March 27, 2018, 8.

4. For the two seminal papers summarizing cryptographers' views on the dangers of weakening encryption, see Harold Abelson, Ross Anderson, Steven M. Bellovin, Josh Benaloh, et al., "Keys under Doormats: Mandating Insecurity by Requiring Government Access to All Data and Communications," Computer Science and Artificial Intelligence Laboratory Technical Report, Massachusetts Institute of Technology, July 6, 2015; and Hal Abelson et al., "The Risks of Key Recovery, Key Escrow, and Trusted Third-Party Encryption," Columbia University Academic Commons, May 27, 1997.

5. *Last Week Tonight with John Oliver,* "Encryption," Season 3, Episode 5, directed and written by John Oliver, HBO, March 14, 2016.

6. Katie Benner and Eric Lichtblau, "U.S. Says It Has Unlocked iPhone without Apple," *New York Times*, March 28, 2016.

7. Pat Milton, "Source: Nothing Significant Found on San Bernardino iPhone So Far," *CBS News*, April 13, 2016.

8. The United States military named its system the M-94 and used it in the early twentieth century. Rachel B. Doyle, "The Founding Fathers Encrypted Secret Messages, Too," *Atlantic*, March 30, 2017.

9. For more on this unit, see Patrick Beesly, *Room 40: British Naval Intelligence 1914–1918* (New York: Harcourt Brace Jovanovich, 1982).

10. For more, see F. W. Winterbotham, *The Ultra Secret: The Inside Story of Operation Ultra, Bletchey Park and Enigma* (London: Orion, 2000).

11. David Leech, Stacey Ferris, and John Scott, "The Economic Impacts of the Advanced Encryption Standard, 1996–2017," National Institute of

Standards and Technology, US Department of Commerce, September 2018.

12. Permanent Select Committee on Intelligence (Larry Combest, Chair), "IC21: The Intelligence Community in the 21st Century," US Congress, House of Representatives, One Hundred Fourth Congress, Staff Study, June 5, 1996.

13. Nicole Perlroth, Jeff Larson, and Scott Shane, "N.S.A. Able to Foil Basic Safeguards of Privacy on Web," *New York Times*, September 5, 2013.

14. James Risen and Laura Poitras, "N.S.A. Report Outlined Goals for More Power," *New York Times*, November 22, 2013. Within this article can be found National Security Agency, "SIGINT Strategy," February 23, 2012, NSA internal document. See page 4.

15. National Security Agency, "SIGINT Strategy," 4.

16. Some earlier versions of this informal standard spell it as "Nobody But US," referring to the United States; "Nobody But Us" can refer to efforts that include Five Eyes partners. For more on the development and challenges of NOBUS, see Ben Buchanan, "Nobody But Us: The Rise and Fall of the Golden Age of Signals Intelligence," Aegis Series Paper No. 1708, Hoover Institution, Stanford, CA, August 30, 2017; David Aitel, "Hope Is Not a NOBUS Strategy," *CyberSecPolitics*, May 13, 2019.

17. When some decryption programs became public, a major review commission pointed out the severe risk of blowback and unintended consequences. Richard A. Clarke, Michael J. Morell, Geoffrey R. Stone, Cass R. Sunstein, and Peter Swire, "Liberty and Security in a Changing World," President's Review Group on Intelligence and Communications Technologies report, December 12, 2013, 36.

18. Barton Gellman and Greg Miller, "'Black Budget' Summary Details U.S. Spy Network's Successes, Failures and Objectives," *Washington Post*, August 29, 2013. Kevin Poulsen, "New Snowden Leak Reports 'Groundbreaking' NSA Crypto-Cracking," *Wired*, August 29, 2013.

19. "BULLRUN," Government Communications Headquarters presentation, n.d.; and "BULLRUN CoI–Briefing Sheet," Government Communications Headquarters memorandum, both published alongside Spiegel Staff, "Inside the NSA's War on Internet Security," *Der Spiegel*, December 28, 2014.

20. For more on the interplay between encryption and state sovereignty, see Ben Buchanan, "Cryptography and Sovereignty," *Survival* 58, no. 5 (2016): 95–122.

21. David Adrian, Karthikeyan Bhargavan, Zakir Durumeric, Pierrick Gaudry, et al., "Imperfect Forward Secrecy: How Diffie-Hellman Fails in Practice," *Communications of the ACM* 62, no. 1 (2019): 106–114; Alex Halderman and Nadia Heninger, "How Is NSA Breaking So Much Crypto?" *Freedom to Tinker* blog, Princeton University Center for Information Technology Policy, October 14, 2015; LetoAms, "66% of VPN's Are Not in Fact Broken," No Hats blog, October 17, 2015.

22. "SIGINT Enabling—Project Description," National Security Agency internal document, published alongside Jeff Larson, "Revealed: The NSA's Secret Campaign to Crack, Undermine Internet Security," *ProPublica*, September 5, 2013.

23. Michelle Wagner, "The Inside Scoop on Mathematics at the NSA," *Math Horizons* 13, no. 4 (2006): 20–23.

24. Halderman and Heninger, "How Is NSA Breaking So Much Crypto?" Leaked files from the NSA support this claim, too. A compartment of highly classified files indicates that the NSA tries to "exploit [signals intelligence] targets by attacking the hard mathematical problems underlying public key cryptography," presumably including Diffie-Hellman. "Exceptionally Controlled Information (ECI) as of 12 September 2003," National Security Agency, published alongside Peter Maass and Laura Poitras, "Core Secrets: NSA Saboteurs in China and Germany," *The Intercept*, October 10, 2014, 5.

25. Andrea Peterson, "Why Everyone Is Left Less Secure When the NSA Doesn't Help Fix Security Flaws," *Washington Post*, October 4, 2013.

26. The GSM originally stood for *Groupe Spéciale Mobile*, a name that is now almost never used.

27. "IR.21—A Technology Warning Mechanism," National Security Agency paper delivered at 2010 Five Eyes SIGDEV conference, published alongside Ryan Gallagher, "Operation Auroragold: How the NSA Hacks Cellphone Networks Worldwide," *The Intercept*, December 4, 2014.

28. Other Five Eyes agencies do this, too. For further discussion, see "TLS Trends: A Roundtable Discussion on Current Usage and Future Directions," Communications Security Establishment Canada presentation,

2012, published alongside Spiegel Staff, "Prying Eyes: Inside the NSA's War on Internet Security," *Der Spiegel*, December 28, 2014; "Crypt Discovery Joint Collaboration Activity," National Security Agency / Government Communications Headquarters joint research paper, January 20, 2011, published alongside Ryan Gallagher, "Profiled: From Radio to Porn, British Spies Track Web Users' Online Identities," *The Intercept*, September 25, 2015.

29. "AURORAGOLD Working Group," National Security Agency paper presented at Five Eyes SIGDEV conference, 2012, published alongside Ryan Gallagher, "Operation Auroragold: How the NSA Hacks Cellphone Networks Worldwide," *The Intercept*, December 4, 2014, 3.

30. "AURORAGOLD," National Security Agency presentation to Five Eyes SIGDEV conference, 2011; and "AURORAGOLD Working Aid," National Security Agency briefing document, May 2012, both published alongside Gallagher, "Operation Auroragold," *The Intercept*, December 4, 2014, 3.

31. "AURORAGOLD Working Group," 3. See also Gallagher, "Operation Auroragold."

32. NSA budgeting documents thus say that one of the agency's goals is to "Anticipate future encryption technologies of [signals intelligence] targets and prepare strategies to exploit those technologies." "Crypt-analysis and Exploitation Services—Analysis of Target Systems," National Security Agency "black budget" extract, January 1, 2013, published alongside Jeremy Scahill and Josh Begley, "The CIA Campaign to Steal Apple's Secrets," *The Intercept*, March 10, 2015, 1.

33. "Site Makes First-Ever Collect of High-Interest 4G Cellular Signal," SIDToday [National Security Agency newsletter], February 23, 2010, published alongside Gallagher, "Operation Auroragold." For an excellent discussion of some of the vulnerabilities in cellular encryption, see Matthew Green, "On Cellular Encryption," *A Few Thoughts on Cryptographic Engineering* blog, May 14, 2013.

34. "A5 / 3 Crypt Attack Proof-of-Concept Demonstrator," Government Communications Headquarters internal document, September 8, 2009, published alongside Gallagher, "Operation Auroragold"; "WOLFRAMITE Encryption Attack," Government Communications Headquarters internal document March 9, 2011, published alongside Gallagher, "Operation Auroragold."

35. Craig Timberg and Ashkan Soltani, "By Cracking the Cellphone Code, NSA Has Ability to Decode Private Conversations," *Washington Post*, December 13, 2013.

36. It is not just SIM cards that the Five Eyes target. For more on key theft in general, see Perlroth, Larson, and Shane, "N.S.A. Able to Foil Basic Safeguards of Privacy on Web."

37. "Where Are These Keys?" Government Communications Headquarters presentation deck, 2010, published alongside Jeremy Scahill and Josh Begley, "How Spies Stole the Keys to the Encryption Castle," *The Intercept*, February 19, 2015.

38. "PCS Harvesting at Scale," Government Communications Headquarters report, April 2010, published alongside Scahill and Begley, "How Spies Stole the Keys"; "CNE Access to Core Mobile Networks," Government Communications Headquarters presentation, 2010, published alongside Scahill and Begley; "CCNE Successes Jan10-Mar10 Trial," Government Communications Headquarters presentation, 2010, published alongside Scahill and Begley, "How Spies Stole the Keys." Note that a report by the cybersecurity firm Gemalto disputes that the operation affected millions of keys: "Gemalto Presents the Findings of its Investigations into the Alleged Hacking of SIM Card Encryption Keys by Britain's Government Communications Headquarters (GCHQ) and the U.S. National Security Agency (NSA)," February 25, 2015, press release, Gemalto.com.

39. Peter Koop, "NSA and GCHQ Stealing SIM Card Keys: A Few Things You Should Know," *Electrospaces* blog, February 23, 2015.

40. Jeremy Scahill and Josh Begley, "The Great SIM Heist," *The Intercept*, February 19, 2015.

41. John Napier Tye, "Meet Executive Order 12333: The Reagan Rule That Lets the NSA Spy on Americans," *Washington Post*, July 18, 2014. For an archived final version of the speech, see Scott Busby, "State Department on Internet Freedom at RightsCon," *RightsCon*, March 4, 2014.

42. US Department of Defense Deputy Chief Management Officer, "DoD Manual 5240.01: Procedures Governing the Conduct of DOD Intelligence Activities," August 8, 2016.

43. "Security," Google, 2014, https://web.archive.org/web/20140117211659 /http:/www.google.com/apps/intl/en-GB/trust/security.html.

44. Craig Timberg, "Google Encrypts Data amid Backlash against NSA Spying," *Washington Post*, September 6, 2013.

45. "Current Efforts—Google," National Security Agency—Special Source Operations, presentation deck, February 28, 2013, published alongside Barton Gellman and Ashkan Soltani, "NSA Infiltrates Links to Yahoo, Google Data Centers Worldwide, Snowden Documents Say," *Washington Post*, October 30, 2013.

46. For the first reporting of this effort, see Gellman and Soltani, "NSA Infiltrates Links." For the specific statistic on collected data, using DS-200B as the identifier for the program, see "WINDSTOP—Last 30 Days," National Security Agency, published alongside Barton Gellman, Ashkan Soltani, and Andrea Peterson, "How We Know the NSA Had Access to Internal Google and Yahoo Cloud Data," *Washington Post*, November 4, 2013.

47. "Wyden & Tech Leaders Discuss Mass Surveillance & the Digital Economy," *YouTube*, October 8, 2014.

48. Gellman and Soltani, "NSA Infiltrates Links."

49. Brandon Downey, "This Is the Big Story in Tech Today," Google Plus blog, October 30, 2013.

50. Tye, "Meet Executive Order 12333."

51. Recommendation 12 of the report opaquely refers to Executive Order 12333 as a "legal authority that justifies the interception of a communication on the ground that it is directed at a non-United States person who is located outside the United States" and argues that the NSA should delete any information collected on Americans using that authority unless it has specific intelligence value. Clarke et al., "Liberty and Security in a Changing World," 145–146.

52. For the then-current guidelines, see "Legal Compliance and U.S. Persons Minimization Procedures," Signals Intelligence Directorate, National Security Agency, 2011. For the 2015 law, including the exception for understanding foreign intelligence, see "H.R. 4681 (113th): Intelligence Authorization Act for Fiscal Year 2015," *GovTrack*, December 9, 2014.

53. "BULLRUN," 4.

54. "BULLRUN," 4.

55. Risen and Poitras, "N.S.A. Report Outlined Goals for More Power."

3. BUILDING A BACKDOOR

1. Ben Macintyre, *Agent Zigzag: The True Wartime Story of Eddie Chapman: Lover, Betrayer, Hero, Spy* (London: Bloomsbury, 2007), 1.

2. "Classification Guide for Cryptanalysis, 2-12," National Security Agency internal document, November 23, 2004, published alongside James Ball, Julian Borger, and Glenn Greenwald, "Revealed: How US and UK Spy Agencies Defeat Internet Privacy and Security," *Guardian*, September 6, 2013, 3; "Classification Guide [Project Bullrun]" National Security Agency internal document, June 16, 2010, published alongside Ball, Borger, and Greenwald, "Revealed"; "National Initiative Protection Program—Sentry Eagle," National Security Agency internal document, published alongside Peter Maass and Laura Poitras, "Core Secrets: NSA Saboteurs in China and Germany," *The Intercept*, October 10, 2014, 9; Nicole Perlroth, Jeff Larson, and Scott Shane, "N.S.A. Able to Foil Basic Safeguards of Privacy on Web," *New York Times*, September 5, 2013.

3. The NSA sets a goal to "insert vulnerabilities into commercial encryption systems, IT systems, networks, and endpoint communications devices used by targets." "Computer Network Operations SIGINT Enabling," National Security Agency internal document, 2012, published alongside Ball, Borger, and Greenwald, "Revealed," 1.

4. For a good discussion of the relevant math, see Matthew Green, "On the Juniper Backdoor," *A Few Thoughts on Cryptographic Engineering* blog, December 22, 2015; Dan Shumow and Niels Ferguson, "On the Possibility of a Back Door in the NIST SP800-90 Dual EC PRNG," presentation to Microsoft *Crypto* conference, Santa Barbara, CA, August 2007; Daniel J. Bernstein, Tanja Lange, and Ruben Niederhagen, "Dual EC: A Standardized Back Door," in *The New Codebreakers: Essays Dedicated to David Kahn on the Occasion of His 85th Birthday,* 256–281 (Berlin: Springer-Verlag, 2016).

5. Zaria Gorvett, "The Ghostly Radio Station That No One Claims to Run," *BBC News*, August 2, 2017.

6. Ellen Airhart, "How a Bunch of Lava Lamps Protect Us from Hackers," *Wired*, July 29, 2018.

7. Properly speaking, these standards were for nonmilitary government use. Some work had been done in this area before this point, but it did not amount to a major effort.

8. Matthew Green, "The Many Flaws of Dual_EC_DRBG," *A Few Thoughts on Cryptographic Engineering* blog, September 18, 2013.

9. Green, "The Many Flaws of Dual_EC_DRBG"; Berry Schoenmakers and Andrey Sidorenko, "Cryptanalysis of the Dual Elliptic Curve Pseudorandom Generator," *IACR Cryptology ePrint Archive,* January 1, 2006; Bernstein, Lange, and Niederhagen, "Dual EC: A Standardized Back Door."

10. Daniel R. L. Brown and Scott A. Vanstone, "Elliptic Curve Random Number Generation," US Patent 20070189527, filed 2005 and issued July 27, 2006; Matthew Green, "A Few More Notes on NSA Random Number Generators," *A Few Thoughts on Cryptographic Engineering* blog, December 28, 2013.

11. Elaine B. Barker and John M. Kelsey, "Recommendation for Random Number Generation Using Deterministic Random Bit Generators," National Institute of Standards and Technology Special Publication, US Department of Commerce, March 14, 2007.

12. Barker and Kelsey, "Recommendation for Random Number Generation," 76.

13. Shumow and Ferguson, "On the Possibility of a Back Door."

14. The most significant warning came from Bruce Schneier, a well-known cryptographer. Bruce Schneier, "Did NSA Put a Secret Backdoor in New Encryption Standard?" *Wired*, November 15, 2007; Bruce Schneier, "The Strange Story of Dual_EC_DRBG," *Schneier on Security*, November 15, 2007.

15. Kim Zetter, "How a Crypto 'Backdoor' Pitted the Tech World against the NSA," *Wired*, September 24, 2013.

16. Perlroth, Larson, and Shane, "N.S.A. Able to Foil Basic Safeguards of Privacy on Web."

17. A later presentation by one of the members of the standards committee for Dual_EC_DRBG indicated that the P and Q points provided in the standard came from the NSA. John Kelsey, "800-90 and Dual EC DRBG," NIST presentation, December 2013, posted publicly at

https://csrc.nist.gov/csrc/media/events/ispab-december-2013
-meeting/documents/nist_cryptography_800-90.pdf.

18. Perlroth, Larson, and Shane, "N.S.A. Able to Foil Basic Safeguards of Privacy on Web."

19. Zetter, "How a Crypto 'Backdoor' Pitted the Tech World against the NSA."

20. Steve Marquess, "Flaw in Dual EC DRBG (No, Not That One)," accessible via Mailing list ARChives (MARC.info) website, December 19, 2013.

21. Joseph Menn, "Exclusive: Secret Contract Tied NSA and Security Industry Pioneer," Reuters, December 20, 2013; Matthew Green, "The Strange Story of 'Extended Random,'" *A Few Thoughts on Cryptographic Engineering* blog, December 19, 2017.

22. Art Coviello, "Keynote," speech, RSA Conference 2014, San Francisco, February 25, 2014.

23. "Assessment of Intelligence Opportunity–Juniper," Government Communications Headquarters internal report, February 3, 2011, published alongside Ryan Gallagher and Glenn Greenwald, "NSA Helped British Spies Find Security Holes in Juniper Firewalls," *The Intercept*, December 23, 2015, 4–5.

24. "Juniper Network Firewall Maintenance Renewal," Request for Quote issued by the US Office of Personnel Management, posted on govtribe.com, September 4, 2013.

25. Andy Ozment, "Written Testimony of NPPD Office of Cybersecurity and Communications Assistant Secretary Andy Ozment for a House Committee on Oversight and Government Reform, Subcommittee on Information Technology Hearing Titled 'Federal Cybersecurity Detection, Response, and Mitigation,'" Washington, DC, April 20, 2016.

26. Juniper Networks, "Customer Success," corporate website page, https://www.juniper.net/us/en/company/case-studies-customer-success/.

27. Stephen Checkoway, Christina Garman, Joshua Fried, Shaanan Cohney, et al., "A Systematic Analysis of the Juniper Dual EC Incident," *Proceedings of the 2016 ACM SIGSAC Conference on Computer and Communications Security,* Vienna, Austria, October 24-28, 2016, 468–479.

28. Green, "On the Juniper Backdoor"; Chris Kemmerer, "The Juniper Backdoor: A Summary," SSL.com, January 16, 2016.

29. Green, "On the Juniper Backdoor."

30. "Juniper Networks Product Information about Dual_EC_DRBG," Juniper Networks, 2013.

31. Stephen Checkoway, Jake Maskiewicz, Christina Garman, Joshua Fried, et al., "Where Did I Leave My Keys? Lessons from the Juniper Dual EC Incident," *Communications of the ACM* 61, no. 11 (2018): 145–155.

32. "Assessment of Intelligence Opportunity: Juniper."

33. Kim Zetter, "Researchers Solve Juniper Backdoor Mystery; Signs Point to NSA," *Wired*, December 22, 2015.

34. Zetter, "Researchers Solve Juniper Backdoor Mystery."

35. For example, "Southeast Asia: An Evolving Cyber Threat Landscape," FireEye Special Report, March 2015, 9.

36. Gallagher and Greenwald, "NSA Helped British Spies."

37. Chris C. Demchak and Yuval Shavitt, "China's Maxim—Leave No Access Point Unexploited: The Hidden Story of China Telecom's BGP Hijacking," *Military Cyber Affairs* 3, no. 1 (2018); Dan Goodin, "Strange Snafu Misroutes Domestic US Internet Traffic through China Telecom," *ArsTechnica*, November 6, 2018; Dan Goodin, "BGP Event Sends European Mobile Traffic through China Telecom for 2 Hours," *ArsTechnica*, June 8, 2019.

38. Green, "On the Juniper Backdoor."

39. HD Moore, "CVE-2015-7755: Juniper ScreenOS Authentication Backdoor," *Rapid7* blog, December 20, 2015.

40. Kemmerer, "The Juniper Backdoor: A Summary."

41. Michael Hayden, "The Making of America's Cyberweapons," *Christian Science Monitor*, February 24, 2016.

42. Juniper Networks, "2015-12 Out of Cycle Security Bulletin: ScreenOS: Multiple Security Issues with ScreenOS (CVE-2015-7755, CVE-2015-7756)," December 20, 2015; Bob Worrall, "Important Juniper Security Announcement," Juniper Security Incident Response Blog, December 17, 2015.

43. Andy Ozment, "Written Testimony," 3–4, 9–13.

44. For more on cryptography policy, Nicole Perlroth, "Tech Giants Urge Obama to Reject Policies That Weaken Encryption," *New York Times*,

May 19, 2015; Ellen Nakashima and Barton Gellman, "As Encryption Spreads, U.S. Grapples with Clash between Privacy, Security," *Washington Post*, April 10, 2015; Ben Buchanan, "Cryptography and Sovereignty," *Survival* 58, no. 5 (2016): 95–122.

45. Edward Snowden [@Snowden], "@tqbf Many *are* talking about all exploits without any nuance. Juniper's Dual EC point change unlikely to be NSA—USG notified them!" Twitter post, December 24, 2015.

46. Kemmerer, "The Juniper Backdoor: A Summary"; Zetter, "Researchers Solve Juniper Backdoor Mystery."

47. National Institute of Standards and Technology, "NIST Cryptographic Standards and Guidelines Development Process," report prepared by Visiting Committee on Advanced Technology, July 2014.

48. Michael Wertheimer, "The Mathematics Community and the NSA," *Notices of the American Mathematical Society* 62, no. 2 (2015): 165–167, 166.

49. For example, see Joseph Menn, "Distrustful U.S. Allies Force Spy Agency to Back Down in Encryption Fight," Reuters, September 21, 2017.

50. Bob Worrall, "Juniper Networks Completes ScreenOS Update," Juniper Networks website, April 6, 2016.

4. STRATEGIC ESPIONAGE

1. Scott Pelley, "FBI Director on Threat of ISIS, Cybercrime," *CBS News*, October 5, 2014.

2. Daniel Ellsberg, *Secrets: A Memoir of Vietnam and the Pentagon Papers* (New York: Penguin, 2002), 290–308.

3. Dennis C. Blair and Jon M. Huntsman, Jr., "Update to the IP Commission Report," Commission on the Theft of American Intellectual Property / National Bureau of Asian Research, February 27, 2017, 9.

4. Josh Rogin, "NSA Chief: Cybercrime Constitutes the 'Greatest Transfer of Wealth in History,'" *Foreign Policy*, July 9, 2012.

5. Defense Science Board Task Force, "Resilient Military Systems and the Advanced Cyber Threat," US Department of Defense, January 2013, 4; Ariana Eunjung Cha and Ellen Nakashima, "Google China Cyberattack Part of Vast Espionage Campaign, Experts Say," *Washington Post*, January 14, 2010.

6. Benjamin Pimentel, "Juniper Networks Investigating Cyber-Attacks," *MarketWatch*, January 15, 2010.

7. David Drummond, "A New Approach to China," *Google Official Blog*, January 12, 2010.

8. Jamil Anderlini, "The Chinese Dissident's 'Unknown Visitors,'" *Financial Times*, January 14, 2010.

9. Drummond, "A New Approach to China."

10. Philip Bethge, "'It Was a Real Step Backward,'" *Der Spiegel*, March 30, 2010.

11. John P. Carlin, *Dawn of the Code War: America's Battle against Russia, China, and the Rising Global Cyber Threat* (New York: PublicAffairs, 2018), 180.

12. Michael Joseph Gross, "Enter the Cyber-Dragon," *Vanity Fair*, August 2, 2011.

13. Kim Zetter, "'Google' Hackers Had Ability to Alter Source Code," *Wired*, March 3, 2010.

14. William T. Eliason, "An Interview with Paul M. Nakasone," *Joint Force Quarterly* 92, no. 1 (2019): 4–9, 5.

15. Kevin Mandia, "APT1: Exposing One of China's Cyber Espionage Units," report published by Mandiant (now FireEye) consultancy, February 18, 2013, 7–19.

16. Mandia, "APT1," 22.

17. Mandia, "APT1," 20–21.

18. Mandia, "APT1," 24.

19. Mandia, "APT1," 25.

20. Mandia, "APT1," 27–38.

21. For a photo from the event, see Stephen Shaver, "Westinghouse and China Signing Ceremony for Nuclear Power Plants," UPI, July 24, 2007.

22. *United States of America v. Wang Dong, Sun Kailiang, Wen Xinyu, Huang Zhenyu, Gu Chunhui*, Criminal Nr 14–118, District Court Western District of Pennsylvania, May 1, 2014, 13–16.

23. Diane Cardwell and Jonathan Soble, "Westinghouse Files for Bankruptcy, in Blow to Nuclear Power," *New York Times*, March 29, 2017.

24. *United States of America v. Wang Dong et al.*, 17–19.

25. *United States of America v. Wang Dong et al.*, 19–21.

26. *United States of America v. Wang Dong et al.*, 23–26.

27. *United States of America v. Wang Dong et al.*, 23–26.
28. For the link to the NSA, see Garrett Graff, "How the US Forced China to Quit Stealing—Using a Chinese Spy," *Wired*, October 11, 2018.
29. For a summary of the United States' investigation, not as complete as the details revealed in John Carlin's later book, see the indictment: *United States of America v. Su Bin,* Department of Justice, August 14, 2014.
30. Carlin, *Dawn of the Code War*, 273–274.
31. Carlin, *Dawn of the Code War*, 273–274.
32. Carlin, *Dawn of the Code War*, 274–277.
33. Ellen Nakashima, "Businessman Admits Helping Chinese Military Hackers Target U.S. Contractors," *Washington Post*, March 23, 2016.
34. Ellen Nakashima, "Confidential Report Lists U.S. Weapons System Designs Compromised by Chinese Cyberspies," *Washington Post*, May 27, 2013; Caitlin Dewey, "The U.S. Weapons Systems That Experts Say Were Hacked by the Chinese," *Washington Post*, May 28, 2013.
35. For more on system vulnerabilities, see "Weapon Systems Cybersecurity: DOD Just Beginning to Grapple with Scale of Vulnerabilities," US Government Accountability Office, October 19, 2018.
36. "BYZANTINE HADES: An Evolution of Collection," National Security Agency presentation to SIGDEV conference, published alongside Jacob Appelbaum, Aaron Gibson, Claudio Guarnieri, Andy Müller-Maguhn, et al., "The Digital Arms Race: NSA Preps America for Future Battle," *Der Spiegel*, January 17, 2015, 3.
37. "Chinese Exfiltrate Sensitive Military Technology," National Security Agency presentation deck, published alongside Jacob Appelbaum, Aaron Gibson, Claudio Guarnieri, Andy Müller-Maguhn, et al., "The Digital Arms Race: NSA Preps America for Future Battle," *Der Spiegel*, January 17, 2015, 3.
38. "Inquiry into Cyber Intrusions Affecting U.S. Transportation Command Contractors," Committee on Armed Services, United States Senate Report 113–258, September 18, 2014, 7–10.
39. For the definitive report on this series of intrusions and the failure to alert relevant authorities, see "Inquiry into Cyber Intrusions Affecting U.S. Transportation Command Contractors."
40. Kim Zetter and Andy Greenberg, "Why the OPM Breach Is Such a Security and Privacy Debacle," *Wired*, June 11, 2015; US Office of

Personnel Management, "Federal Information Security Management Act Audit FY 2014: Final Audit Report," Office of the Inspector General / Office of Audits Report Number 4A-CI-00-14-016, November 12, 2014, 10; Aliya Sternstein, "Here's What OPM Told Congress the Last Time Hackers Breached Its Networks," *NextGov*, June 15, 2015.

41. David Sanger, "Hackers Took Fingerprints of 5.6 Million U.S. Workers, Government Says," *New York Times*, September 23, 2015. Also see Brendan L. Koerner, "Inside the Cyberattack That Shocked the US Government, " *Wired*, October 23, 2016.

42. Ellen Nakashima, "Hacks of OPM Databases Compromised 22.1 Million People, Federal Authorities Say," *Washington Post*, July 9, 2015.

43. Sanger, "Hackers Took Fingerprints of 5.6 Million U.S. Workers."

44. Mark Mazzetti and David Sanger, "U.S. Fears Data Stolen by Chinese Hacker Could Identify Spies," *New York Times*, July 24, 2015.

45. Nakashima, "Hacks of OPM Databases Compromised 22.1 Million People."

46. Brian Krebs, "China to Blame in Anthem Hack?" *Krebs on Security*, February 6, 2015; *United States of America v. Fujie Wang, John Doe,* US District Court Southern District of Indiana, indictment filed May 7, 2019.

47. Brian Krebs, "Premera Blue Cross Breach Exposes Financial, Medical Records," *Krebs on Security*, March 17, 2015.

48. Krebs, "China to Blame in Anthem Hack?"

49. Aruna Viswanatha and Kate O'Keefe, "Before It Was Hacked, Equifax Had a Different Fear: Chinese Spying," *Wall Street Journal*, September 12, 2018.

50. For strong initial coverage of the breach, see Brian Krebs, "Breach at Equifax May Impact 143M Americans," *Krebs on Security*, September 7, 2017. The eventual number of affected Americans reached 145 million. Stacy Cowley, "2.5 Million More People Potentially Exposed in Equifax Breach," *New York Times*, October 2, 2017.

51. Kate Fazzini, "The Great Equifax Mystery: 17 Months Later, the Stolen Data Has Never Been Found, and Experts Are Starting to Suspect a Spy Scheme," *CNBC*, February 13, 2019.

5. COUNTERINTELLIGENCE

1. William Shirer, *The Rise and Fall of the Third Reich* (New York: Simon and Schuster, 1959), 872. For a concurring opinion, see Carl Boyd, *Hitler's Japanese Confidant* (Lawrence: University Press of Kansas, 1993), 38.

2. For more on the Japanese confidence in PURPLE and the Allied effort to break it, see David Kahn, *The Codebreakers* (London: Weidenfeld and Nicolson, 1974), ch. 1.

3. George Marshall, "Letter to Thomas E. Dewey," September 27, 1944, George C. Marshall Papers, Pentagon Office Collection, Selected Materials, George C. Marshall Research Library, Lexington, VA.

4. For more about the case, see Boyd, *Hitler's Japanese Confidant*.

5. Allen Dulles, *The Craft of Intelligence* (New York: Harper and Row, 1963; Guilford CT: Lyons Press 2016).

6. William T. Eliason, "An Interview with Paul M. Nakasone," *Joint Force Quarterly* 92, no. 1 (2019): 7.

7. "BYZANTINE HADES: An Evolution of Collection," National Security Agency presentation to SIGDEV conference, published alongside Jacob Appelbaum, Aaron Gibson, Claudio Guarnieri, Andy Müller-Maguhn, et al., "The Digital Arms Race: NSA Preps America for Future Battle," *Der Spiegel*, January 17, 2015, 3.

8. The Five Eyes use hop points, as well, which they call Operational Relay Boxes. Two or three times per year, some Five Eyes employees conduct a one-day push to obtain access to as many of these machines in non-Five Eyes countries as they can for use in future operations. "What Is HACIENDA?" UK Government Communications Headquarters internal presentation, published online alongside Jacob Appelbaum, Monika Ermert, Julian Kirsch, Henrik Moltke, Laura Poitras, and Christian Grothoff, "The HACIENDA Program for Internet Colonization," *Heise / c't Magazin*, August 15, 2014.

9. Passive collection can be useful for this task, especially when other intelligence agencies do not practice good operational security. An effort by the Canadian signals intelligence agency against Russian hackers suggests as much. "Hackers Are Humans Too," Communications Security Establishment Canada presentation, 2011, published

alongside Sam Biddle, "White House Says Russia's Hackers Are Too Good to Be Caught but NSA Partner Called Them 'Morons,'" *The Intercept*, August 2, 2017.

10. "BYZANTINE HADES: An Evolution in Collection," 3–27.

11. For more on the link between these efforts and cyber defense, see "TUTELAGE 411," National Security Agency presentation deck, published alongside Jacob Appelbaum, Aaron Gibson, Andy Müller-Maguhn, Claudio Guarnieri, et al., "The Digital Arms Race: NSA Preps America for Future Battle," *Der Spiegel*, January 17, 2015; Ben Buchanan, *The Cybersecurity Dilemma* (New York: Oxford University Press, 2017).

12. Juan Andres Guerrero-Saade and Costin Raiu, "Walking in Your Enemy's Shadow: When Fourth Party Collection Becomes Attribution Hell," *SecureList*, October 2017, 8.

13. The cybersecurity industry often takes a similar approach, sharing dozens and sometimes hundreds of indicators among network defenders about particular actors.

14. The TeDi effort also tracks malicious code orchestrated by the NSA partners in the Five Eyes, likely for the purposes of deconflicting friendly operations and avoiding unintentional interference. It also includes signatures for Stuxnet, which appears to have been part of an effort to monitor the worm's unintentional spread and contribute to a clean-up effort. Kim Zetter, "Leaked Files Show How the NSA Tracks Other Countries' Hackers," *The Intercept*, March 6, 2018.

15. For the best analysis of the TeDi files, see Boldizsár Bencsáth, "Territorial Dispute," *CrySyS*, March 2018.

16. "SNOWGLOBE: From Discovery to Attribution," Communications Security Establishment Canada presentation, 2011, published alongside Appelbaum et al., "Digital Arms Race." See also "Pay Attention to That Man behind the Curtain: Discovering Aliens on CNE Infrastructure," Communications Security Establishment Canada presentation to CSEC conference, June 2010, published alongside Appelbaum et al., "Digital Arms Race."

17. "The Wizards of Oz II: Looking over the Shoulder of a Chinese C2C Operation," NSA Special Deployments Division *SIDToday* memo, August 8, 2006, published alongside Margot Williams, Henrik Moltke, Micah Lee, and Ryan Gallagher, "Meltdown Showed Extent of NSA

Surveillance—And Other Tales from Hundreds of Intelligence Documents, " *The Intercept*, May 29, 2019.

18. Zetter, "Leaked Files Show How the NSA Tracks Other Countries' Hackers."

19. "Fourth Party Opportunities," National Security Agency, internal presentation, n.d., published alongside Appelbaum et al., "Digital Arms Race."

20. For brief media coverage of fourth-party collection, see Appelbaum et al., "Digital Arms Race."

21. For additional conceptualization of the fourth-party collection concept beyond NSA documents, see Guerrero-Saade and Raiu, "Walking in Your Enemy's Shadow."

22. "Fourth Party Opportunities," 1-9.

23. "TRANSGRESSION Overview for Pod58," National Security Agency internal presentation, February 7, 2010, published alongside Appelbaum et al., "Digital Arms Race."

24. "NSA's Offensive and Defensive Missions: The Twain Have Met," NSA / CSS Threat Operations Center (NTOC) Hawaii, *SIDToday* post, April 26, 2011, published alongside Appelbaum et al., "Digital Arms Race."

25. "Is There Fifth Party Collection?," National Security Agency, discussion board post, n.d., published alongside Applebaum et al., "Digital Arms Race."

26. "'4th Party Collection': Taking Advantage of Non-Partner Computer Network Exploitation Activity," National Security Agency Menwith Hill Station, *Horizon* [internal newsletter], published alongside Appelbaum et al., "Digital Arms Race."

6. STRATEGIC SABOTAGE

1. For the most complete account of the secret air assault, see David Makovsky, "The Silent Strike," *New Yorker*, September 17, 2012.

2. David Sanger, *Confront and Conceal: Obama's Secret Wars and Surprising Use of American Power* (New York: Crown, 2012), 193.

3. Jonathan Steele, "Israel Asked US for Green Light to Bomb Nuclear Sites in Iran," *Guardian*, September 25, 2008.

4. Zahra Hosseinian and Edmund Blair, "Iran Aims for 50,000 Atomic Centrifuges in 5 Years," Reuters, December 11, 2007.

5. This name was first reported by David Sanger. See Sanger, *Confront and Conceal*, ch. 8. See also Kim Zetter and Huib Modderkolk, "Revealed: How a Secret Dutch Mole Aided the U.S.-Israeli Stuxnet Cyberattack on Iran," *Yahoo News,* September 2, 2019.

6. Fanny both preceded and, in terms of its code architecture, heavily overlapped with the versions of Stuxnet that came later, strongly suggesting that the two were part of the same operation. The only suggestion that the situation might be more complex was that, curiously, researchers eventually found a significant number of Fanny infections in Pakistan. Perhaps this can be explained by Fanny's use in another cyber espionage operation, or by an inadvertent proliferation of Fanny beyond targeted networks due to its self-propagating nature. For more, see Kaspersky Lab, "A Fanny Equation: 'I Am Your Father, Stuxnet,'" February 17, 2015.

7. For this reason, there is no mention of Fanny in David Sanger's seminal reporting on Stuxnet or in Kim Zetter's excellent history. Sanger, *Confront and Conceal*; Kim Zetter, *Countdown to Zero Day: Stuxnet and the Launch of the World's First Digital Weapon* (New York: Crown, 2014).

8. For a much more detailed technical discussion of Fanny and related pieces of malicious code, see Kaspersky Lab, "A Fanny Equation"; Kaspersky Lab, "Equation: The Death Star of Malware Galaxy," February 16, 2015; Kaspersky Lab, "Equation Group: Questions and Answers," February 2015.

9. For the first reporting of this test, see William Broad, John Markoff, and David Sanger, "Israeli Test on Worm Called Crucial in Iran Nuclear Delay," *New York Times*, January 15, 2011.

10. Sanger, *Confront and Conceal*, 197.

11. For the first reporting of this order, see Sanger, *Confront and Conceal*, ch. 8.

12. For a good discussion of this propagation, see Zetter, *Countdown to Zero Day*, 91. See also Zetter and Modderkolk, "Revealed."

13. Zetter, *Countdown to Zero Day*, 97. For more detailed technical analysis of this point, see Kaspersky Lab, "Stuxnet: Victims Zero," November 18, 2014. Note that not all five contractors were used to spread each version of Stuxnet.

14. The two command-and-control sites used the domain names mypremierfutbol.com and todaysfutbol.com.

15. For example, contrast Stuxnet to Flame. sKyWIper Analysis Team, "sKyWIper (a.K.a. Flame a.K.a. Flamer): A Complex Malware for Targeted Attacks," *CrySys*, May 31, 2012; Alexander Gostev, "The Flame: Questions and Answers," *SecureList*, May 28, 2012.

16. For more on Stuxnet's target verification, see Zetter, *Countdown to Zero Day*, 167–175.

17. Ron Rosenbaum, "Richard Clarke on Who Was behind the Stuxnet Attack," *Smithsonian*, April 2012.

18. For the seminal work on this part of the Stuxnet operation, see Ralph Langner, "Stuxnet's Secret Twin," *Foreign Policy*, November 19, 2013. For expanded later analysis, see Ralph Langner, "To Kill a Centrifuge: A Technical Analysis of What Stuxnet's Creators Tried to Achieve," Langner Group report, 2013, quote on 10.

19. Sanger, *Confront and Conceal*, 199–203.

20. Langner, "To Kill a Centrifuge," 9–10. Later, officials would see benefits to the attack becoming public.

21. Langner, "To Kill a Centrifuge," 10–14; Eric Chien, "Stuxnet: A Breakthrough," Symantec, November 12, 2010; Ralph Langner, "Can You HEAR Stuxnet Damaging Centrifuges at Natanz?" YouTube, July 27, 2017.

22. For discussion of the number of centrifuges destroyed and the effects, see Ivanka Barzashka, "Are Cyber-Weapons Effective? Assessing Stuxnet's Impact on the Iranian Enrichment Programme," *RUSI Journal* 158, no. 2 (2013); Sanger, *Confront and Conceal*, 207.

23. Sanger, *Confront and Conceal*, 200.

24. For the initial infection report, see Jarrad Shearer, "W32.Stuxnet," Symantec Security Center (website), July 13, 2010. Other firms reported greater infection numbers as time went on.

25. David Sanger, "Obama Order Sped Up Wave of Cyberattacks against Iran," *New York Times*, June 1, 2012.

26. Sanger, *Confront and Conceal*, 205.

27. Eugene Kaspersky, "The Man Who Found Stuxnet: Sergey Ulasen in the Spotlight," Kaspersky Lab blog, November 2, 2011.

28. Brian Krebs, "Experts Warn of New Windows Shortcut Flaw," *Krebs on Security*, July 15, 2010.

29. One of these companies was Siemens, which made the industrial controllers that Stuxnet targeted. But after a July statement, the firm was curiously silent. Zetter, *Countdown to Zero Day*, 168.

30. For a good discussion of Stuxnet's relative size, see Zetter, *Countdown to Zero Day*, 20.

31. Symantec posted a series of blog posts throughout the summer and fall of 2010 updating what it knew about Stuxnet. For an archived list of these posts as of early 2011, see "Security Response (Posts Tagged with W32.Stuxnet)," Symantec, January 20, 2011, https://web.archive .org/web/20110120133017/https://www.symantec.com/connect /symantec-blogs/security-response/11761/all/all/all/all.

32. Emphasis in the original. Kim Zetter, "How Digital Detectives Deciphered Stuxnet, the Most Menacing Malware in History," *Wired*, July 11, 2011.

33. Zetter, *Countdown to Zero Day*, 173.

34. Zetter, *Countdown to Zero Day*, 177.

35. Ralph Langner, "Stuxnet Is a Directed Attack: 'Hack of the Century,'" Langner Group, September 13, 2010.

36. Ralph Langner, "Stuxnet Logbook, Sep 16 2010, 1200 Hours MESZ," Langner Group, September 16, 2010.

37. Kaspersky Global Research & Analysis Team (GReAT), "What Was That Wiper Thing?" Kaspersky Lab SecureList, August 29, 2012.

38. Thomas Erdbrink, "Facing Cyberattack, Iranian Officials Disconnect Some Oil Terminals from Internet," *New York Times*, April 23, 2012.

39. Erdbrink, "Facing Cyberattack."

40. Erdbrink, "Facing Cyberattack."

41. One kind of file Wiper deleted was the type of file used in Stuxnet, leading some to speculate that it may have been a cleanup operation of sorts. But this file type, known as .INF, is also used by Windows—and the Stuxnet code had already been widely studied by the time Wiper began. Meanwhile, Wiper's specific targeting of the Iranian oil industry— at a time when the West was launching a campaign to undermine and isolate Iran's economy—undercuts the notion that the operation's goal was solely to remove the evidence of Stuxnet and instead supports the notion of a sabotage attempt.

42. For the best technical analysis of the little that is known about Wiper, see Kaspersky Global Research & Analysis Team (GReAT), "What Was That Wiper Thing?"

43. The phrase was often used by Thomas Schelling. See for example Thomas C. Schelling, *Arms and Influence* (New Haven, CT: Yale University Press, 1966), 33.

44. David Sanger, "Diplomacy and Sanctions, Yes. Left Unspoken on Iran? Sabotage," *New York Times*, January 19, 2016.
45. Zetter, *Countdown to Zero Day*.
46. Sanger, *Confront and Conceal*.

7. TARGETED DISRUPTION

1. Chris Kubecka, "How to Implement IT Security after a Cyber Meltdown," YouTube, August 6, 2015; Jose Pagliery, "The Inside Story of the Biggest Hack in History," *CNN*, August 5, 2015.
2. David Sanger and Annie Lowrey, "Iran Threatens to Block Oil Shipments, as U.S. Prepares Sanctions," *New York Times*, December 27, 2011.
3. For more on the series of wiping attacks that followed Shamoon, see Saher Naumaan, "Now You See It, Now You Don't: Wipers in the Wild," *Virus Bulletin*, October 3, 2018.
4. "Iran—Current Topics, Interaction with GCHQ," National Security Agency internal memorandum, April 12, 2013, published alongside Glenn Greenwald, "NSA Claims Iran Learned from Western Cyberattack," *The Intercept,* February 10, 2015, 1.
5. The exact date of this is unclear. One technical after-action analysis suggests that the date is unknown, while other media reporting places the event in mid-2012. Pagliery, "The Inside Story of the Biggest Hack in History"; Kubecka, "How to Implement IT Security after a Cyber Meltdown," 4:20. For the slides of Kubecka's presentation, see Chris Kubecka, "How to Implement IT Security after a Cyber Meltdown," presentation to Black Hat USA conference, Las Vegas, NV, August 6, 2015.
6. Symantec Security Response, "The Shamoon Attacks," *Symantec*, August 16, 2012; "Shamoon the Wiper: Copycats at Work," Kaspersky Lab, August 16, 2012.
7. Nicole Perlroth, "Among Digital Crumbs from Saudi Aramco Cyberattack, Image of Burning U.S. Flag," *New York Times*, August 24, 2012.
8. Cutting Sword of Justice, untitled guest post claiming responsibility for Saudi Aramco hack, *Pastebin*, August 15, 2012, https://pastebin.com/HqAgaQRj.
9. Kubecka, "How to Implement IT Security after a Cyber Meltdown."

10. Kubecka, "How to Implement IT Security," 9.

11. Angry Internet Lovers, "Saudi Aramco Hug, Another One," guest-posted on *Pastebin*, August 27, 2012.

12. Pagliery, "The Inside Story of the Biggest Hack in History."

13. For more on the case, see Dan Verton, *The Hacker Diaries: Confessions of Teenage Hackers* (Berkeley, CA: McGraw-Hill Education, 2002), ch. 3.

14. Joshua Davis, "Hackers Take Down the Most Wired Country in Europe," *Wired*, August 21, 2007; "Project Grey Goose Phase I Report: Russia / Georgia Cyber War—Findings and Analysis," Project Grey Goose open-source intelligence initiative, October 17, 2008.

15. John Bumgarner and Scott Borg, "Overview by the US-CCU of the Cyber Campaign Against Georgia in August of 2008," US Cyber Consequences Unit special report, August 2009; "Project Grey Goose Phase II Report: The Evolving State of Cyber Warfare," Greylogic [consultancy] special report, March 20, 2009.

16. Qassam Cyber Fighters, "Bank of America and New York Stock Exchange under Attack," guest-posted on *Pastebin*, September 18, 2012.

17. Qassam Cyber Fighters, "Operation Ababil: Second Step over Chase .Com," guest-posted on *Pastebin*, September 19, 2012.

18. *United States of America v. Ahmad Fathi, Hamid Firoozi, Amin Shokohi, Sadegh Ahmadzadegan, Omid Ghaffarinia, Sina Keissar, and Nader Saedi*, US District Court, Southern District of New York, indictment filed March 24, 2016, 4.

19. Qassam Cyber Fighters, "The Fourth Week, Operation Ababil," guest-posted on *Pastebin*, October 8, 2012.

20. Ellen Nakashima, "Iran Blamed for Cyberattacks on U.S. Banks and Companies," *Washington Post*, September 21, 2012.

21. Jim Garamone, "Panetta Spells Out DOD Roles in Cyberdefense," US Department of Defense American Forces Press Service, October 11, 2012.

22. *United States of America v. Ahmad Fathi, et al.*, 4.

23. Qassam Cyber Fighters, "The 5th Week, Operation Ababil : 8 $=$ 0 !," guest-posted on *Pastebin*, October 16, 2012.

24. Qassam Cyber Fighters, "The 6th Week, Operation Ababil," guest-posted on *Pastebin*, October 23, 2012.

25. For example, see Qassam Cyber Fighters, "P2 / W5, Operation Ababil : 2*2 = 4," guest-posted on *Pastebin*, January 8, 2013.

26. Qassam Cyber Fighters, "Operation Ababil Suspended Due to Removal of Insulting Movie," guest-posted on *Pastebin*, January 29, 2013.

27. Qassam Cyber Fighters, "Phase 2 Operation Ababil," guest-posted on *Pastebin*, December 10, 2012.

28. Yaakov Katz, "Iran Embarks on $1B Cyber-Warfare Program," *Jerusalem Post*, December 18, 2011; "Iran—Current Topics, Interaction with GCHQ," 1.

29. "Iran—Current Topics, Interaction with GCHQ."

30. Sands Casino, "Casino Locations," https://www.sandscasino.com /global/casino-locations.html, accessed August 14, 2019.

31. Eric Lipton, "GOP's Israel Support Deepens as Political Contributions Shift," *New York Times*, April 5, 2015.

32. Raviv Drucker, "The Real Connection Between Netanyahu and Adelson's Israel Hayom," *Haaretz*, June 13, 2015.

33. Sheldon Adelson, remarks at Yeshiva University, New York City, October 22, 2013, posted by Philip Weiss on YouTube as "Sheldon Adelson Calls on Obama to Fire a Nuclear Weapon at Iran, Not Negotiate," October 22, 2013.

34. Ben Elgin and Michael Riley, "Now at the Sands Casino: An Iranian Hacker in Every Server," *Bloomberg*, December 11, 2014.

35. Waqas Amir, "Iran Hacked Vegas Casino Wiping Hard Drives, Shutting Down Email," *HackRead*, December 19, 2014.

36. Elgin and Riley, "Now at the Sands Casino: An Iranian Hacker in Every Server."

37. This account of the Sands operation is drawn from in-depth media reporting. Many details were confirmed by individuals in the information security community with direct knowledge of the case and the attackers. Jose Pagliery, "Iran Hacked an American Casino, U.S. Says," *CNN*, February 27, 2015; Elgin and Riley, "Now at the Sands Casino: An Iranian Hacker in Every Server."

38. Joseph Marks, "The Cybersecurity 202: Iran's the Scariest Cyber Adversary, Former NSA Chief Says," *Washington Post*, May 3, 2019.

39. Elgin and Riley, "Now at the Sands Casino: An Iranian Hacker in Every Server."

8. COERCION

1. David Sanger, *The Perfect Weapon: War, Sabotage, and Fear in the Cyber Age* (New York: Crown, 2018), 142.

2. Mark Seal, "An Exclusive Look at Sony's Hacking Saga," *Vanity Fair*, February 4, 2015.

3. "DPRK FM Spokesman Blasts U.S. Moves to Hurt Dignity of Supreme Leadership of DPRK," *Korean Central News Agency,* June 25, 2014.

4. Sony Pictures executives sought advice from a North Korea expert at RAND Corporation. As part of his response, that analyst referenced a conversation with the State Department's special envoy for North Korean human rights issues, saying the envoy was not particularly worried about the threat because it sounded like "typical North Korean bullying." Seal, "An Exclusive Look at Sony's Hacking Saga."

5. Seth Rogen (@Sethrogen), tweet, June 25, 2014, 10:48 AM.

6. Sanger, *The Perfect Weapon*, 129.

7. For contemporaneous coverage of two previous North Korean cyber operations, see Choe Sang-Hun and John Markoff, "Cyberattacks Jam Government and Commercial Web Sites in U.S. And South Korea," *New York Times*, July 8, 2009; and Choe Sang-Hun, "Computer Networks in South Korea Are Paralyzed in Cyberattacks," *New York Times*, March 20, 2013. For technical analysis, see Sergei Shevchenko, "Two Bytes to $951m," *BAE Systems Threat Research Blog*, April 25, 2016; Kate Kochetkova, "What Is Known About the Lazarus Group: Sony Hack, Military Espionage, Attacks on Korean Banks and Other Crimes," *Kaspersky Daily,* February 24, 2016; "Operation Blockbuster," *Novetta*, 2016.

8. Choe Sang-Hun, "North Korea Urgently Needs Food Aid After Worst Harvest in Decade, U.N. Says," *New York Times*, May 3, 2019.

9. Cyber coercion has been the subject of a great deal of academic discussion. For examples, see Thomas Rid, *Cyber War Will Not Take Place* (New York: Oxford University Press, 2013); Erik Gartzke, "The Myth of Cyberwar: Bringing War in Cyberspace Back Down to Earth," *International Security* 38, no. 2 (2013): 41–73; Brandon Valeriano, Benjamin Jensen, and Ryan C. Maness, *Cyber Strategy: The Evolving*

Character of Power and Coercion (New York: Oxford University Press, 2018).

10. *United States of America v. Park Jin Hyok*, US District Court, Central District of California, criminal complaint filed June 8, 2018, 45–53.

11. Kurt Baumgartner, "Sony / Destover: Mystery North Korean Actor's Destructive and Past Network Activity: Comparisons with Shamoon and DarkSeoul," Kaspersky Lab *SecureList* blog, December 4, 2014.

12. Peter Elkind, "Sony Pictures: Inside the Hack of the Century, Part Three," *Fortune*, June 27, 2015.

13. Seal, "An Exclusive Look at Sony's Hacking Saga."

14. Elkind, "Sony Pictures: Inside the Hack."

15. Baumgartner, "Sony / Destover."

16. Seal, "An Exclusive Look at Sony's Hacking Saga."

17. Sanger, *The Perfect Weapon*, 141.

18. Kevin Roose, "Inside Sony Pictures, Employees Are Panicking About Their Hacked Personal Data," *Splinter News*, December 3, 2014.

19. Roose, "Inside Sony Pictures."

20. Elkind, "Sony Pictures: Inside the Hack"; Seal, "An Exclusive Look at Sony's Hacking Saga."

21. Sanger, *The Perfect Weapon*, 138–141.

22. Seal, "An Exclusive Look at Sony's Hacking Saga."

23. Elkind, "Sony Pictures: Inside the Hack."

24. Andrew Wallenstein and Brent Lang, "Sony's New Movies Leak Online Following Hack Attack," *Variety*, November 29, 2014.

25. Roose's work would later be incorporated under the *Splinter News* umbrella; the references that follow are to its archived copies of his articles.

26. Kevin Roose, "Hacked Documents Reveal a Hollywood Studio's Stunning Gender and Race Gap," *Splinter News*, December 1, 2014.

27. Seal, "An Exclusive Look at Sony's Hacking Saga."

28. Roose, "Hacked Documents Reveal a Hollywood Studio's Stunning Gender and Race Gap."

29. Roose, "Hacked Documents."

30. Kevin Roose, "More from the Sony Pictures Hack: Budgets, Layoffs, HR Scripts, and 3,800 Social Security Numbers," *Splinter News,* December 2, 2014.

31. Seal, "An Exclusive Look at Sony's Hacking Saga."

32. Roose, "More from the Sony Pictures Hack."

33. Kevin Roose, "Sony Pictures Hack Spreads to Deloitte: Thousands of Audit Firm's Salaries Are Leaked," *Splinter News*, December 3, 2014.

34. Roose, "Inside Sony Pictures, Employees Are Panicking."

35. Sony executives released another memo outlining what the company was doing to help employees. For a copy, see *THR* Staff, "Michael Lynton and Amy Pascal Call Sony Hack 'Brazen Attack' in Staff Memo," *Hollywood Reporter*, December 2, 2014.

36. Roose, "Inside Sony Pictures, Employees Are Panicking About Their Hacked Personal Data."

37. Seal, "An Exclusive Look at Sony's Hacking Saga." Emphasis in the original.

38. Anna Fifield, "North Korea Denies Hacking Sony but Calls the Breach a 'Righteous Deed,'" *Washington Post*, December 7, 2014.

39. The original message has been removed, but an archived copy is available on the Internet Archive. GOP [Guardians of Peace], "Gift of GOP for 4th Day: Their Privacy," guest-posted to GitHub, December 8, 2014.

40. Kevin Roose, "Even More Sony Pictures Data Is Leaked: Scripts, Box Office Projections, and Brad Pitt's Phone Number," *Splinter News*, December 8, 2014.

41. Sam Biddle, "Leaked: The Nightmare Email Drama behind Sony's Steve Jobs Disaster," *Gawker*, December 9, 2014.

42. Seal, "An Exclusive Look at Sony's Hacking Saga."

43. Matthew Zeitlin, "Leaked Emails Suggest Maureen Dowd Promised to Show Sony Exec's Husband Column before Publication," *Buzzfeed*, December 12, 2014.

44. Margaret Sullivan, "Hacked Emails, 'Air-Kissing'—and Two Firm Denials," *New York Times*, December 12, 2014.

45. For two examples, see Biddle, "Leaked: The Nightmare Email Drama behind Sony's Steve Jobs Disaster"; Zeitlin, "Leaked Emails Suggest Maureen Dowd Promised to Show Sony Exec's Husband Column before Publication."

46. Pascal's dismissal was likely for reasons beyond just the email leaks. For examples of the news coverage, see Michael Cieply and Brooks Barnes,

"Sony Hack Reveals Email Crossfire over Angelina Jolie and Steve Jobs Movie," *New York Times*, December 10, 2014; Ben Fritz, "Hack of Amy Pascal Emails at Sony Pictures Stuns Industry," *Wall Street Journal*, December 11, 2014; Amy Kaufman, "The Embarrassing Emails That Preceded Amy Pascal's Resignation," *Los Angeles Times*, February 5, 2015.

47. Aaron Sorkin, "The Sony Hack and the Yellow Press," *New York Times*, December 14, 2014.

48. Sullivan, "Hacked Emails, 'Air-Kissing'—and Two Firm Denials."

49. For a notable example, see Brooks Barnes, "Amy Pascal's Hollywood Ending, Complete with Comeback Twist," *New York Times*, July 8, 2017.

50. Kevin Roose, "Sony Pictures Hackers Make Their Biggest Threat Yet: 'Remember the 11th of September 2001,'" *Splinter News*, December 16, 2014.

51. Jace Lacob, "Theater Chains Pull 'The Interview,' Press Appearances Canceled Amid Threats," *Buzzfeed*, December 16, 2014.

52. Gregg Kilday, "Top Five Theater Circuits Drop 'The Interview' after Sony Hack," *Hollywood Reporter*, December 17, 2014.

53. Brent Lang, "Sony Weighing Premium VOD Release for 'The Interview,'" *Variety*, December 17, 2014.

54. Brooks Barnes and Michael Cieply, "Sony Drops 'The Interview' Following Terrorist Threats," *New York Times*, December 17, 2014.

55. Brian Stelter, "Hackers to Sony: We'll Stand Down If You Never Release the Movie," *CNN*, December 19, 2014.

56. FBI National Press Office, "Update on Sony Investigation," Federal Bureau of Investigation press release, December 19, 2014.

57. One widely cited story that ran before the FBI's announcement but after other cybersecurity research had suggested a link to North Korea was Kim Zetter, "The Evidence That North Korea Hacked Sony Is Flimsy," *Wired*, December 17, 2014. Norse, a cybersecurity company, directly challenged the FBI and was publicly rebutted after meeting with agents. See Pamela Brown and Mary Kay Mallonee, "North Korea Did It: FBI Not Budging on Sony Hack Culprit," *CNN*, December 30, 2014; and Michael Schmidt, Nicole Perlroth, and Matthew Goldstein, "F.B.I. Says Little Doubt North Korea Hit Sony," *New York Times*,

January 7, 2015. For general discussion of the idea of attribution in cybersecurity, see Thomas Rid and Ben Buchanan, "Attributing Cyber Attacks," *Journal of Strategic Studies* 39, no. 1 (2015): 4–37; Sergio Caltagirone, Andrew Pendergast, and Christopher Betz, "The Diamond Model of Intrusion Analysis," Center for Cyber Intelligence Analysis and Threat Research Hanover, MD, July 5, 2013; Herb Lin, "Attribution of Malicious Cyber Incidents: From Soup to Nuts," *Journal of International Affairs* 70, no. 1 (2016). For a discussion of the 2014 debate's flaws, see Kevin Collier, "The Indictment of North Korea for The Sony Hack Shows How Cybersecurity Has Evolved," *Buzzfeed*, September 7, 2018.

58. David Sanger and Martin Fackler, "N.S.A. Breached North Korean Networks before Sony Attack, Officials Say," *New York Times*, January 18, 2015. In 2018, the United States government issued its indictment *United States of America v. Park Jin Hyok*, revealing some of what it knew about how the North Korean hack took place.

59. Barack Obama, "Year-End Press Conference," White House Press Briefing Room, Washington, DC, December 19, 2014.

60. Michael J. Lynton, comments in broadcast interview with Fareed Zakaria, "Would Sony Entertainment Make 'The Interview' Again?," *Fareed Zakaria GPS, CNN,* December 20, 2014.

61. Seal, "An Exclusive Look at Sony's Hacking Saga."

62. "North Korea Berates Obama over The Interview Release," *BBC News*, December 27, 2014.

63. Mike Fleming, Jr., "North Korea-Based Thriller With Gore Verbinski and Steve Carell Canceled," *Deadline*, December 17, 2014.

9. TESTING AND DEMONSTRATION

1. Jon Wellinghoff, "Performance and Accountability Report: Fiscal Year 2011," US Federal Energy Regulatory Commission, Washington, DC, 2011; National Research Council, *Terrorism and the Electric Power Delivery System* (Washington, DC: National Academies Press, 2012).

2. Lloyd's of London and University of Cambridge Centre for Risk Studies, "Business Blackout: The Insurance Implications of a Cyber Attack on the US Power Grid," Emerging Risk Report Series, July 8, 2015. Ted

Koppel, *Lights Out: A Cyberattack, A Nation Unprepared, Surviving the Aftermath* (New York: Broadway Books, 2016).

3. "Aurora Generator Test," video of demonstration by Idaho National Laboratory, Department of Homeland Security, March 4, 2007, accessible on YouTube at https://youtu.be/LM8kLaJ2NDU; or see the prose "Video Summary" among Operation Aurora documents obtained by Freedom of Information Act request: https://s3.amazonaws.com/s3 .documentcloud.org/documents/1212530/14f00304-documents.pdf, 58–59.

4. Trend Micro, "Frequently Asked Questions: BlackEnergy," TrendMicro Security News, February 11, 2016; Udi Shamir, "Analyzing a New Variant of BlackEnergy 3," *SentinelOne*, January 26, 2016, 13.

5. For an example of the NSA and GCHQ working together to detect and exploit firewall weaknesses, see Ryan Gallagher and Glenn Greenwald, "NSA Helped British Spies Find Security Holes in Juniper Firewalls," *The Intercept,* December 23, 2015.

6. For good technical discussion of the attack's components, see Robert Lee, Michael Assante, and Tim Conway, "Analysis of the Cyber Attack on the Ukrainian Power Grid," report, Electricity Information Sharing and Analysis Center, March 18, 2016; and Robert Lipovsky and Anton Cherepanov, "BlackEnergy Trojan Strikes Again: Attacks Ukrainian Electric Power Industry," ESET *WeLiveSecurity* blog, January 4, 2016. For a more narrative overview, see Kim Zetter, "Inside the Cunning, Unprecedented Hack of Ukraine's Power Grid," *Wired*, March 3, 2016.

7. The video can be seen online. For one posting, see Andy Greenberg, Watch Hackers Take Over the Mouse of a Power-Grid Computer, *Wired*, June 28, 2017.

8. Zetter, "Inside the Cunning, Unprecedented Hack of Ukraine's Power Grid."

9. Kelly Jackson Higgins, "Lessons from the Ukraine Electric Grid Hack," *Dark Reading*, March 3, 2016.

10. The reference to Moscow comes from Zetter, "Inside the Cunning, Unprecedented Hack of Ukraine's Power Grid."

11. Dragos, "CRASHOVERRIDE: Analysis of the Threat to Electric Grid Operations," Dragos report, June 13, 2017, 10.

12. Andy Greenberg, *Sandworm: A New Era of Cyberwar and the Hunt for the Kremlin's Most Dangerous Hackers* (New York: Doubleday, 2019), 130.
13. For more on the notion of sophistication in cyber operations, see Ben Buchanan, "The Legend of Sophistication in Cyber Operations," Belfer Center for Science and International Affairs, January 2017.
14. Rebecca Smith, "Cyberattacks Raise Alarm for U.S. Power Grid," *Wall Street Journal*, December 30, 2016.
15. For more on Havex, also known as Dragonfly, see Nell Nelson, "The Impact of Dragonfly Malware on Industrial Control Systems," SANS Technology Institute Graduate Student paper, January 18, 2016.
16. For more on BlackEnergy2's exploitation of human-machine interfaces, see Industrial Control Systems Cyber Emergency Readiness Team, "Ongoing Sophisticated Malware Campaign Compromising ICS (Update E)," ICS Alert 14,281-01E, National Cybersecurity and Communications Integration Center, rev. December 9, 2016.
17. Joe Slowik, "CRASHOVERRIDE: Reassessing the 2016 Ukraine Electric Power Event as a Protection-Focused Attack," Dragos report, August 15, 2019.
18. For excellent technical overviews of CRASHOVERRIDE, also known as Industroyer, see Dragos, "CRASHOVERRIDE: Analysis of the Threat to Electric Grid Operations"; Michael J. Assante, Robert M. Lee, and Tim Conway, "ICS Defense Use Case No. 6: Modular ICS Malware," report, SANS Institute, Electricity Information Sharing and Analysis Center, August 2, 2017; Anton Cherepanov, "Industroyer: Biggest Threat to Industrial Control Systems Since Stuxnet," ESET *WeLiveSecurity* blot, June 12, 2017; Greg Masters, "Industroyer Can Knock Out Power Grid, ESET," SC Magazine, June 12, 2017; Joe Slowik, "Anatomy of an Attack: Detecting and Defeating CRASH-OVERRIDE," Dragos, October 12, 2018.
19. Assante, Lee, and Conway, "ICS Defense Use Case No. 6: Modular ICS Malware," 14.
20. Ellen Nakashima, "Russia Has Developed a Cyberweapon That Can Disrupt Power Grids, According to New Research," *Washington Post*, June 12, 2017; iSight Partners, "Microsoft Windows Zero-Day: Targeting NATO, EU, Telecom and Energy Sectors (CVE-2014-4114)," report, iSight Russian Cyber Espionage Campaign, Sandworm Team, 2014.

21. FireEye, "Cyber Attacks on the Ukrainian Grid: What You Should Know," FireEye Industry Intelligence Report, 2016.

22. Ivan Nechepurenko and Neil MacFarquhar, "As Sabotage Blacks Out Crimea, Tatars Prevent Repairs," *New York Times*, November 23, 2015.

23. Zetter, "Inside the Cunning, Unprecedented Hack of Ukraine's Power Grid."

24. Assante, Lee, and Conway, "ICS Defense Use Case No. 6: Modular ICS Malware," 5.

25. Alyza Sebenius, "Will Ukraine Be Hit by Yet Another Holiday Power-Grid Hack?," *Atlantic*, December 13, 2017.

26. Andy Greenberg, "How An Entire Nation Became Russia's Test Lab for Cyberwar," *Wired*, June 20, 2017; Greenberg, *Sandworm*, 137.

27. Greenberg, *Sandworm*, 145. For more on Russian threats to infrastructure generally, see Scott J. Shackelford, Michael Sulmeyer, Amanda N. Craig Deckard, Ben Buchanan, and Brian Micic, "From Russia with Love: Understanding the Russian Cyber Threat to US Critical Infrastructure and What to Do about It," *Nebraska Law Review* 96, no. 2 (2017).

28. William M. Arkin, Ken Dilanian, and Robert Windrem, "CIA Prepping for Possible Cyber Strike against Russia," *NBC News*, October 14, 2016; Ken Dilanian, William M. Arkin, Cynthia McFadden, and Robert Windrem, "U.S. Govt. Hackers Ready to Hit Back If Russia Tries to Disrupt Election," *NBC News*, November 4, 2016.

29. Probably the most dramatic narrative of this sort comes from Richard A. Clarke and Robert Knake, *Cyber War: The Next Threat to National Security and What to Do About It* (New York: HarperCollins, 2010). See also Joel Brenner, *America the Vulnerable: Inside the New Threat Matrix of Digital Espionage, Crime, and Warfare* (New York: Penguin, 2011).

10. ELECTION INTERFERENCE

1. The quote is from staffer Sydney Morrell in a memo defining the work of his group. Nicholas John Cull, *Selling War: The British Propaganda Campaign against American "Neutrality"* (Oxford: Oxford University Press, 1995), 132. See also Steve Usdin, "When a Foreign Government

Interfered in a U.S. Election—to Reelect FDR," *Politico*, January 16, 2017; William Samuel Stephenson and Nigel West, *British Security Coordination: The Secret History of British Intelligence in the Americas, 1940–1945* (London: Fromm International, 1999); Philip M. Taylor, "Techniques of Persuasion: Basic Ground Rules of British Propaganda during the Second World War," *Historical Journal of Film, Radio and Television* 1, no. 1 (1981): 57–66.

2. For a detailed study on this point, see Dov H. Levin, "When the Great Power Gets a Vote: The Effects of Great Power Electoral Interventions on Election Results," *International Studies Quarterly* 60, no. 2 (2016): 189–202.

3. Kenneth Geers, ed., *Cyber War in Perspective: Russian Aggression against Ukraine* (Tallinn, Estonia: NATO Cooperative Cyber Defence Center of Excellence, 2015), ch. 6; Ben Buchanan and Michael Sulmeyer, "Hacking Chads: The Motivations, Threats, and Effects of Electoral Insecurity," paper, Cyber Security Project, Belfer Center for Science and International Affairs, October 2016; Mark Clayton, "Ukraine Election Narrowly Avoided 'Wanton Destruction' from Hackers," *Christian Science Monitor*, June 17, 2014; Andy Greenberg, *Sandworm: A New Era of Cyberwar and the Hunt for the Kremlin's Most Dangerous Hackers* (New York: Doubleday, 2019): 46–47.

4. Ryan Naraine, "Obama, McCain Campaigns Hacked by 'Foreign Entity'," *Newsweek*, November 5, 2008.

5. Mark Halperin and John Heilemann, "The Hunt for Pufferfish: A Double Down Excerpt," *Time*, November 2, 2013.

6. Jens Gluesing, Laura Poitras, Marcel Rosenbach, and Holger Stark, "Fresh Leak on US Spying: NSA Accessed Mexican President's Email," *Der Spiegel*, October 20, 2013. For a broader look at the NSA's activities against political targets, see Scott Wilson and Anne Gearan, "Obama Didn't Know about Surveillance of U.S.-Allied World Leaders until Summer, Officials Say," *Washington Post*, October 28, 2013.

7. Laura Poitras, Marcel Rosenbach, and Holger Stark, "'A' for Angela: GCHQ and NSA Targeted Private German Companies and Merkel," *Der Spiegel*, March 29, 2014.

8. FireEye Threat Intelligence, "HAMMERTOSS: Stealthy Tactics Define a Russian Cyber Threat Group," FireEye Threat Research blog, July 29, 2015; Huib Modderkolk, "Dutch Agencies Provide Crucial

Intel about Russia's Interference in US-Elections," *Volkskrant*, January 25, 2018.

9. This account is drawn from Eric Lipton, David Sanger, and Scott Shane, "The Perfect Weapon: How Russian Cyberpower Invaded the U.S.," *New York Times*, December 13, 2016.

10. FireEye Threat Intelligence, "APT28: A Window into Russia's Cyber Espionage Operations?," FireEye Threat Research blog, October 27, 2014.

11. Robert S. Mueller III, "Report on the Investigation into Russian Interference in the 2016 Presidential Election," Department of Justice Special Counsel Report, Washington, DC, March 2019, 45.

12. For a good discussion of this dynamic, see Mark Galeotti, "Putin's Hydra: Inside Russia's Intelligence Services," paper, European Council on Foreign Relations (May 11, 2016).

13. *United States of America v. Viktor Borisovich Netyksho, Boris Alekseyevich Antonov, Dmitriy Sergeyevich Badin, Ivan Sergeyevich Yermakov, Aleksey Viktorovich Lukashev, Sergey Aleksandrovich Morgachev, Nikolay Yuryevich Kozachek, Pavel Vyacheslavovich Yershov, Artem Andreyevich Malyshev, Aleksandor Vladimirovich Osadchuk, Aleksey Aleksandrovich Potemkin, and Anatoliy Sergeyevich Kovalev,* US District Court, District of Columbia, indictment filed July 13, 2018, 8.

14. Lipton, Sanger, and Shane, "The Perfect Weapon."

15. For the seminal analysis of this activity, see Thomas Rid, "Disinformation: A Primer in Russian Active Measures and Influence Campaigns," Hearing before Select Committee on Intelligence, US Senate, March 30, 2017, 4.

16. Thomas Rid, "How Russia Pulled Off the Biggest Election Hack in U.S. History," *Esquire*, October 20, 2016.

17. *United States of America v. Viktor Borisovich Netyksho et al.,* 7.

18. *United States of America v. Viktor Borisovich Netyksho et al.,* 4–5; "En Route with Sednit," research paper series, ESET [IT security company], October 20, 2016.

19. *United States of America v. Viktor Borisovich Netyksho et al.,* 9.

20. *United States of America v. Viktor Borisovich Netyksho et al.,* 10.

21. *United States of America v. Viktor Borisovich Netyksho et al.,* 11–12. Much of this activity was first noted in the seminal analysis of the two sets of hackers and their different activities inside the DNC's networks. Dmitri Alperovitch, "Bears in the Midst: Intrusion into the Democratic National Committee," CrowdStrike blog, June 15, 2016.

22. Raphael Satter, "Inside Story: How Russians Hacked the Democrats' Emails," AP, November 4, 2017.

23. *United States of America v. Viktor Borisovich Netyksho et al.*, 9–10.

24. *United States of America v. Viktor Borisovich Netyksho et al.*, 11.

25. *United States of America v. Viktor Borisovich Netyksho et al.*

26. *United States of America v. Viktor Borisovich Netyksho et al.*, 13.

27. The site has since been taken down, but it is possible to reconstruct its appearance from the Internet Archive. "DC Leaks / About," Internet Archive, June 20, 2016, https://web.archive.org/web/20160620202602 /http:/dcleaks.com:80/index.php/about.

28. Alperovitch, "Bears in the Midst"; Ellen Nakashima, "Russian Government Hackers Penetrated DNC, Stole Opposition Research on Trump," *Washington Post*, June 14, 2016.

29. For a good summary of Guccifer's activity and the cybersecurity community analysis by one of its participants, see Rid, "How Russia Pulled Off the Biggest Election Hack in U.S. History."

30. Lorenzo Franceschi-Bicchierai, "We Spoke to DNC Hacker 'Guccifer 2.0,'" *Motherboard*, June 21, 2016.

31. Mueller, "Report on the Investigation into Russian Interference in the 2016 Presidential Election," 47–52; Raffi Khatchadourian, "What the Latest Mueller Indictment Reveals about WikiLeaks' Ties to Russia—and What It Doesn't," *New Yorker*, July 24, 2018; Marshall Cohen, Kay Guerrero, and Arturo Torres, "Exclusive: Security Reports Reveal How Assange Turned an Embassy into a Command Post for Election Meddling," *CNN*, July 15, 2019.

32. *United States of America v. Viktor Borisovich Netyksho et al.*, 17–18.

33. Mueller, "Report on the Investigation into Russian Interference in the 2016 Presidential Election," 46.

34. Satter, "Inside Story: How Russians Hacked the Democrats' Emails."

35. Elias Groll, "Turns Out You Can't Trust Russian Hackers Anymore," *Foreign Policy*, August 22, 2016; Scott Shane, "When Spies Hack Journalism," *New York Times*, May 12, 2018.

36. "Full Transcript: Michael Cohen's Opening Statement to Congress," *New York Times*, February 27, 2019.

37. *United States of America v. Roger Jason Stone, Jr.*, US District Court, District of Columbia, indictment filed January 24, 2019, 2. Mueller,

"Report on the Investigation into Russian Interference in the 2016 Presidential Election," 173.

38. *United States of America v. Roger Jason Stone, Jr.*, 4–9.

39. Michael Schmidt, "Trump Invited the Russians to Hack Clinton. Were They Listening?," *New York Times*, July 13, 2018.

40. *United States of America v. Viktor Borisovich Netyksho et al.,* 7–8; Mueller, "Report on the Investigation into Russian Interference in the 2016 Presidential Election."

41. Alexandra Berzon and Rob Barry, "How Alleged Russian Hacker Teamed Up with Florida GOP Operative," *Wall Street Journal*, May 25, 2017.

42. Berzon and Barry, "How Alleged Russian Hacker Teamed Up."

43. Michael Isikoff, "Obama Cyber Chief Confirms 'Stand Down' Order Against Russian Cyberattacks in Summer 2016," *Yahoo News*, June 20, 2018.

44. Adam Entous, Ellen Nakashima, and Greg Miller, "Secret CIA Assessment Says Russia Was Trying to Help Trump Win White House," *Washington Post*, December 9, 2016.

45. Mark Landler and David Sanger, "Obama Says He Told Putin: 'Cut It Out' on Hacking," *New York Times*, December 16, 2016.

46. Department of Homeland Security and Office of the Director of National Intelligence, "Joint Statement on Election Security," Department of Homeland Security release, October 7, 2016.

47. David Corn, "Secret Video: Romney Tells Millionaire Donors What He Really Thinks of Obama Voters," *Mother Jones*, September 17, 2012; Chris Cillizza, "Why Mitt Romney's '47 Percent' Comment Was So Bad," *Washington Post*, March 4, 2013; Katharine Q. Seelye and Jeff Zeleny, "On the Defensive, Obama Calls His Words Ill-Chosen," *New York Times,* April 13, 2008.

48. Aaron Sharockman, "It's True: WikiLeaks Dumped Podesta Emails Hour after Trump Video Surfaced," *Politifact*, December 18, 2016.

49. For one example, see Zachary Crockett, "WikiLeaks Reveals John Podesta's Secret for Making Creamy Risotto," *Vox*, October 12, 2016.

50. *United States of America v. Roger Jason Stone, Jr.*, 4–9.

51. David Sanger, "White House Confirms Pre-Election Warning to Russia Over Hacking," *New York Times*, November 16, 2016.

52. Mueller, "Report on the Investigation into Russian Interference in the 2016 Presidential Election," 14, fn. 2.

53. *United States of America v. Internet Research Agency LLC*, US District Court, District of Columbia, indictment filed February 16, 2018, 12–16.

54. *United States of America v. Internet Research Agency LLC*, 13.

55. *United States of America v. Internet Research Agency LLC*, 14.

56. *United States of America v. Internet Research Agency LLC*, 15.

57. *United States of America v. Internet Research Agency LLC*, 16.

58. *United States of America v. Internet Research Agency LLC*, 14.

59. *United States of America v. Internet Research Agency LLC*, 15.

60. *United States of America v. Internet Research Agency LLC*, 14.

61. *United States of America v. Internet Research Agency LLC*, 17.

62. *United States of America v. Internet Research Agency LLC*, 17–18.

63. *United States of America v. Internet Research Agency LLC*, 18. Emphasis in the original.

64. *United States of America v. Internet Research Agency LLC*.

65. Colin Stretch, "Testimony of Colin Stretch, General Counsel, Facebook" Hearing before the US Senate Committee on the Judiciary Subcommittee on Crime and Terrorism, Washington, DC, October 31, 2017.

66. Craig Silverman, "This Analysis Shows How Viral Fake Election News Stories Outperformed Real News On Facebook," *Buzzfeed*, November 16, 2016.

67. Andrew Guess, Brendan Nyhan, and Jason Reifler, "Selective Exposure to Misinformation: Evidence from the Consumption of Fake News During the 2016 U.S. Presidential Campaign," European Research Council working paper, January 9, 2018.

68. Craig Silverman and Jeremy Singer-Vine, "Most Americans Who See Fake News Believe It, New Survey Says," *Buzzfeed*, December 6, 2016; Ipsos Public Affairs, "BuzzFeed Fake News," December 6, 2016. See also Hunt Allcott and Matthew Gentzkow, "Social Media and Fake News in the 2016 Election," *Journal of Economic Perspectives* 31, no. 2 (2018) 211–236.

69. *United States of America v. Internet Research Agency LLC*, 18.

70. *United States of America v. Internet Research Agency LLC*, 17.

71. *United States of America v. Internet Research Agency LLC*, 19.

72. For a detailed account of this period and its aftermath, see Nicholas Thompson and Fred Vogelstein, "Inside the Two Years That Shook Facebook—and the World," *Wired*, February 12, 2018.

73. *United States of America v. Internet Research Agency LLC*, 19.

74. *United States of America v. Internet Research Agency LLC*, 19–20. For copies of all of the ads, see "Social Media Advertisements," webpage, House Permanent Select Committee on Intelligence, May 10, 2018, https://intelligence.house.gov/social-media-content/social-media -advertisements.htm.

75. Facebook Business, "Success Story: Toomey for Senate," webpage promoting Facebook's services "to significantly shift voter intent," https://www.facebook.com/business/success/toomey-for-senate.

76. Mueller, "Report on the Investigation into Russian Interference in the 2016 Presidential Election," 29–31.

77. Mueller, "Report on the Investigation into Russian Interference in the 2016 Presidential Election," 29–31; *United States of America v. Internet Research Agency LLC*, 22–23.

78. Scott Shane, "How Unwitting Americans Encountered Russian Operatives Online," *New York Times*, February 18, 2018.

79. John D. Gallacher and Marc W. Heerdink, "Measuring the Effect of Russian Internet Research Agency Information Operations in Online Conversations," *Defence Strategic Communications* 6 (2019): 155–198.

80. Mueller, "Report on the Investigation into Russian Interference in the 2016 Presidential Election," 149.

81. Donald J. Trump (@realDonaldTrump), "Russia, Russia, Russia! That's all you heard at the beginning of this Witch Hunt Hoax . . . And now Russia has disappeared because I had nothing to do with Russia helping me to get elected. It was a crime that didn't exist. So now the Dems and their partner, the Fake News Media, ...," tweet, May 30, 2019, 7:57 AM. Also see Adam Gabbatt, "Trump Says Russia Helped Elect Him—Then Quickly Backtracks," *Guardian*, May 30, 2019.

82. Nate Silver, "How Much Did Russian Interference Affect The 2016 Election?," *FiveThirtyEight*, February 16, 2018; Lucam Ahmad Way and Adam Casey, "Russia Has Been Meddling in Foreign Elections for Decades. Has It Made a Difference?," *Washington Post*, January 8, 2018; Jane Mayer, "How Russia Helped Swing the Election for Trump," *New Yorker*, September 24, 2018.

83. For an analysis of the Comey letter, see Nate Silver, "The Comey Letter Probably Cost Clinton The Election," *FiveThirtyEight*, May 3, 2017. Among other possibly serious missteps, Clinton never campaigned in

Wisconsin during the general election, a state she narrowly lost. Nate Silver, "Donald Trump Had a Superior Electoral College Strategy," *FiveThirtyEight*, February 6, 2017. For a discussion of turnout in various demographic groups, see Bernard L. Fraga, Sean McElwee, Jesse Rhodes, and Brian Schaffner, "Why Did Trump Win? More Whites—and Fewer Blacks—Actually Voted," *Washington Post Monkey Cage Blog*, May 8, 2017.

84. For the definitive history of Soviet active measures, see Thomas Rid, *Active Measures: The Secret History of Disinformation and Political Warfare* (New York: Farrar, Strauss, and Giroux, 2020).

85. Mueller, "Report on the Investigation into Russian Interference in the 2016 Presidential Election," 42.

86. The phrase "de facto instrument of Russian intelligence" originates with Scott Shane, a *New York Times* reporter who reflected after the election on how the Russians had managed to "hack journalism." Chozick repeated it in her retrospective essay and said of the charges, "they were right." Amy Chozick, "'They Were Never Going to Let Me Be President,'" *New York Times*, April 20, 2018. Shane, "When Spies Hack Journalism."

87. Gabrielle Healy, "Did Trump Really Mention WikiLeaks Over 160 Times in the Last Month of the Election Cycle?," *Politifact*, April 21, 2017.

88. This was one of many different explanations offered by Trump; in others, he said the perpetrators could have been China, the DNC, "some guy in New Jersey," or "other people and other countries." Krishnadev Calamur, "Some of the People Trump Has Blamed for Russia's 2016 Election Hack," *Atlantic*, July 18, 2018.

89. Rebecca Sinderbrand, "How Kellyanne Conway Ushered in the Era of 'Alternative Facts,'" *Washington Post*, January 22, 2017. For more on challenges in democracy, see Scott J. Shackelford, Bruce Schneier, Michael Sulmeyer, Anne Boustead, and Ben Buchanan, "Making Democracy Harder to Hack," *University of Michigan Journal of Law Reform* 50, no. 3 (2016).

11. EXPOSURE

1. David Sanger, "'Shadow Brokers' Leak Raises Alarming Question: Was the N.S.A. Hacked?," *New York Times*, August 16, 2016; Ellen Na-

kashima, "Powerful NSA Hacking Tools Have Been Revealed Online," *Washington Post*, August 16, 2016.

2. Ellen Nakashima, "Pentagon and Intelligence Community Chiefs Have Urged Obama to Remove the Head of the NSA," *Washington Post*, November 19, 2016.

3. Ellen Nakashima and Craig Timberg, "NSA Officials Worried about the Day Its Potent Hacking Tool Would Get Loose. Then It Did," *Washington Post*, May 16, 2017.

4. Scott Shane, Nicole Perlroth, and David Sanger, "Security Breach and Spilled Secrets Have Shaken the NSA to Its Core," *New York Times*, November 12, 2017.

5. Matt Suiche was one of the first in the information security community to draw out this connection. Matt Suiche, "Shadow Brokers: NSA Exploits of the Week," *Medium*, August 15, 2016.

6. Sam Biddle, "The NSA Leak Is Real, Snowden Documents Confirm," *The Intercept*, August 19, 2016.

7. theshadowbrokers, "Equation Group Cyber Weapons Auction—Invitation," *Pastebin*, August 13, archived at 2016, https://swithak .github.io/SH20TAATSB18/Archive/Pastebin/JBcipKBL/.

8. Some of the messages have been deleted and are accessible through the internet archive. "The Shadow Brokers Twitter History," https://swithak .github.io/SH20TAATSB18/Archive/Tweets/TSB/TSBTwitterHistory/.

9. theshadowbrokers, "Equation Group Cyber Weapons Auction."

10. theshadowbrokers, "Equation Group Cyber Weapons Auction."

11. Kim Zetter, "Exclusive: How a Russian Firm Helped Catch an Alleged NSA Data Thief," *Politico*, January 9, 2019.

12. Jo Becker, Adam Goldman, Michael S. Schmidt, and Matt Apuzzo, "NSA Contractor Arrested in Possible New Theft of Secrets," *New York Times*, October 5, 2016; Ellen Nakashima, "Prosecutors to Seek Indictment against Former NSA Contractor as Early as This Week," *Washington Post*, February 6, 2017.

13. theshadowbrokers, "New Message from TheShadowBrokers," *Pastebin*, August 28, 2016, archived at https://swithak.github.io/SH20TAATSB18 /Archive/Pastebin/5R1SXJZp/.

14. theshadowbrokers, "TheShadowBrokers Message #3," *Medium*, October 1, 2016.

15. William N. Arkin, Ken Dilanian, and Robert Windrem, "CIA Prepping for Possible Cyber Strike against Russia," NBC News, October 14, 2016.

16. Becker et al., "NSA Contractor Arrested in Possible New Theft of Secrets."

17. This original message and others from this period appear to have been taken down, but reposts are visible on the Shadow Brokers' account on *Steemit*, a blockchain-based messaging site, which the Shadow Brokers later used for their communications and which is the best compendium of their messages in one place. theshadowbrokers, "Repost: TheShadowBrokers Message#4 - October 2016," *Steemit*, October 15, 2016.

18. theshadowbrokers, "Message#5— Trick or Treat?," *Medium*, October 30, 2016.

19. theshadowbrokers, "Message#5."

20. Amy B. Wang, "'Post-Truth' Named 2016 Word of the Year by Oxford Dictionaries," *Washington Post*, November 16, 2016.

21. Boceffus Cleetus, "Are the Shadow Brokers Selling NSA Tools on ZeroNet?," *Medium*, December 14, 2016.

22. Joseph Cox, "A Brief Interview with The Shadow Brokers, The Hackers Selling NSA Exploits," *Motherboard*, December 15, 2016; "The Shadow Brokers Twitter History."

23. thegrugq, "The Great Cyber Game: Commentary (3)," *Medium*, December 16, 2016.

24. Cox, "A Brief Interview with The Shadow Brokers."

25. "The Shadow Brokers Twitter History."

26. theshadowbrokers, "Repost: TheShadowBrokers Message#7 - January 2017," *Steemit*, January 11, 2017.

27. theshadowbrokers, "Repost: TheShadowBrokers Message#8 - January 2017," *Steemit*, January 12, 2017.

28. Dan Goodin, "NSA-Leaking Shadow Brokers Lob Molotov Cocktail Before Exiting World Stage," *Ars Technica*, January 12, 2017.

29. theshadowbrokers, "Don't Forget Your Base," *Steemit*, April 8, 2017.

30. theshadowbrokers, "Grammer Critics: Information vs Knowledge," *Steemit*, April 9, 2017.

31. David Aitel, "Naming / Shaming Iran Was a Huge Mistake," *CyberSecPolitics*, April 13, 2016; Jake Williams, "DOJ Indictments of Foreign Hackers Are Bad for US Gov Employees," MalwareJake, March 26, 2016.

32. "The Shadow Brokers Twitter History."

33. theshadowbrokers, "Lost in Translation," *Steemit*, April 15, 2017.

34. "Analyzing the DOUBLEPULSAR Kernel DLL Injection Technique," Countercept blog, April 19, 2017; theshadowbrokers, "Lost in Translation"; Dune Lawrence, "Seriously, Beware the 'Shadow Brokers,'" *Bloomberg*, May 4, 2017.

35. "Doublepulsar," BinaryEdge blog, April 21, 2017.

36. Nakashima and Timberg, "NSA Officials Worried about the Day Its Potent Hacking Tool Would Get Loose. Then It Did."

37. Ryan McCombs, Jason Barnes, Karan Sood, and Ian Barton, "WannaMine Cryptomining: Harmless Nuisance or Disruptive Threat?," Crowdstrike blog, January 25, 2018.

38. Catalin Cimpanu, "Shadow Brokers Release New Files Revealing Windows Exploits, SWIFT Attacks," *BleepingComputer*, April 14, 2017.

39. theshadowbrokers, "OH LORDY! Comey Wanna Cry Edition," *Steemit*, May 16, 2017.

40. theshadowbrokers, "TheShadowBrokers Monthly Dump Service— July 2017," *Steemit*, June 28, 2017.

41. Matt Suiche, "Shadow Brokers: The Insider Theory," Comae Technologies, August 16, 2016.

42. LexingtonAluminum (@LexingtonAl), "TheShadowBrokers is a group of insiders, from within the USG. You dont know our names, we dont work for another country, and we weren't in it for profit. If course you shitbird charlatans had all your stupid fucking theories that sound like a script from some shitty spy movie," February 16, 2019, tweet.

43. Bruce Schneier, "Who Are the Shadow Brokers?," *The Atlantic*, May 23, 2017; Matt Tait, Benjamin Wittes, and Matthew Kahn, "The *Lawfare* Podcast: Matt Tait on Recent Events in Cybersecurity," *Lawfare*, July 8, 2017.

44. Among other citations in this chapter, see Shane Harris, Gordon Lubold, and Paul Sonne, "How Kaspersky's Software Fell under Suspicion of Spying on America."

45. See Vindu Goel and Eric Lichtblau, "Russian Agents Were behind Yahoo Hack, U.S. Says," *New York Times*, March 15, 2017; Ben Buchanan and Michael Sulmeyer, "Russia and Cyber Operations: Challenges and Opportunities for the Next U.S. Administration," white paper, Carnegie Endowment for International Peace, November 2016. More generally

on cross-pollination, see Ben Buchanan, "The Life Cycles of Cyber Threats," *Survival* 58, no. 1 (2016): 39–58.

46. As one security analyst noted, "there is simply too much here" for this to have come from a hack of a staging server. thegrugq, "The Great Cyber Game: Commentary (3)," *Medium*, December 16, 2016.

47. Nakashima, "Prosecutors to Seek Indictment against Former NSA Contractor."

48. Gordon Lubold and Shane Harris, "Russian Hackers Stole NSA Data on U.S. Cyber Defense," *Wall Street Journal*, October 5, 2017.

49. Once again referred to as the Equation Group.

50. Nicole Perlroth and Scott Shane, "How Israel Caught Russian Hackers Scouring the World for U.S. Secrets," *New York Times*, October 10, 2017.

51. Michael S. Rogers, "Re: *United States v. Nghia Hoang Pho*," letter to the Honorable George L. Russell III, March 5, 2018, published alongside Josh Gerstein, "NSA Curbs Spying After Security Breach," *Politico*, September 20, 2018.

52. Department of Justice, "Former NSA Employee Sentenced to Prison for Willful Retention of Classified National Defense Information," Office of Public Affairs press release, September 25, 2018.

53. "Preliminary Results of the Internal Investigation into Alleged Incident Reported by US Media," Kaspersky Lab blog, October 24, 2017; Kim Zetter, "NSA Worker's Software Piracy May Have Exposed Him to Russian Spies," *The Intercept*, October 25, 2017; "Investigation Report for the September 2014 Equation Malware Detection Incident in the US," Kaspersky Lab blog, November 16, 2017.

54. The firm later promised to move its data centers to Switzerland. "Kaspersky Lab Moving Core Infrastructure from Russia to Switzerland; Opening First Transparency Center," Kaspersky Lab blog, May 15, 2018.

55. For one articulation of this idea, see Thomas Rid, "How Russia Pulled Off the Biggest Election Hack in U.S. History," *Esquire*, October 20, 2016.

56. Shane, Perlroth, and Sanger, "Security Breach and Spilled Secrets Have Shaken NSA to Its Core."

57. For the full review, see Ash Carter, "A Lasting Defeat: The Campaign to Destroy ISIS," paper, Belfer Center for Science and International Affairs, October 2017.

58. Brad Smith, "The Need for Urgent Collective Action to Keep People Safe Online: Lessons from Last Week's Cyberattack," Microsoft blog, May 14, 2017.

59. For discussion of some of this behind-the-scenes negotiating, see Michael V. Hayden and Barton Gellman, "National Security Agency and Privacy Debate," American University School of Public Affairs event, Washington, DC, April 3, 2014. The staged debate can be viewed on C-Span, https://www.c-span.org/video/?318674-1/debate-nsa-privacy-laws.

60. theshadowbrokers, "OH LORDY! Comey Wanna Cry Edition."

61. theshadowbrokers, "OH LORDY!"

62. Jacob Appelbaum, Judith Horchert, and Christian Stoecker, "Shopping for Spy Gear: Catalog Advertises NSA Toolbox," *Der Spiegel*, December 29, 2013.

63. Jacob Appelbaum, Nikolaus Blome, Hubert Gude, Ralf Neukirch, et al., "Embassy Espionage: The NSA's Secret Spy Hub in Berlin," November 4, 2013; Jacob Appelbaum, A. Gibson, J. Goetz, V. Kabisch, et al., "NSA Targets the Privacy-Conscious," *Das Erste*, July 3, 2014. For more on these non-Snowden leaks, see Peter Koop, "Leaked Documents That Were Not Attributed to Snowden," *Electrospaces*, December 13, 2015; Peter Koop, "Are the Shadow Brokers Identical with the Second Source?," *Electrospaces*, September 14, 2017.

64. Former GCHQ employee Matt Tait tweeted: "They don't care if anyone pays. The whole point of this is to bait the NSA into burning [capabilities] that [the Shadow Brokers don't] have out of excessive caution." Matt Tait (@pwnallthethings), May 31, 2017, 5:27 PM, tweet.

65. James Risen, "U.S. Secretly Negotiated with Russians to Buy Stolen NSA Documents, and the Russians Offered Trump-Related Material, Too," *The Intercept*, February 9, 2018; Matthew Rosenberg, "U.S. Spies, Seeking to Retrieve Cyberweapons, Paid Russian Peddling Trump Secrets," *New York Times*, February 9, 2018.

12. THEFT, RANSOM, AND MANIPULATION

1. Sheena Chestnut Greitens, *Illicit: North Korea's Evolving Operations to Earn Hard Currency* (Washington, DC: Committee for Human Rights in North Korea, 2014). See also Sheena Chestnut, "Illicit Activity and Proliferation: North Korean Smuggling Networks," *International Security* 32, no. 1 (2007): 80–111; Stephen Mihm, "No Ordinary Counterfeit," *New York Times*, July 23, 2006.

2. Liana Sun Wyler and Dick K. Nanto, "North Korean Crime-for-Profit Activities," Congressional Research Service report for US Congress, August 25, 2008, 8.

3. For example, see Isaac Stone Fish, "Inside North Korea's Crystal Meth Trade," *Foreign Policy*, November 21, 2013.

4. Wyler and Nanto, "North Korean Crime-for-Profit Activities," 3-4.

5. Greg Walters, "North Korea's Counterfeit Benjamins Have Vanished," *Vice News*, March 16, 2016. See also Dick K. Nanto, "North Korean Counterfeiting of U.S. Currency," Congressional Research Service report for US Congress, June 12, 2009.

6. For a good summary of the North Korean hacking program, see David Sanger, David Kirkpatrick, and Nicole Perlroth, "The World Once Laughed at North Korean Cyberpower. No More," *New York Times*, October 15, 2017.

7. "The World Factbook: Korea, North," Central Intelligence Agency, continually updated at https://www.cia.gov/library/publications/the-world-factbook/geos/kn.html, accessed September 15, 2017. See also Michelle Nichols, "North Korea Took $2 Billion in Cyberattacks to Fund Weapons Program: U.N. Report," Reuters, August 5, 2019.

8. John Markoff and Thom Shanker, "Halted '03 Iraq Plan Illustrates U.S. Fear of Cyberwar Risk," *New York Times*, August 1, 2009.

9. Richard A. Clarke, Michael J. Morell, Geoffrey R. Stone, Cass R. Sunstein, and Peter Swire, "Liberty and Security in a Changing World," President's Review Group on Intelligence and Communications Technologies, report, December 12, 2013, 221.

10. Steven D. Levitt and Stephen J. Dubner, *When to Rob a Bank* (New York: HarperCollins, 2015).

11. Associated Press, "Suspect in Major Brazil Robbery Is Found Dead," *New York Times*, October 22, 2005.

12. Serajul Quadir, "Bangladesh Bank Exposed to Hackers by Cheap Switches, No Firewall: Police," Reuters, April 21, 2016.

13. Sergei Shevchenko and Adrian Nish, "Cyber Heist Attribution," BAE Systems blog, May 13, 2016; "Lazarus Under the Hood," Kaspersky Lab blog, April 3, 2017; Sergei Shevchenko, "Two Bytes to $951m," *BAE Systems Threat Research Blog*, April 25, 2016.

14. Kim Zetter, "That Insane, $81M Bangladesh Bank Heist? Here's What We Know," *Wired*, May 17, 2016.

15. This was a different intrusion in a different country than the North Koreans' breach of TPBank in Vietnam, which also occurred in late 2015.

16. Jose Pagliery, "North Korea-Linked Hackers Are Attacking Banks Worldwide," *CNN*, April 4, 2017.

17. Elizabeth Shim, "North Korea Targeted Bitcoin Exchange in Hacking Attempt, Expert Says," *UPI*, August 24, 2017; Timothy W. Martin, Eun-Young Joeng, and Steven Russolillo, "North Korea Is Suspected in Bitcoin Heist," *Wall Street Journal*, December 20, 2017.

18. Because the thefts are of cryptocurrency, their estimated dollar values fluctuate with the price of the currency. David Canellis, "North Korean Hacker Crew Steals $571M in Cryptocurrency across 5 Attacks," *The Next Web (TNW) News*, October 19, 2018.

19. Kaspersky Lab Global Research and Analysis Team, "Lazarus Under the Hood," report, April 3, 2017; Dmitry Volkov, "Lazarus Arisen Architecture, Techniques, and Attribution," Group-IB Threat Intelligence Department, May 30, 2017; Kate Kochetkova, "What Is Known About the Lazarus Group: Sony Hack, Military Espionage, Attacks on Korean Banks and Other Crimes," *Kaspersky Daily,* February 24, 2016.

20. David Sanger and Michael Schmidt, "More Sanctions on North Korea After Sony Case," *New York Times,* January 2, 2015.

21. Symantec Security Response, "WannaCry: Ransomware Attacks Show Strong Links to Lazarus Group," Symantec blog, May 22, 2017.

22. At some level, the idea of the worm dated back to a famous work in computer science written in 1966. John Von Neumann and Arthur W. Burks, "Theory of Self-Reproducing Automata," *IEEE Transactions on Neural Networks* 5, no. 1 (1966): 3–14.

23. Details are not abundant about the initial infection vector for Wanna-Cry. For one view, see thegrugq, "The Triple A Threat: Aggressive Autonomous Agents," presentation deck, Comae Technologies, 2017, 22.

24. Nicole Perlroth and David Sanger, "Hackers Hit Dozens of Countries Exploiting Stolen N.S.A. Tool," *New York Times*, May 12, 2017.

25. Sam Petulla, "Ransomware Attack: This Is the Total Paid and How the Virus Spread," *NBC News*, May 15, 2017.

26. Symantec Security Response, "WannaCry."

27. For technical discussion of the WannaCry code, see Kaspersky Lab Global Research and Analysis Team, "WannaCry and Lazarus Group: The Missing Link?," *SecureList*, May 15, 2017; John Miller and David Mainor, "WannaCry Ransomware Campaign: Threat Details and Risk Management," FireEye blog, May 15, 2017; Sergei Shevchenko and Adrian Nish, "WanaCrypt0r Ransomworm," BAE Systems Threat Research Blog, May 16, 2017.

28. His best guess was that this was not meant to be a kill switch at all, but rather something to help the code hide from security researchers. Marcus Hutchins, "How to Accidentally Stop a Global Cyber Attack," *MalwareTech*, May 13, 2017.

29. One estimate placing the costs between $4 and $8 billion is Andy Greenberg, "The Untold Story of NotPetya, the Most Devastating Cyberattack in History," *Wired*, August 22, 2018.

30. Dan Strumpf, "North Korean Cybercriminals Implicated in Taiwan Bank Theft," *Wall Street Journal*, October 17, 2017. Some initial reporting placed the figure at $60 million, but sources with direct knowledge of the case indicated that was too high by a factor of four.

31. Sergei Shevchenko, Hirman Muhammad bin Abu Bakar, and James Wong, "Taiwan Heist: Lazarus Tools and Ransomware," BAE Systems blog, October 16, 2017. For local reporting on the case, see "Shalila

Moonasinghe Removed as Litro Gas Chairman," *Daily News*, October 11, 2017.

32. Taipei Times Staff, "Lai Orders Information Security Review," *Taipei Times*, October 8, 2017.

33. Brian Krebs, "Hackers Breached Virginia Bank Twice in Eight Months, Stole $2.4M," *Krebs on Security*, July 24, 2018.

34. Brian Krebs, "FBI Warns of 'Unlimited' ATM Cashout Blitz," *Krebs on Security*, August 12, 2018.

35. The best discussion of the mechanics of the entire Cosmos case comes from Saher Naumaan, a central member of the BAE team. See Saher Naumaan, "Lazarus On The Rise: Insights from SWIFT Bank Attacks," presentation to BSides Belfast 2018, Belfast, Ireland, September 27, 2018; Adrian Nish and Saher Naumaan, "The Cyber Threat Landscape: Confronting Challenges to the Financial System," Carnegie Endowment for International Peace, paper, March 25, 2019.

36. Gitesh Shelke, "Cosmos Bank Data from Nine Years Compromised in Rs 94.42 Crore Heist," *Times of India*, August 19, 2018.

37. Brian Krebs, "Indian Bank Hit in $13.5M Cyberheist after FBI ATM Cashout Warning," *Krebs on Security*, August 17, 2018.

38. Screenshots taken nine days after the incident suggested key online systems were still inaccessible to customers at that time.

13. WIDESPREAD DISRUPTION

1. Andy Greenberg, "The Untold Story of NotPetya, the Most Devastating Cyberattack in History," *Wired,* August 22, 2018.

2. For an excellent discussion of the benefits and perils of updating software, see Matt Tait, "Updating How We Think About Security," *Vimeo*, May 1, 2018.

3. Anton Cherepanov and Robert Lipovsky, "New TeleBots Backdoor: First Evidence Linking Industroyer to NotPetya," *ESET*, October 11, 2018.

4. Jack Stubbs and Matthias Williams, "Ukraine Scrambles to Contain New Cyber Threat After 'NotPetya' Attack," Reuters, July 5, 2017.

5. For an excellent discussion of how the hackers extended Petya and why NotPetya is thought to be the work of a different author, see "EternalPetya: Yet Another Stolen Piece in the Package?," *Malwarebytes Labs* blog, June 30, 2017.

6. Andy Greenberg, *Sandworm: A New Era of Cyberwar and the Hunt for the Kremlin's Most Dangerous Hackers* (New York: Doubleday, 2019), 181.

7. Greenberg, "The Untold Story of NotPetya."

8. For a good technical analysis of NotPetya, see Anton Cherepanov, "Analysis of TeleBots' Cunning Backdoor," *ESET*, July 4, 2017; David Maynor, Aleksandar Nikolic, Matt Olney, and Yves Younan, "The MeDoc Connection," *Threatsource* [Cisco Talos newsletter], July 5, 2017; Microsoft Defender ATP Research Team, "New Ransomware, Old Techniques: Petya Adds Worm Capabilities," Microsoft Security blog, June 27, 2017; Karan Sood and Shaun Hurley, "NotPetya Technical Analysis—A Triple Threat: File Encryption, MFT Encryption, Credential Theft," *CrowdStrike*, June 29, 2017; Symantic Security Response, "Petya Ransomware Outbreak: Here's What You Need to Know," Symantec blog, October 24, 2017.

9. It did not launch this attack if antivirus from Symantec, Norton, or Kaspersky was present. Microsoft Defender ATP Research Team, "New Ransomware, Old Techniques: Petya Adds Worm Capabilities," 8–9.

10. Greenberg, *Sandworm,* 151–153.

11. Greenberg, "The Untold Story of NotPetya."

12. Catalin Cimpanu, "Maersk Reinstalled 45,000 PCs and 4,000 Servers to Recover from NotPetya Attack," *BleepingComputer*, January 25, 2018.

13. Greenberg, "The Untold Story of NotPetya"; Greenberg, *Sandworm,* 190–195.

14. "Maersk 2017 Annual Report," Maersk, February 9, 2018, 8.

15. Jeff Berman, "FedEx Acquisition of TNT Is Made Official," *Logistics Management,* May 25, 2016.

16. "FedEx Q1 FY18 Earnings Call Transcript," FedEx, September 19, 2017.

17. The executives did not specify a precise cost for the increased integration of computer systems, but the overall integration project cost almost a billion dollars. For more details, see "FedEx Corporation

10-K," FedEx, July 16, 2018, 53; "FedEx Q1 FY18 Earnings Call Transcript."

18. Greenberg, *Sandworm*, 198.

19. Kim S. Nash, Sara Castellanos, and Adam Janofsky, "One Year after NotPetya Cyberattack, Firms Wrestle With Recovery Costs," *Wall Street Journal*, June 27, 2018.

20. For examples, see Kat Hall, "Largest Advertising Company in the World Still Wincing after NotPetya Punch," *The Register*, July 7, 2017; Ry Crozier, "DLA Piper Paid 15,000 Hours of IT Overtime after NotPetya Attack," *ITNews*, May 8, 2018; "Mondelēz International, Inc 10-K," Mondelēz International, February 9, 2018, 24–25; "Nuance Communications, Inc. 10-Q," Nuance Communications, May 10, 2018, 23; "First-Half 2017 Results," Saint-Gobain, July 27, 2017, 2; John Leyden, "Nothing Could Protect Durex Peddler from NotPetya Ransomware," *The Register*, July 6, 2017.

21. Greenberg, *Sandworm*, 185–189. For two other good contemporaneous news accounts of the damage, see Lizzie Dearden, "Ukraine Cyber Attack: Chaos as National Bank, State Power Provider and Airport Hit by Hackers," *The Independent*, June 27, 2017; Christian Borys, "Ukraine Braces for Further Cyber-Attacks," *BBC News*, July 26, 2017.

22. Ken Dilanian, "Can the CIA and NSA Be Trusted with Cyber Hacking Tools?," *NBC News*, June 30, 2017.

23. Mikko Hypponen, chief research officer at Finnish information security firm F-Secure, said: "I believe that NotPetya was the single most expensive computer security incident in history. I believe it created bigger losses than any malware outbreak ever, or any hacking incident ever, or any data leak ever. It was historic." John Leyden, "A Year after Devastating NotPetya Outbreak, What Have We Learnt? Er, Not A Lot, Says Blackberry Bod," *The Register*, June 27, 2018. Also see Greenberg, *Sandworm*, 199.

24. Greenberg, "The Untold Story of NotPetya."

25. Greenberg, *Sandworm*, 215.

26. Robert Jervis, "Hypotheses on Misperception," *World Politics* 20, no. 3 (1968): 454–479, 474.

27. Sarah Sanders, "Statement from the Press Secretary," White House Press Office release, February 15, 2018.

28. For a good discussion of the penalty, or lack thereof, levied on Russia, see Greenberg, *Sandworm*, 243–245.

29. Kaspersky sKyWIper Analysis Team, "sKyWIper (a.K.a. Flame a.K.a. Flamer): A Complex Malware for Targeted Attacks," report, Laboratory of Cryptography and System Security, Budapest University of Technology and Economics, May 31, 2012; Alexander Gostev, "The Flame: Questions and Answers," *Securelist*, May 28, 2012; Kaspersky Lab, "Unveiling 'Careto'—The Masked APT," report, February 6, 2014; Josh Chin, "Chinese Firm Behind Alleged Hacking Was Disbanded This Month," *Wall Street Journal*, November 29, 2017.

30. *United States of America v. Ahmad Fathi, Hamid Firoozi, Amin Shokohi, Sadegh Ahmadzadegan, Omid Ghaffarinia, Sina Keissar, and Nader Saedi*, US District Court, Southern District of New York, indictment filed March 24, 2016; *United States of America v. Wang Dong, Sun Kailiang, Wen Xinyu, Huang Zhenyu, Gu Chunhui*, United States District Court, Western District of Pennsylvania, indictment filed May 1, 2014; *United States of America v. Park Jin Hyok*, US District Court, Central District of California, criminal complaint filed June 8, 2018.

31. Jack Goldsmith and Robert D. Williams, "The Failure of the United States' Chinese-Hacking Indictment Strategy," *Lawfare* blog, December 28, 2018.

CONCLUSION

1. US Cyber Consequences Unit, "Overview by the US-CCU of the Cyber Campaign against Georgia in August of 2008," special report, August 2009; Greylogic [Jeff Carr, principal investigator], "Project Grey Goose Phase II Report: The Evolving State of Cyber Warfare," report, March 20, 2009.

2. For more on this, see Sean Naylor, *Relentless Strike: The Secret History of Joint Special Operations Command* (New York: St. Martin's Press, 2015).

3. For examples of conceptual and threat-specific frameworks, see Michael J. Assante and Robert M. Lee, "The Industrial Control System

Cyber Kill Chain," SANS Institute, report, October 2015; Eric M. Hutchins, Michael J. Cloppert, and Rohan M. Amin, "Intelligence-Driven Computer Network Defense Informed by Analysis of Adversary Campaigns and Intrusion Kill Chains," Lockheed Martin white paper, 2010; Ben Buchanan, *The Cybersecurity Dilemma*, ch. 2–3; Katie Nickels, "Getting Started with ATT&CK: Threat Intelligence," *Medium*, June 10, 2019.

4. Danny Vinik, "America's Secret Arsenal," *Politico*, December 9, 2015.

5. Thomas C. Schelling, *Arms and Influence* (New Haven: Yale University Press, 1966), 69–70.

6. Robert Jervis, "Hypotheses on Misperception," World Politics 20, no. 3 (1968): 454–479.

7. Xenophon, *Anabasis* in *Xenophon* Volume III, Book VI, Chapter V, trans. Carleton L. Brownson and John Dillery (Cambridge, MA: Harvard University Press, 1998).

8. For discussion of some of these operations, see Andy Ozment, "The DHS Role in Federal Cybersecurity and the Recent Compromise at the Office of Personnel Management," written testimony to Committee on Oversight and Government Reform, US House of Representatives, 2015; Christopher Drew and John Markoff, "Data Breach at Security Firm Linked to Attack on Lockheed," *New York Times*, May 27, 2011; Nathan Hodge and Ian Scherr, "Lockheed Martin Hit by Security Breach," *Wall Street Journal*, May 27, 2011; Adrian Nish and Tom Rowles, "APT10—Operation Cloud Hopper," BAE Systems blog, April 3, 2017; Andy Greenberg, "A Mysterious Hacker Group Is on a Supply Chain Hijacking Spree," *Wired*, May 3, 2019; Gordon Lubold and Dustin Volz, "Navy, Industry Partners Are 'Under Cyber Siege' by Chinese Hackers, Review Asserts," *Wall Street Journal*, March 12, 2019; Jack Stubbs, Joseph Menn, and Christopher Bing, "Inside the West's Failed Fight against China's 'Cloud Hopper' Hackers," Reuters, June 26, 2019.

9. James Stavridis, "China's Next Naval Target Is the Internet's Under-water Cables," *Bloomberg*, April 8, 2019; "PRC Information Warfare & Huawei," National Security Agency internal presentation deck, published alongside Micah Lee and Henrik Moltke, "Everybody Does

It: The Messy Truth about Infiltrating Computer Supply Chains," *The Intercept*, January 24, 2019.

10. Nicole Perlroth, "D.N.C. Says It Was Targeted Again by Russian Hackers after '18 Election," *New York Times*, January 18, 2019; United States Computer Emergency Readiness Team, "Advanced Persistent Threat Activity Targeting Energy and Other Critical Infrastructure Sectors," Department of Homeland Security release, October 20, 2017; Tara Seals, "APT29 Re-Emerges after 2 Years with Widespread Espionage Campaign," *ThreatPost*, November 20, 2018; Kaspersky Lab Global Research and Analysis Team, "Shedding Skin—Turla's Fresh Faces," *SecureList*, October 4, 2018.

11. Joseph Cox, "Experts Doubt Russian Claims That Cryptographic Flaw Was a Coincidence," *Motherboard*, May 8, 2019; Léo Parrin, "Partitions in the S-Box of Streebog and Kuznyechik," *IACR Transactions on Symmetric Cryptology*, January 29, 2019.

12. David E. Sanger, "U.S. Cyberattacks Target ISIS in a New Line of Combat." *New York Times,* April 24, 2016.

13. Ash Carter, "A Lasting Defeat: The Campaign to Destroy ISIS," report, Belfer Center for Science and International Affairs, October 2017, 32–33.

14. Costin Raiu, Mohamad Amin Hasbini, Sergey Belov, and Sergey Mineev, "From Shamoon to StoneDrill," Kaspersky *SecureList*, March 6, 2017; Bill Marczak, Nicholas Weaver, Jakub Dalek, Roya Ensafi, et al., "China's Great Cannon," research brief, Munk School of Global Affairs, Citizen Lab, April 10, 2015.

15. Kaspersky Lab Global Research and Analysis Team, "OlympicDestroyer Is Here to Trick the Industry," *SecureList*, March 8, 2018; Greenberg, *Sandworm*, 257–265.

16. Nicole Perlroth and Clifford Krauss, "A Cyberattack in Saudi Arabia Had a Deadly Goal. Experts Fear Another Try," *New York Times*, March 15, 2018; Raiu, Hasbini, Belov, Mineev, "From Shamoon to StoneDrill"; Blake Sobczak, "The Inside Story of the World's Most Dangerous Malware," *E&E News,* March 7, 2019; FireEye Intelligence "TRITON Attribution: Russian Government-Owned Lab Most Likely Built Custom Intrusion Tools for TRITON Attackers," FireEye Threat

Research blog, October 23, 2018; Dragos, "TRISIS Malware: Analysis of Safety System Targeted Malware," Dragos report, December 13, 2017.

17. Craig Silverman, "Facebook Removed over 2 Billion Fake Accounts, But the Problem Is Getting Worse," *BuzzFeed*, May 24, 2019; Melanie Amann and Pavel Lokshin, "German Populists Forge Ties with Russia," *Der Spiegel*, April 27, 2016.

18. Josh Gerstein, "U.S. Brings First Charge for Meddling in 2018 Midterm Elections," *Politico*, October 19, 2018; Twitter Safety, "Information Operations Directed at Hong Kong," Twitter blog, August 19, 2019.

19. The Dutch government made many of these activities public. See, for example, "Russia Denies Western Accusations of Attacks," *CNN Video*, October 4, 2018.

20. "Facebook's Sputnik Takedown—In Depth," report, Atlantic Council Digital Forensics Research Lab, January 17, 2019; Philip N. Howard, Bharath Ganesh, Dimitra Liotsiou, John Kelly, and Camille François, "The IRA, Social Media and Political Polarization in the United States, 2012–2018," University of Oxford, Computational Propaganda Research Project, report, December 2018; Kevin Roose, "Is a New Russian Meddling Tactic Hiding in Plain Sight?," *New York Times*, September 25, 2018.

21. Gabrielle Lim, Etienne Maynier, John Scott-Railton, Alberto Fittarelli, Ned Moran, and Ron Deibert, "Burned after Reading: Endless Mayfly's Ephemeral Disinformation Campaign," Citizen Lab threat research report, May 14, 2019; "Taking Down More Coordinated Inauthentic Behavior," Facebook corporate communications news release, August 21, 2018; Jack Stubbs and Christopher Bing, "Exclusive: Iran-Based Political Influence Operation–Bigger, Persistent, Global," Reuters, August 28, 2018.

22. Andy Greenberg, "A Mystery Agent Is Doxing Iran's Hackers and Dumping Their Code," *Wired*, April 18, 2019.

23. Shannon Vavra, "Why Cyber Command's Latest Warning Is a Win for the Government's Information Sharing Efforts," *Cyberscoop*, July 10, 2019.

24. Joseph Cox, "Meet 'Intrusion Truth,' the Mysterious Group Doxing Chinese Intel Hackers," *Motherboard*, August 21, 2018.

25. Karen DeYoung and Ellen Nakashima, "UAE Orchestrated Hacking of Qatari Government Sites, Sparking Regional Upheaval, According to U.S. Intelligence Officials," *Washington Post*, July 16, 2017; Kevin Poulsen, "Hackers Vow to Release Apparent Trove of U.A.E. Ambassador's Emails," *Daily Beast*, June 2, 2017; Adam Hulcoop, John Scott-Railton, Peter Tanchak, Matt Brooks, and Ron Deibert, "Tainted Leaks: Disinformation and Phishing with a Russian Nexus," *Citizen Lab*, May 25, 2017; Scott Shane, "The Age of Big Leaks," *New York Times*, February 2, 2019.

26. David Ignatius, "How a Chilling Saudi Cyberwar Ensnared Jamal Khashoggi," *Washington Post*, December 7, 2018.

27. For examples, see Kim Zetter, "Hacking Team Leak Shows How Secretive Zero-Day Exploit Sales Work," *Wired*, July 24, 2015; Bill Marczak, Claudio Guarnieri, Morgan Marquis-Boire, and John Scott-Railton, "Hacking Team and the Targeting of Ethiopian Journalists," *Citizen Lab*, February 12, 2014; Alex Kane, "How Israel Became a Hub for Surveillance Technology," *The Intercept*, October 17, 2017; Joel Schechtman and Christopher Bing, "UAE Used Cyber Super-Weapon to Spy on iPhones of Foes," Reuters, January 30, 2019.

28. John Scott-Railton, Bill Marczak, Claudio Guarnieri, and Masashi Crete-Nishihata, "Bitter Sweet: Supporters of Mexico's Soda Tax Targeted With NSO Exploit Links," report, Citizen Lab Targeted Threats Research, February 11, 2017.

29. "H.R.5515—John S. McCain National Defense Authorization Act for Fiscal Year 2019," bill introduced April 13, 2018, passed as Public Law 115–232, 115th Congress, August 13, 2018. See Section 1632, "Affirming the Authority of the Secretary of Defense to Conduct Military Activities and Operations in Cyberspace."

30. United States Cyber Command, "Achieve and Maintain Cyberspace Superiority: Command Vision for US Cyber Command," March 23, 2018; Michael P. Fischerkeller and Richard J. Harknett, "Persistent Engagement, Agreed Competition, Cyberspace Interaction Dynamics, and Escalation," report, Institute for Defense Analyses, May 2018; Michael P. Fischerkeller and Richard J. Harknett, "Persistent Engage-

ment and Tacit Bargaining: A Path toward Constructing Norms in Cyberspace," Lawfare blog, November 9, 2018.

31. Paul M. Nakasone, "A Cyber Force for Persistent Operations," *Joint Forces Quarterly*, 92 (2019), 10–14: 11.

32. Greenberg, *Sandworm*, 288.

33. For more on this case, see Thomas Rid, *Rise of the Machines: A Cybernetic History* (New York: WW Norton, 2016), ch. 8.

34. Blake Sobczak, "Ex-NSA Official Urges Utilities to Beware of Russian Hackers," *E&E News*, May 22, 2019.

Acknowledgments

I am deeply indebted to Georgetown University, which has provided me with two degrees, a host of friends, a soulmate, an engagement spot, a wedding venue, a professorship, and the world's best colleagues. Among the people who animate the campus and help provide such a welcoming intellectual home are Dan Byman, Fr. Matthew Carnes, Tarun Chhabra, Joel Hellman, Keir Lieber, Jason Matheny, Rebecca Patterson, and the rest of the Security Studies department and the Center for Security and Emerging Technology. Elizabeth Arsenault and Crouton deserve special recognition for making every day in the townhouse so much fun. Wonderful friends from my time as a student at Georgetown include Scott Fligor, Alex Guyton, Nathalie Lawyer, Charlotte Markson, Charlie Morton, Greg Ouellette, Dani Soldin, and John Weidinger. From ambulances to Arabic and so much since, Taylor Miller makes everything fun (and a little ridiculous).

I am indebted to the teachers throughout my life who made this book and so much else possible, especially those at Regis High School. My friends from Regis, especially Kevin Keogh, Antonio Loccisano, Casey Quinn, and Colin Ross, will be stuck with me for a long time.

The Marshall Scholarship changed my life and career. I am deeply grateful for the three years I spent at King's College London. My PhD advisor, Thomas Rid, is a remarkable scholar but an even better person. Other great friends from the United Kingdom not mentioned elsewhere in these acknowledgments include Adi Ashok, Alex Baron, Will Berdanier, Alyssa Bilinski, Kenzie Bok, Alex Chaitoff, Emily Coker, Natalia Emanuel, Shea Houlihan, Rahul Rekhi, and Heather Williams.

From start to finish, Michael Sulmeyer made this book possible. He recruited me as a post-doctoral fellow to Harvard's Belfer Center for Science and International Affairs and gave me the time to think about a large project like this. When I had produced a first draft, even though I was no longer at Harvard, he offered an exceptionally detailed review, carefully marking up hundreds of pages by hand. Our country is lucky to have him as a public servant but, most important to me, I am proud to call him a friend.

Gabriella Roncone was also there from the beginning. She was an invaluable research assistant who quickly became as excited as I was about what this book could be. For the first year of the project, she helped track down important facts and offered incredibly perceptive feedback on my drafts. She is well on her way to becoming a rock star in the information security world. Later on, Roxanne Heston continued in Gabby's footsteps, providing important research support and helping me revise drafts of key chapters. She, too, has a bright future ahead of her.

This book was made better by the candid feedback from others who read part or all of it and provided detailed comments. I am grateful to Jerod Coker, Teddy Collins, Matthew Green, Matthew Harries, Trey Herr, John Hultquist, Hilary Hurd, Kevin Keogh, Jack Lucas, Taylor Miller, Alex Palmer, Ben Read, Thomas Rid, Chris Rohlf, Joe Slowik, Bruce Schneier, Bryan Vadheim, and the anonymous peer reviewers. More generally, I have benefited from my conversations on cybersecurity and other subjects with Brian Bartholomew, Chris Bing, Jack Clark, Grayson Clary, Jack Goldsmith, Andy Greenberg, Richard Harknett, Eli Jellenc, Robert M. Lee, Danny Moore, Ned Moran, Saher Naumaan, Adrian Nish, Joseph Nye, David Sanger, Conrad Stosz, Matt Tait, Michael Thomas, and JD Work.

At the Woodrow Wilson Center, I am grateful to Jane Harman, Meg King—the woman who makes everything happen—Jake Rosen, and Spencer Stucky.

Jeff Dean at Harvard University Press believed in this book from the very beginning. Time and time again, he offered perceptive suggestions, talking me out of my worst ideas in the process. Joy de Menil, Julia Kirby, and the rest of the team at Harvard continued in Jeff's footsteps, taking the book over the finish line with care. When I needed one more set of eyes, Brian Bergstein stepped up, offering hard-earned wisdom from his many years writing about technology. Without Matt Mahoney's thorough fact-checking, I would not sleep well at night.

My agents, Michael Carlisle and William Callahan of Inkwell Management, also saw potential in this project early on. They offered valuable insights when my ideas were only beginning to form, and helped guide the book to market. I am glad to know they are in my corner.

I owe a debt of gratitude to the intelligence officers and national security officials in the United States and United Kingdom who shared their perspectives with me, both for this book and for other projects. The shadowy world of international cyber competition can be vexing, but my conversations with current and former practitioners helped me understand and tell the story as well as it can currently be told. Given the nature of their work, these individuals cannot be thanked publicly, but I hope they know that I value their friendship and expertise. All errors remain mine alone.

My family deserves special recognition. My parents, Bruce and Laura, show unconditional love every single day. Mary Buchanan is an amazing editor and an even better younger sister. Annie and Gerard are the best godparents around.

Kelly Buchanan is the love of my life. She has been a partner in this project and so much else. No day is complete without her uproarious laugh. This book is dedicated to her.

Index